Sampler

A Cookbook
Published by the Women's Art Guild
of
Laguna Gloria Art Museum

The purpose of the Women's Art Guild is to support the Laguna Gloria Art Museum by organizing fund raising events; by providing volunteer services throughout the year; and by encouraging interest in the activities and cultural programs available through the Museum. Proceeds from the sale of this book will be given to the Laguna Gloria Art Museum for their many projects.

First Printing   April 1986   10,000 copies

Copyright© 1986
by the

Women's Art Guild of Laguna Gloria Art Museum, Inc.
Austin, Texas

ISBN 0-9616348-0-4
Library of Congress No.: 86-50116

Copies of *Sampler* are available for $14.95, plus $1.50 postage and handling. Texas residents please add $.92 sales tax. Send to:

Sampler
P.O. Box 5705
Austin, Texas 78763

Cover Art: "Cooks Gathering"   Laguna Gloria Art Museum:
Oil on Canvas   15"x30"   Pen and Ink   15³/₄"x11"
LuAnn Barrow   Ed Jordan

Printed by Hart Graphics, Inc.
8000 Shoal Creek
Austin, TX 78767

LAGUNA GLORIA ART MUSEUM

The two young students at St. Mary's Academy were not going to the dance, unfortunately, but if they listened carefully from their upstairs window, they could hear the faint notes of a popular dance tune. They imagined they could even hear the laughter, the conversations, the click of the carriage wheels on their trip up to the high bluff overlooking a lagoon on the Colorado River, to the home of Clara Driscoll and her husband Henry Hume Sevier. The Seviers loved to dance, loved to give dances. In the 20's that is where eager young ladies met the eligible young men of Austin, Texas.

Stephen F. Austin had loved the place. In 1832, he sent a speedy post from Saltillo, Mexico to his private secretary in the States, instructing him to purchase 28-1/2 acres situated at the foot of Mount Bonnell, a 775-foot mountain overlooking Austin, a site with the enviable advantage of natural terraces and beautiful vistas. He dreamed of a home there, "I shall fix a place on the Colorado at the foot of the mountains to live", but died in 1836 before the dream could become a reality. Some 80 years would pass before the bluff would provide residence. Those who took up residence there would be as rich in history as the land itself.

At San Antonio's first Fiesta in 1896, they crowned a sixteen-year-old queen, hazel eyed with red-black hair and flawless skin, who could speak four languages and handle a lariat with admirable skill. Clara Driscoll had been educated at Miss Peebles and Thompson's School in New York, would complete her education at a convent outside of Paris - an accomplished young lady of her day, certainly, yet with fire and spirit and boundless energy for those pursuits she found worthy of her time. In 1904, she put up the money needed to save a Texas shrine, the Alamo, after a lengthy battle over its future she began with a letter to the San Antonio Express in 1901. By 1906, she was a published author, having written a novel *The Girl From La Gloria* and a comic opera *Mexicana* produced on Broadway. In that same year she married a young Texas legislator Henry Hulme Sevier at St. Patrick's Cathedral in New York City, beginning their life together touring Europe and finally settling in Austin in 1914. Stephen F. Austin's proposed homesite would become their Laguna Gloria ("Heavenly Lagoon"), chosen because it reminded them of a honeymoon stop at Lake Como.

From 1916 to 1929 this 15-room house would become well-known as a center of international hospitality. The tower serving as a study, Hal Sevier would direct his newly founded Austin American Statesman newspaper and Clara would conduct duties as a Democratic National Committee woman from Texas. Mrs. Sevier would also devote extensive time to her dream villa and its grounds, imbuing it with her romantic view of life.

Built on the highest of four terraces, the house faced the Colorado River, with steps down to the water framed in trellisses of yellow Lady Banksia roses. There would be mountain laurel, redbuds, flowering peach, lavender and white iries, crape myrtle for hedges, five acres of formal gardens and thirteen acres remaining in a naturally wooded state. Former gates from the State Capitol greeted visitors to a world as lush and lively as Clara's imagination. In 1929, Clara and Hal Sevier would leave their Laguna Gloria forever, moving to Corpus Christi to manage family business there, leaving their Austin home in the care of Galvan, a Mexican caretaker who had been on the property since its construction and would remain until his death.

The Texas Fine Arts Association, a statewide organization devoted to the purpose of stimulating interest in art throughout the state, counted among its charter members in 1911 Clara Driscoll. In 1943, two years before her death, Clara would convey Laguna Gloria and the surrounding acres to the TFAA with the provision that it be maintained as an art museum. In addition, she donated the capital necessary for rennovation and the continued salary of caretaker Galvan. Remaining on the property would be an Italian chandelier in the living room, an elegant table, and a wood carving of "The Battle of the Alamo", made from an original rafter of the historical mission.

The newly organized Laguna Gloria Art Museum would receive title on the property from TFAA in 1966, with no endownment. Laguna Gloria has depended upon membership subscriptions, private donations, and a few fund raising activities. Among those activities would be an annual arts and crafts fiesta, first held by TFAA in the City Coliseum in 1951 and five years later transferred to the newly formed Women's Art Guild and the Laguna Gloria grounds, where it remains as a significant financial contributer today. "Fiesta" would prove to be so financially successful that guild representatives from around the country seek Austin's guidance in founding their own fiestas.

Laguna Gloria Art Museum has continued Clara Driscoll's legacy not only with exhibitions of major trends in art but through a museum school offering classes year round, geared to persons of all ages and backgrounds. May in Austin still means Fiesta, when hundreds of volunteers transform Clara's heavenly lagoon into a festive marketplace for artists and craftsmen, a weekend event of art, music, food and entertainment. The tower retains its dominance, visible from distant views. The palms that Clara planted still stand, the majestic oaks she cared for remain, the property can even today evoke moods as expansive and inspiring as Clara Driscoll's vision. Like Austin itself, Laguna Gloria remains a distinctive blend of ease and grace.

ACKNOWLEDGEMENTS

LuAnn Barrow, who painted the cover picture, "Cooks Gathering", is of Irish-German ancestry, from a small Texas community. She decided early that her life's ambition was to become an artist.

She was fortunate to become a student of William Lester, (now retired), a former chairman of The University of Texas Art Department. His influence was to teach her to be comfortable with and in charge of her talents. While at The University of Texas, where she earned her B.F.A. ('56), she won the honorable mention award in a national art contest sponsored by Madamoiselle magazine.

Art became a secondary part of her life after she became the bride of David Barrow, Jr., an Austin architect. Two other happy events again placed her work on the "simmering burner" with the births and "raising" of sons, David III and Thomas.

LuAnn has displayed her art at exhibitions such as the prestigious Laguna Gloria Fiesta and invitation-only shows in Oklahoma City and Albuquerque. LuAnn said, "I soon found this was not my thing. I respect all artists who enjoy being on-the-go; but I am a home-lover and my home studio is my delight."

"As a younger artist I worried about filling a small 9"x12" canvas. Today my 30"x40" canvases are full. I find myself looking once more for a space to use an image I had stored in my memory years before", she added.

When one sees her works one may wonder why they have not seen a Barrow original or heard of her previously. She has a limited amount of time available for painting, and numbers of finished canvases are not her goal.

Ed Jordan, Austin, ink and serigraph artist, whose drawing of the Laguna Gloria Art Museum is included in this cookbook, is respected as one of the innovators of serious serigraph work.

Ed earned his Bachelor of Fine Arts degree from The University of Texas, Austin. In 1978, he was nominated for "Who's Who in American Art". He enjoys a diverse career in advertising, public relations and graphic design. His subject matter ranges from drawings of Victorian architecture and allied themes to the whimsical.

"Other diversions designed to keep me whole", Jordan remarked, "are drawings of devious cats, innocent chickens, shy pigs and a cow or elephant here and there. These make me and my customers laugh and I enjoy the humor in life," he added.

His work is shown at his Austin studio and in shops in Texas and one in California. Jordan is represented in Dallas by Kaye Locke-Spaces.

Table of Contents

The **Womens' Art Guild of Laguna Gloria Art Museum** continues a long tradition o successful growth since its formation in 1956. Today, there are over 500 member The Guild undertook sponsorship of Fiesta as its principal fundraising effort for th Museum in 1957. From those devoted charter members with great vision to th membership of today, the Women's Art Guild has given more than financial suppor to Laguna Gloria Art Museum. The Guild enjoys hosting exhibition opening acquainting the public with the activities and cultural enrichment programs available and volunteering support for Austin's Art Museum.

With its rich history, the Women's Art Guild is very pleased to offer its firs cookbook, *Sampler*, for you to use and enjoy. We hope that you will have fun cookin, and sampling the more than 500 recipes in the book. We have brought together diverse mixture of recipes, some new and some "handed down" favorites. Our collec tion will hopefully bring back the pleasures of "plain fun and fancy cooking."

We are especially proud of the wide variety of Central Texas art included as chapte dividers. We owe a special thanks to those artists who graciously donated origina works and to those who allowed us to reproduce their work: LuAnn Barrow, Malo Flato, Manuel Garza, Daryl Howard, Ed Jordan, Robert L. Levers, Jr., Alberto Meza Melissa Miller, William B. Montgomery, and Amado Maurilio Peña, Jr. Many artist involved with Fiesta and the Laguna Gloria Art Museum have contributed thei favorite recipes. Biographical sketches are included for each artist, but not necessaril under each recipe. Look for your favorite artist in our special chapter.

The Cookbook Committee wishes to thank those Guild members who took time t submit their favorite recipes. We are especially indebted to those members wh helped test and organize them. A very special thanks to Mrs. David Ferris who wrot the history of the Laguna Gloria Art Museum, and to Paul Loftin who spent man hours compiling and writing the delightful artist biographical sketches included in th book.

COOKBOOK COMMITTEE

Co-Chairmen:

Mrs. Larry Hall   Mrs. Paul Loftin
Mrs. Marcus Bone

Committee

Mrs. Bill Balcezak	Mrs. David Hart
Mrs. Robert Bluntzer	Mrs. Chris John
Mrs. Charlie Cantwell	Deborah Kaster
Mary Coneway	Mrs. Fred Markham
Mrs. Don Davis	Mrs. Ted Nagel
Mrs. David Ferris	Mrs. David Todd
Mrs. Rowland V. Firth	Mrs. Pat Whaley

"Practicing for the Half-Time
Ceremonies at the Burning Stadium"

Robert L. Levers, Jr., judged by many of his peers as the foremost imaginary satirist in the Southwest, has allowed the Women's Art Guild to include his recent work "Practicing for the Half-Time Ceremonies at the Burning Stadium", in its Cookbook.

Levers, who is in his 24th year as a professor of art at The University of Texas, used the eye-catching greens, browns, reds, blues and yellows in this extraordinary work done in oils. The glazes readily show his B.F.A. and M.F.A. from Yale were earned with care. His restricted field of art does not allow dabs of mud - but very carefully balanced colors.

Eighteen one-man shows, five two-man shows, and 46 selected group exhibits, including the Venice Biennale, first held in 1895 at Venice, Italy; add honors to The University of Texas, Laguna Gloria Art Museum and Texas.

Levers gallery affiliations include: Watson Gallery, Houston, and Patrick Gallery, Austin.

Although satirists rarely paint the "literal appearance of things", just think of the artist's fanciful humor as he tells fellow U.T. cronies, "the burning stadium is not at College Station!".

Artist Recipes

Appetizers

Naccios

Texas French bread
Melted garlic butter or olive oil

Montrachet or Mozzarella
cheese, sliced
Pesto sauce

Cut bread into 1/4 inch slices and brush with melted garlic butter or olive oil. Top each piece with cheese, then pesto sauce. Broil until bubbly and hot. *This is an Italo/Yuppie version of nachos. This original recipe placed second in the Second Annual Pesto Cook-Off in Austin, Texas.*

Gay Fay
Mixed Media

Gay Fay, Austin, who has had a successful artistic fling at all the conventional mediums, has a ribbon to prove her culinary skill. Gay was an exhibitor at a recent Laguna Gloria Art Museum New Works Show. She earned her B.A. from Rice University.

Lake Country Dip

1   bunch green onions, tops
    and all, chopped
6   ripe tomatoes, chopped
2   (4 1/2 ounce) cans chopped
    green chilies
2   (4 1/2 ounce) cans chopped
    ripe olives

2   tablespoons vinegar
4   tablespoons oil
Garlic powder to taste
Tortilla chips

Combine onions, tomatoes, green chilies and ripe olives. Toss with vinegar and oil. Add garlic powder to taste. Serve with tortilla chips or fajitas. Yields 3 1/2 cups.

Randy Smith Huke
Drawings and Sculptures

John and Randy Hukes' paintings, drawing and sculptures, have been in many Laguna Gloria Art Museum exhibits. Recently their collaborative drawings were seen at the Waco Art Center, and the Mary Ryan Gallery, New York City. A November count of mouths to feed, Lake Country Dip, at their hill country home revealed: John, Randy; sons Jared and Graham, three dogs, and a cat and 13 chickens.

Shrimply Divine Dip

3	ounces cream cheese, softened	1	(5/8 ounce) package Italian salad dressing mix
1	cup sour cream	1/2	cup finely chopped shrimp
2	teaspoons lemon juice		Potato chips

Blend all ingredients together, mixing well. Chill at least 1 hour before serving. Serve with potato chips. Yields 1 2/3 cups.

Daryl Howard
Woodblock Prints and Collages

Daryl Howard has exhibited her collage art work internationally and is an 11-year veteran of Laguna Gloria's Fiesta. Her work may be seen at Garner-Smith Gallery, Austin. Daryl is always looking for a "just right" article, even a unique color of dirt, to complete her collages. She is also a cook "ready to share" choice recipes which she has done with Shrimply Divine Dip and Mexican Rice.

Soaked Mushrooms

1/3	cup red wine	2	teaspoons prepared mustard
1/3	cup vegetable oil	2	(6 ounce) cans mushrooms, drained
1	small onion, diced		
2 to 4	cloves garlic, minced	1	(8 ounce) can sliced water chestnuts
1	teaspoon salt		
2	teaspoons parsley	1/3	cup wine vinegar

Combine red wine, oil, onion, garlic, salt, parsley and mustard in a saucepan and bring to a boil. Add mushrooms and water chestnuts and continue to boil for a few minutes. Reduce heat and add wine vinegar. Remove from heat and chill.

Joe McMordie
Whittlin'

Whittlin' Joe McMordie, Elgin, Texas; is an important part of Laguna Gloria Art Museum's Fiesta. He does an eminent chore as an exhibitor; but he may also be welcoming artists, shoveling hay, remembering where seldom used electrical outlets are hidden, or assuring a "first-timer" that "this little wind and shower will be gone in no time". Joe's Soaked Mushrooms should be served chilled. He also recommends that these not be used as ice cream toppings.

• *The oldest known recipe books were carved in stone around 1700 B.C. in an ancient Babylonian language. The stones were thought to contain pharmaceutical symbols until they were translated recently by French scholar Jean Bottero. According to Meat Board Reports, the best preserved tablets feature 25 recipes, with a heavy emphasis on aromatic meat stews.*
Texas Agricultural Extension Service

Hot Sauce

4   tablespoons butter
1   onion, chopped
Juice of 2 lemons
1   (16 ounce) can peeled
     tomatoes
1/2 cup white vinegar

3   jalapeños, chopped
Dash of oregano
Dash of coriander
Dash of cumin
Dash of salt

Sauté onions in butter until golden. Add lemon juice and process all ingredients in a blender until coarsely chopped. Add more jalapeños and cumin to taste. Yields 1 pint.

Michael Obranovich
Clay

Michael Obranovich, Dallas, a Laguna Gloria Art Museum Fiesta exhibitor, is an exciting purist in clay and one may see his works in select museums, galleries, and shops throughout the Southwest.

Chile Con Queso

Butter
1   onion, chopped
1   (10 ounce) can tomatoes
     and green chiles
2   pounds Velveeta cheese,
     cubed

8   ounces Monterey Jack
     cheese, cubed
Half and half cream
Tortilla chips to serve

Sauté onions in butter until tender. Add tomatoes and green chiles, and simmer until most of the liquid is boiled off. Add cheeses, stirring until melted. Add enough cream to desired consistency. *Chile con queso is excellent served with chips or as a topping on casseroles, eggs, beans, or anything you may come up with.*

Amado Maurilio Peña, Jr.
Mixed Media, Lithographs, Etchings, Embossures

Amado Maurilio Peña, Jr., who headquarters at his Austin "El Taller Gallery" is internationally recognized as a master printmaker in the serigraphy process. He has contributed many works for the benefit of Laguna Gloria Fiesta and Art Museum. His recipes for Migas and Chile Con Queso are exquisite and superb.

• *Fiesta of Laguna Gloria is indeed a city wide effort. We have many business and individuals in the community who contribute equipment and man hours in helping to create our Fiesta. We thank them all.*

Salmon Paté

1   (15½ ounce) can red
    sockeye salmon
12 ounces cream cheese
3 to 6 ounces garlic cheese
    spread
Dash of Tabasco
Dash of Liquid Smoke

Dash of lemon or lime juice
1 to 2 tablespoons mayonnaise,
    optional
Stuffed green olives, optional
Ripe pitted olives, optional
Green bell peppers, optional
Romaine lettuce, garnish

Blend salmon, cream cheese, garlic cheese, Tabasco, Liquid Smoke and lemon juice thoroughly to a stiff paste consistency. Use a tablespoon or two of mayonnaise to thin if necessary. Shape like a fish using fish mold as a basic model, or make it freestyle. For garnish slice 2 green olives for eyes, slivers of green bell pepper for the nose and tail and semi-circles of ripe olives for scales. Garnish with lettuce. Serves 8. *Lasts well for 4 to 5 days in the refrigerator.*

Louise LaBauve Saxon
Acrylic Painting, Collages, Serigraphs

Louise LaBauve Saxon, Austin, is a five-year Laguna Gloria Art Museum Fiesta exhibitor. She is best known for her acrylic works. Louise earned her M.F.A. from The University of Texas and has taught at Elisabet Ney Museum and two secondary Austin Schools. Her Salmon Paté will bring ovations and requests for this elegant culinary art!

Aztec Pie

4   corn tortillas
Cream cheese
2   (4 ounce) cans green chiles

Half and half cream
Salt to taste

Spread cream cheese in half inch layers over the entire surface of 3 tortillas. Slice green chiles into bits and embed in the cream cheese. Stack the 3 tortillas in a 7 inch baking dish, cheese side up. Pour in enough cream to cover the top layer of cheese. Place the last tortilla on top and bake at 350° until the cream is absorbed. Keep adding cream until a firm consistency is achieved. The pie should be thick enough to cut with a knife, hold a wedge shape, and still be moist. Serves 4.

Hills Snyder
Wood, Drawing, Mixed Media

Hills Snyder, Austin, whose artistic appeal combines: wood, drawing and one or more mediums to "finish" the piece. He exhibited at Laguna Gloria Art Museum New Works in '84. His audience is growing and recently he had solo shows in Dallas and Tyler. Hill's Aztec Pie will bring him "best of show" honors for many moons. P.S. Do not freeze.

Artist Soups

Green Soup

1/2 cup chopped green bell pepper	1 cup evaporated milk
2 cups chopped broccoli	1/2 cup buttermilk
1/4 cup chopped onion	Salt to taste
1 tablespoon butter	1/2 teaspoon curry powder
	Lemon slices to garnish

Simmer vegetables 20 minutes in 1½ cups water. Purée vegetables and water in blender, return to saucepan. Add butter, milk, buttermilk, salt and curry. Heat through. Garnish with lemon slices. Serves 4. *This soup is also good with the addition of 1 cup cooked and peeled shrimp.*

Ave Bonar
Photographer

Ave Bonar, Austin, Laguna Gloria Art Museum exhibitor, has earned more than enough kudos to have graduated from a camera bug to serious photography. However, after her cameras have been carefully packed, Ave goes to her kitchen where she is a creator of soups, salads and homemade breads.

Autumn Soup

1 pound ground beef	1 teaspoon brown bouquet sauce
1 cup chopped onion	
4 cups water	1/4 teaspoon pepper
1 cup chopped carrots	1 bay leaf
1 cup diced celery	1/8 teaspoon basil
1 cup cubed pared potatoes	6 tomatoes, chopped
2 tablespoons salt	

In a large saucepan, cook and stir meat until brown. Drain off excess fat. Cook and stir in remaining ingredients except tomatoes; heat to boiling. Reduce heat, cover and simmer 20 minutes. Add tomatoes, cover and simmer 10 more minutes. Remove bay leaf, serves 6. *Leftovers can be placed in freezer bags for future meals when you are too busy to cook.*

Peggy Byars
Oils

Peggy Byars, Austin, whose oils have been shown at Laguna Gloria Art Museum's Fiesta, Corpus Christi, and at Kerrville's Cowboy Artists of America Museum, is "coming-of-age" in her profession. Peggy has recently studied with Gary Carter and James Boren. Her summer Chicken Fried Rice is "a great cold lunch grabber"; and Autumn Soup loses no nerve when "too busy to cook" times arrive.

Autumn Vegetable Soup

1	large carrot, chopped		Oil
1	butternut squash, diced	3	quarts water or stock
1	acorn squash, diced	1/4	pound buckwheat noodles
1	large onion, sliced		Soy sauce to taste
2	ribs celery, chopped		

Cut carrot and butternut squash into matchsticks. Dice acorn squash. Slice onion and celery. Heat a small amount of oil and stir fry vegetables. Add hot water or stock. Bring to a boil. Stir in noodles and simmer for 5 minutes. Add soy sauce. Serves 8.

Ave Bonar
Photographer

Green Tomato Soup

3	tablespoons butter	1	tablespoon flour
1	large onion, chopped	2	tablespoons tamari or soy
10	medium green tomatoes, chopped		sauce
2	cups milk	2	tablespoons honey

In a saucepan, melt butter and sauté the onion and tomatoes until they are cooked but still somewhat firm. Blend milk, flour, tamari and honey together in a blender. Combine the 2 mixtures and cook over low heat about 10 to 15 minutes. Serves 4 to 6.

Janet Engle Kastner
Clay

Janet Engle Kastner, Austin, artist whose clay sculptures were part of the Laguna Gloria Art Museum's New Work 1985 exhibit, is an avid gardener. Her recipes help keep the "ho, hum" out of her galley offerings.

Cold Tomato And Horseradish Soup

1	onion, diced	2	sprigs parsley, chopped
1	carrot, diced	1	teaspoon thyme
3	ribs celery, diced	1	cup buttermilk
2	tablespoons oil		Tamari to taste, or soy sauce
4	large or 6 small tomatoes, chopped		Pepper to taste
		3	tablespoons horseradish

Sauté onion, carrot and celery in oil until crisp tender. Add tomatoes and cook 5 more minutes. Add parsley and thyme and cook over very low heat for 20 minutes. Process in blender with pepper and tamari. Chill. Just before serving add buttermilk and horseradish. Serves 4.

Janet Engle Kastner
Clay

Artist Salads & Sandwiches

Gourmet Potato Salad

1 cup cottage cheese	1 cup chopped green onion
1 cup sour cream	with tops
2 teaspoons prepared mustard	1 cup chopped celery
Salt and freshly ground pepper	½ cup chopped red bell
to taste	pepper
4 cups sliced cooked potatoes	3 hard cooked eggs, chopped

Combine cottage cheese, sour cream, mustard, salt and pepper. Mix potatoes, onion, celery, red bell pepper and eggs. Carefully fold cottage cheese mixture into potato mixture. Chill several hours and serve on a bed of romaine lettuce. Serves 6 to 8.

Ave Bonar
Photographer

Garbanzo Bean Salad

2 cups dry garbanzo beans	1 cup quartered ripe olives
1 cup chopped celery	Vinaigrette dressing
2 green bell peppers, diced	Fresh or dried basil to taste
2 to 3 small tomatoes, chopped	Salt and freshly ground pepper
½ cup chopped sweet onion	to taste
¼ cup chopped parsley	Romaine lettuce

Soak beans in water overnight. Cook, drain and cool. Combine with remaining ingredients and chill for several hours. Serve on a bed of romaine lettuce. Serves 6 to 8.

Ave Bonar
Photographer

Mary Walsh's Potato Salad

8 medium to large red	½ cup mayonnaise
potatoes, diced	Salt and pepper to taste
8 strips bacon, cooked and	
crumbled	

Cook red potatoes for about 15 minutes. When the potatoes have cooled, add the bacon pieces and toss with mayonnaise. Add salt and pepper to taste. Serves 8. *This potato salad works because of its simplicity. Resist the urge to add other ingredients. It tastes like a baked potato.*

Randy Smith Huke
Drawings and Sculptures

Garlic Lover's Caesar Salad

Salad:

2	large heads romaine lettuce, washed and chilled	½	cup margarine
½	loaf French bread, sliced and dried	1	tablespoon garlic powder
		1	tablespoon dried sweet basil
		¼	cup grated Parmesan cheese

Cut or break dried French bread into 1 inch cubes. In a skillet melt margarine and sauté bread. Add garlic powder and basil. Stir until croutons are well coated and browned. Sprinkle with Parmesan cheese.

Dressing:

5	anchovies	2	eggs
4	large cloves garlic	1	cup oil
2	tablespoons Vermouth	1	cup grated Parmesan cheese
2	teaspoons oil		Juice of 2 lemons

Process anchovies, garlic cloves, Vermouth and oil in a blender until it becomes a smooth paste. Pour into salad bowl. Add eggs, oil, Parmesan cheese and lemon juice and whisk until well blended. Pour dressing into a cup, allowing some dressing to remain in the bowl. Tear romaine lettuce and place in the bowl. Add croutons, toss lightly and add remaining dressing. Toss again. Serves 10 to 12.

Fran Larsen
Watercolor

Hal and Fran Larsen, Santa Fe, New Mexico, internationally known for their watercolors, mixed media and graphics, are friends and exhibitors of Laguna Gloria Art Museum's Fiesta. Hal's Chicken Picata is complimented by Fran's Garlic Lover's Caesar Salad. Fran wrote: "we divide the cooking arts evenly—he sets a beautiful table and I do the food preparation."

Sauerkraut Salad

1	(16 ounce) can sauerkraut	1	cup finely chopped celery
1	cup finely chopped green bell pepper	1	cup water
1	cup chopped white onion	1	cup sugar
		½	cup white vinegar

Thoroughly rinse sauerkraut in tap water. Add green pepper, onion and celery to sauerkraut, and mix thoroughly. Combine water, sugar and vinegar in a saucepan and boil. Pour over sauerkraut mixture. Refrigerate in closed container immediately, while still hot. Let marinate 24 hours. Yields 8 cups. *This salad will keep indefinitely in the refrigerator. It is also very good when served with Fredericksburg or Elgin sausage.*

Ed Jordan
Graphics, Pen and Ink, Watercolor, Serigraphs

Snow Pea Salad

2   large potatoes, cut into 1/2
    inch cubes
2   ears corn, shucked
6   carrots, sliced
1   large bunch broccoli, tops
    diced
1   cup snow peas, cut into 1/2
    inch pieces

6   green onions, chopped
1   red bell pepper, diced
1/4 cup chopped cilantro
White pepper to taste
1   cup plain yogurt
1/2 cup mayonnaise

Using a vegetable steaming rack in the bottom of a large covered pot, add potatoes and place corn cobs on top. Cover and steam until potatoes are tender. Remove from steamer and cool in a large bowl. Steam carrots and broccoli for 10 minutes, add snow peas and steam for 1 more minute. Remove from steamer and cool in bowl. Cut corn kernels off cob and return to bowl. Fold in onions, red pepper and cilantro. Fold in pepper, yogurt and mayonnaise, and chill. Serves 4.

David Haun
Precious Metal Jewelry

David Haun, Austin, who last year was a Laguna Gloria Art Museum Fiesta exhibitor, is a metal jewelry craftsman. David's Snow Pea Salad is at its best when fresh country corn first hits the market. David has been selected to participate in juried shows in Tulsa, Lubbock, Houston, El Paso and recently the Red River Revel, Shreveport, Louisiana.

Hot Chicken Salad

2   cups toasted dried bread
    cubes
2   cups chopped, cooked
    chicken
1   cup chopped celery
1   medium onion, chopped

1   tablespoon lemon juice
3/4 cup mayonnaise
1   cup cream of chicken soup,
    undiluted
1 1/2 cups grated cheese
1/2 cup chopped almonds

Mix all ingredients together. Bake uncovered at 350° for 25 minutes. Serves 4 to 6. *May be frozen and cooked later; allow 1 hour to thaw and bake.*

Winslow Whitehurst and Milton Cloud
Hand Carved Decorative Duck Decoys

Win Whitehurst and Milton Cloud, Richmond Virginia; are Laguna Gloria Art Museum Fiesta wood carvers par excellence. Years ago they reported A.W.O.L. from 8 to 5 management jobs and "went full steam ahead" letting the chips fall-at-will. Win and Milton relish the thoughts of having supper ready when they return from an exhibit: thus this recipe is a fine "prepare ahead" delight.

Curried Rice Salad

1   (6 ounce) package wild
pecan rice
1½ cups mayonnaise
1   tablespoon curry powder,
or to taste
¼   teaspoon garlic powder
Salt to taste
Dash of milk
⅓   cup chopped green bell
pepper

⅓   cup chopped celery
⅓   cup chopped red bell
pepper
⅓   cup chopped yellow bell
pepper
⅓   cup chopped tart apples
⅓   cup dry roasted cashews
⅓   cup raisins
⅓   cup thinly sliced green
onions

Prepare rice according to directions on package and cool. Combine mayonnaise, spices and enough milk to make a creamy consistency. Combine vegetables and rice in large bowl. Add dressing, and mix to coat thoroughly. Chill before serving. Serves 6 to 8.

Bill Dodd
Metal and Stone Sculpture

Tom E. Nichols and Bill L. Dodd, Austin, whose metal works and stone products have been viewed many times by Laguna Gloria Art Museum patrons, are contributors of their piece de resistance treat for this cookbook. These include: Tom's "Potato Torte" and Ginger Lime Chicken and Bill's Curried Rice Salad and Quail: Norman Style.

Claudia's Salad Dressing

1   cup apple cider vinegar
1   cup safflower oil
1   cup olive oil
Dash of cayenne pepper or
Tabasco sauce
Handful of fresh basil, dill or
cilantro, chopped

3   cloves garlic, minced
Fresh ground pepper
Salt to taste
½   cup finely grated Romano
cheese
½   cup finely grated Parmesan
cheese

Mix all ingredients together in a jar. Shake well and pour over salad and enjoy. Yields 4 cups.

Claudia Reese
Clay

Claudia Reese, Austin; B.A. Connecticut College, New London, Connecticut; M.F.A. Indiana University, Bloomington, Indiana, has exhibited at Laguna Gloria Art Museum, the Smithsonian, California and New York to name a few. She has been the visiting artist at L.S.U., Baton Rouge; School of Art, Chicago; Purdue University and the University of Northern Colorado, Greeley. Claudia has a thing about clay—perhaps this earthly love follows through in her iron-skillet onion-corn-cornbread, and her use of basil, garlic, dill, pepper and cider for a salad dressing.

Onion Sandwiches

1 purple Bermuda onion	2 slices dark rye bread
Italian salad dressing	Mayonnaise

Slice onion crosswise as thinly as possible. Pour salad dressing over onions and marinate in the refrigerator for 30 minutes. Spread the bread with mayonnaise and add 3 to 4 drained onion slices. Serves 1. *This recipe has the advantage of being very easy and quick to prepare, which is perfect for the busy artist.*

William B. Montgomery
Oil Paintings and Etchings

Bill B. Montgomery, Austin, is at times a lonely artist and a busy artist because: (1) he relishes onion-on-rye sandwiches; and (2) he swears by Uncle Posh Oltorf's Chicken and Wild Rice. Both recipes are quick and the utensils required are few. Recently Bill had exhibits at Clifford Gallery, Dallas; and Laguna Gloria Art Museum. (P.S. White onions are not an acceptable substitute).

Artist Vegetables

Jimmy's Variable Vegetables

Broccoli, corn, beans, potatoes	1 to 2 cloves garlic, minced
or squash	Parsley, basil, or cilantro
1 tablespoon butter	Dash of cayenne pepper
2 to 3 tablespoons olive oil	Juice of 1 lemon
1/2 cup vegetable oil	Short grain rice or noodles
3 to 4 mushrooms, chopped	

Steam vegetables in a 2 quart steamer with basket. Heat butter and oil in a saucepan and very lightly brown the mushrooms and garlic. Add the green parsley or other herbs and cayenne pepper. Remove from heat and add lemon juice. Serve over vegetables and rice. *You can freeze it and it can be your whole meal or go with some meat dish. It's quick for a busy person, but more nourishing than a frozen dinner.*

Jimmy Jalapeeno
General Art

Jimmy Jalapeeno, Austin, whose first Laguna Gloria Art Museum's show was: New Works '82, has a unique artistic entertainment repertoire. After gaining his B.F.A. at The University of Texas '69, Jimmy continued his studies by earning the M.F.A. from the University of California at Davis. To insure his daily bread, Jimmy is a photographer for the Texas Historical Commission, Austin.

Grandma Jordan Beans

1	(16 ounce) can whole green beans	3	slices bacon
1	cup water	1	medium onion, chopped
1	teaspoon salt	3	tablespoons white vinegar

Rinse beans and add water. Add salt and let steam for a few minutes. Chop bacon, fry until crisp, remove from drippings and set aside. Sauté onion in drippings. Drain water from beans and add to onion. Add vinegar and heat. Sprinkle bacon over beans. Serves 4. *Grandma Jordan had a large and productive garden in Fredericksburg and on a morning she would gather a washtub of fresh string beans. Later in the afternoon she would can them. This recipe is the one she would use later in serving the canned beans.*

Ed Jordan
Graphics, Pen and Ink, Watercolor, Serigraphs

Ed Jordan, Austin, whose pen and ink sketch of Laguna Gloria Art Museum will become a collector's treasure, has weathered 17 years of Fiestas. He is an entrepreneur, windmill man and historian of how "it" happened in the rare style of J. Frank Dobie. Ed's recipes are favorites from German-Fredericksburg lineage. Many got their start from great-great grandmother Pletz (Germany) and grandmother Caroline Pfiester Jordan, recent help from Jewell Jordan, a loving mom.

Apple Snap Beans

1	pound snap beans, tipped and cut	1	tablespoon cider vinegar
2	tablespoons butter	1⅓	cups bean broth
1	medium onion, chopped	1	teaspoon tamari or soy sauce
2	tablespoons flour	2	medium sour green apples, pared and coarsely chopped
2	tablespoons brown sugar		

Steam beans until crisp tender. Drain beans, reserving broth. In a 10 inch skillet, melt butter and sauté onion until softened. Stir in flour slowly, add sugar and vinegar. Be sure there are no lumps at this point. Gradually add broth and tamari stirring constantly over low heat until thickened and bubbling. Stir in beans and apples. Do not let apples cook. Serve immediately. Serves 6 to 8.

Janet Engle Kastner
Clay

• *Cauliflower cooked in an aluminum pot will darken. Use a different kind of pot and add a little sugar, lemon peel or vinegar to the cooking water to keep the cauliflower white.*

Squash Soufflé

2	pounds yellow squash, sliced	3	tablespoons flour
1	onion, chopped	2	eggs, slightly beaten
1	teaspoon salt	1	cup milk
½	teaspoon sugar	¾ to 1	cup grated cheese
3	tablespoons butter, melted		Salt to taste
			Buttered bread crumbs

Combine squash, onion, salt and sugar in a saucepan and simmer about 20 minutes, or until tender. Drain well and mash. Make a white sauce from the butter, flour, eggs, milk, cheese and salt to taste. Combine with squash. Bake in a buttered ½ quart casserole at 350° for 30 minutes. Top with crumbs and bake 10 minutes more. Serves 2 to 4. *This may be frozen before baking. Takes about 1 hour to thaw and bake at 350°.*

Milton Cloud and Winslow Whitehurst
Hand Carved Decorative Duck Decoys

Potato Torte

2	tablespoons olive oil	⅓	cup chopped red bell pepper
2	tablespoons vegetable oil		
4	cloves garlic, minced	⅓	cup choppped yellow bell pepper
1	medium onion, diced		
½	teaspoon salt	4	cups grated raw Idaho potatoes
½	teaspoon ground pepper		
⅓	cup chopped green bell pepper	4	eggs, well beaten

Put oils in a large deep non-stick skillet and heat over medium heat. Add garlic, onion, salt and pepper. Sauté until onions are soft. Add peppers and potatoes and stir thoroughly to coat evenly with oil. Reduce heat and cover, stirring often to insure even cooking. When potatoes are just cooked and begin to brown, stir in eggs, and mix thoroughly and quickly. Smooth and level top of mixture, and continue to cook until torte begins to brown on sides and bottom. Place a large round dish on top of skillet. Invert. Carefully slide torte back into skillet and continue cooking until golden brown. Remove from heat and let stand 5 minutes before serving. Serves 6.

Tom Nichols
Metal and Stone Sculpture

Tom E. Nichols and Bill L. Dodd, Austin, whose metal works and stone products have been viewed many times by Laguna Gloria Art Museum patrons, are contributors of their piece de resistance treat for this cookbook. These include: Tom's "Potato Torte" and Ginger Lime Chicken and Bill's Curried Rice Salad and Quail: Norman Style. Caution: Don't be afraid of their measures—they may need slight changes.

Roberta's Ratatouille

1	pound zucchini, cubed	1	teaspoon salt
1	small eggplant, cubed	1/8	teaspoon pepper
1	onion, sliced	1/4	teaspoon basil
3	cloves garlic	1/4	teaspoon oregano
1/4	cup olive oil		
2	(16 ounce) cans stewed tomatoes		

Cut the zucchini and eggplant into 1 inch cubes. In a large skillet, sauté the zucchini, eggplant, onion and garlic in olive oil. Stir in stewed tomatoes and herbs. Cook covered for 15 minutes or until vegetables are tender. This should serve 6, however if you have 6 *starving* artists, the recipe should be doubled. *I have always felt that a dinner party should be a group experience. The best parties are those where everyone contributes. Since most of my friends are artists also, money is often an object. Then I discovered Ratatouille. A pound of zucchini or a small onion or eggplant was not too much to ask of a friend.*

Roberta St. Paul
Watercolors and Hand Colored Serigraphs

Roberta St. Paul, an Austin and Laguna Gloria Fiesta artist, is active in producing watercolors and hand colored serigraphs. She recommends her super vegetable dish: Roberta's Ratatouille. Financial note: "If you or your friends have sold any paintings, the Ratatouille could be made into crepes and served with caviar and champagne". Her art may be seen at Air Gallery and Arts Warehouse, Austin.

Rice Pilaf

1	cup water	2	tablespoons minced dried onion
1	can condensed chicken broth	1	cup sliced fresh mushrooms
1	cup brown rice		

Bring water and chicken broth to a boil, then add rice and onion. Reduce heat and continue to cook covered for 40 minutes. Add mushrooms and cook covered an additional 5 minutes. Drain off any excess liquid. Serves 4.

Damian Priour
Glass

Damian Priour, glass sculptor, Laguna Gloria Art Museum exhibitor New-Works '82, has gained national acclaim. Damian is the owner of Skylight Glass Studio, Austin. His latest commission, a 22-foot work in glass and marble, will be unveiled in Dallas during the fall of 1986.

Mother's Corn Pudding

1	(16 ounce) can whole kernel corn	1/4	cup sugar
1	(16 ounce) can cream style corn	2	eggs
1	teaspoon salt	2	cups milk
		1/4	cup butter or margarine
		2	slices bread

Mix corn, sugar and salt. Beat eggs, adding milk then add to corn. Pour mixture into a buttered 2 quart casserole. Slice bread into cubes and put on top of corn mixture. Pour butter over bread cubes. Bake at 350° for 45 minutes or until mixture is firm. Serves 10 to 12.

Ed Jordan
Graphics, Pen and Ink, Watercolor, Serigraphs

Mexican Rice

2/3	cup chopped onions	1	(8 ounce) can whole tomatoes
3	tablespoons bacon drippings	2	teaspoons salt
1	cup converted raw white rice		Chopped fresh tomato, to garnish
1	cup chopped green bell pepper		Chopped green pepper, to garnish
1	teaspoon chili powder		

In a heavy skillet with a tight fitting lid, sauté onion in hot bacon drippings. Stir in rice, 1 cup green pepper, chili powder, tomatoes and salt. Add 2 cups water. Bring to a boil, reduce heat and simmer covered 20 minutes; or until liquid is absorbed and rice is cooked. Turn into warm serving dish. Garnish with chopped tomato and green pepper. Serves 6.

Daryl Howard
Woodblock Prints and Collages

- *The Fiesta Auction has expanded and moved over the many years. The big striped tent was first set in the center circle, then moved to the warehouse area, then to the bottom of the stairs and finally is set at the end of the Baja road.*

Artist Main Dishes

Broccoli Frittata

1/2	cup chopped onion	4	large eggs, beaten
1	tablespoon oil	1/2	cup grated Parmesan
1	cup milk		cheese, divided
1/4	cup chopped fresh basil	3	cups chopped fresh
1	teaspoon tamari or soy		broccoli, steamed until
	sauce		crisp tender

Sauté onion in oil until tender, not brown. Add milk, basil and tamari, heat until scalding. Add a small amount of hot mixture to beaten eggs in bowl, stirring constantly. Add remaining hot milk mixture, cooked broccoli and 1/3 of the Parmesan cheese. Mix well. Pour into a greased 8 inch round pan and sprinkle with remaining cheese. Bake at 350° for 45 minutes or until set. Serve immediately. Serves 4 to 6.

Janet Engle Kastner
Clay

Migas

1/2	onion, chopped	1	(4 ounce) can chopped
6	corn tortillas, cut into 1		green chiles
	inch squares	4	eggs, beaten
Butter		Salt and pepper to taste	
1	tomato, chopped		

Sauté onions and tortillas in butter until tortillas are almost crispy on the edges. Add tomato and heat until warm. Add eggs and chiles. Continue to cook, stirring until mixture is evenly cooked. Serves 2.

Amado Maurilio Peña, Jr.
Mixed Media, Lithographs, Etchings, Embossures

Uncle Posh's Chicken And Wild Rice

3 to 4 chicken breasts, halved		1	can water
1	(6 ounce) box white and	Salt and pepper to taste	
	wild rice mix	Garlic salt to taste	
1	can onion soup		

Sprinkle chicken with salt and pepper. Place rice and spices in deep casserole and place chicken on top of rice. Add soup and water. Bake in a 350° oven for 1 hour. Serves 6 to 8.

William B. Montgomery
Oil Paintings and Etchings

Chicken Fried Rice

1 cup diced cooked chicken	1/2 cup chopped onions
1 tablespoon soy sauce	1/4 cup finely chopped green
1/2 teaspoon salt	bell pepper
1 cup uncooked long grain	1/4 cup finely sliced celery
rice	2 eggs, slightly beaten
1/3 cup vegetable oil	1 cup finely shredded lettuce
2 1/2 cups chicken broth	or Chinese cabbage

Combine chicken, soy sauce and salt. Let stand 15 minutes. Cook rice in hot oil in a skillet over medium heat until golden brown; stir frequently. Reduce heat and add chicken with soy sauce and broth. Simmer, covered 20 to 25 minutes, or until rice is tender. Remove cover last few minutes. Stir in onions, green pepper and celery. Cook, uncovered over medium heat until liquid is absorbed. Push rice mixture to sides of skillet. Add eggs and cook until almost set. Blend into rice. Stir in lettuce, and serve at once. Serves 6. *This a great summer one-dish meal.*

Peggy Byars
Oils

Chicken Curry

2 tablespoons oil	2 tablespoons flour
4 cooking apples, chopped	2 cups milk
1 large onion, chopped	Raisins
1/2 cup chopped celery	Salt and pepper to taste
1 whole chicken, cooked and	Cooked rice for 6
deboned	Almonds, shredded coconut,
1 cup chicken broth	unsalted cashews for
2 to 4 tablespoons curry	condiments
powder	

Heat oil and sauté the apples, onion and celery. Cut chicken into bite sized pieces. In a large saucepan combine sautéed mixture and chicken, and stir. Add flour and curry powder. Add chicken broth and milk, and heat slowly, do not boil. Add raisins. Cover and let sit with no heat for a few hours. Reheat before serving. Do not boil. Serve with rice and almonds. Serves 6. *It is best to make the curry 2 to 4 hours in advance. It brings out the flavor and plumps the raisins.*

Laurie Weller
Watercolors, Oils

Laurie Weller, Austin, a former faculty member of Laguna Gloria Art Museum School, is now on the faculty at Southwest Texas State University. Her M.F.A. was earned from the Tyler School of Art, Philadelphia. Laurie paints watercolors as big as Texas' Sesquicentennial (60"x40" to 60"x80"). Artspace, an artist's magazine, reported: "Weller leaves one looking ahead, knowing the present work will hold its own." Her Chicken Curry is big on satisfaction—but is best for six.

My Favorite Chicken Enchiladas

Corn tortillas
1   chicken, cooked and
    deboned, cut into cubes,
    reserve broth
1   onion, chopped
1   cup sour cream

1   (8 ounce) can tomato sauce
1   (4 ounce) can green chiles
8   ounces Longhorn cheese,
    grated
8   ounces Monterey Jack
    cheese

Dip corn tortillas in hot chicken broth to soften and place in a 9x13 inch baking dish. Next, layer chicken and onion. Mix together sour cream, tomato sauce and green chiles and pour over onion. Top with grated cheeses and bake at 350° until cheese has melted. Serves 4 to 6.

Liese Jean Scott
Graphics, Collages

Liese Jean Scott, Austin, is one of a very few artists who produce gallery-quality collages. She has shown in juried exhibitions at Laguna Gloria Art Museum's Fiesta, Houston, Santa Fe, Taos and Scottsdale, Arizona. Her pictures may be seen in Austin's El Taller Gallery. Collage works "with the prayer that the glue is fail proof" have been collected since the Byzantine days and are described as pictures made from a number of original materials which may be changed in color and shape. Liese Jean's recipes are: Capirotada, a mexican bread pudding usually served during Lent, and a quick Chicken Enchilada.

Gary's Chicken Enchiladas

10 flour tortillas
4 to 6 boned chicken breasts
8   slices Monterey Jack cheese
3/4 cup chopped onion
4   tablespoons butter
1/4 cup flour

2   cups chicken broth
1/2 teaspoon cumin
3 to 4 jalapeños, chopped
1   cup sour cream
Salt to taste
Picante sauce to serve

Soften tortillas before rolling by patting a little water on each side. Put some chicken and cheese on each tortilla, roll up and put in a 9x13 inch pan. Make a sauce by melting butter, then stirring in flour. Add chicken broth and cook until thickened. Add cumin, jalapeños and sour cream to the sauce. Heat and pour over tortillas. Top with any leftover cheese and onions. Bake at 425° for 20 minutes. Serves 5.

Gary Washmon
Acrylics

Gary Washmon, Austin, a Laguna Gloria Art Museum New Works (1985) exhibitor, recently was awarded a study grant from the Dallas Museum of Art. While working for and earning his M.F.A. at the University of Illinois, Gary used acrylics on canvas—and today this method is his favorite. His Tex-Mestizo enchilada dish is an Austin influence.

Pollo En Mola

1	medium chicken, cut in pieces	1/8	teaspoon garlic powder
1	small onion, sliced	1	cup chicken broth
2	tablespoons flour	2	tablespoons peanut butter
4	teaspoons chile powder	1/4	teaspoon salt
		1/8	teaspoon ground cloves

Boil chicken and onion in water for about 20 minutes, reserve 1 cup broth. Heat skillet over low heat, add flour and brown. Let stand for a few minutes before adding chile and garlic powders. Add 1/2 cup reserved broth and stir until mixture is dissolved. Blend in remaining broth and mix well. Add peanut butter, salt, ground cloves and chicken pieces; cook for 15 minutes over medium heat. Serves 4 to 6. *This is best when served with baked beans and Mexican fried rice.*

Andrew J. Saldaña
Mixed Media, Acrylics and Graphics

Andrew J. Saldaña, an Austin Community College Art instructor, owns his own Austin studio-gallery. He exhibits at Laguna Gloria Art Museum's Fiesta and is also shown in Houston, Chicago, Colorado and New Mexico. Andrew is pleased to present his Pollo en Mola recipe and is proud of his Mestizo-Lipan (Aztec indian) lineage. This background is responsible for his incredible use of acrylic-gouache mediums.

Padre Pedro's Chicken

5	tablespoons oil	2	onions, chopped
1	chicken, cut into small pieces		Salt to taste
1	pound ripe tomatoes, chopped	2	bay leaves
		2 to 3	cloves garlic
1	green bell pepper, chopped	3/4	cup water

Heat oil in a large heavy skillet. Add chicken, tomatoes, green pepper and onions, and sauté until browned. Add salt and bay leaves, and cook on medium heat for 20 minutes. Add garlic and water and cook until chicken is tender, at least 1 hour. Remove bay leaves and serve. *Serve chicken topped with vegetables and pan liquid. The chicken may be cooked and then frozen.*

Maximo L. Cortina
Oils

Maximo Cortina, Charlotte, Florida; whose oils are displayed in many galleries, gift shops and Laguna Gloria Art Museum's Fiesta has developed this prized recipe from his travels. "Padre Pedro's Chicken" cuts down on the calories by requiring only three-fourths cup of water. This Spanish chicken and sauce assemblage rings the dinner bell with deserved Pedros gusto.

Huntington's Quick Chicken Anchovy Pasta

5 ounces vegetable swirl pasta	1/2 pound boneless chicken breast, cut into small pieces
1 (2 ounce) can fillets of anchovies in oil	2 ounces grated Parmesan cheese
6 cloves garlic, minced	Coarsely ground pepper to taste
1/2 red bell pepper, chopped	

Cook pasta until al dente. Drain and set aside. Heat some of the oil from the anchovies in a frying pan at medium high heat. While oil is heating mince garlic, then sauté until golden brown. Sauté for about 1 minute the bell pepper, adding more anchovy oil if nessecessay. Stir in chicken pieces and sauté until done, about another minute or so. Chop anchovies and add to skillet. Stir in drained pasta, Parmesan cheese and ground pepper. Serves one healthy eater or 2 normal humans.

Jim Huntington
Sculpture

Jim Huntington, Brooklyn, an exhibitor in a recent Laguna Gloria Art Museum's Fiesta, is better known for his sculpture of stone and steel or copper. Jim testifies his "Huntington's Quick Chicken Anchovy Pasta" is a true test of taste buds—but if the buds and guests survive, the combo will cause conversation for the evening and for generations to come.

Lime Glazed Chicken

3/4 cup apple juice	1 teaspoon chopped fresh mint
Juice of 1 lime, divided	
2 teaspoons cornstarch	2 whole large boneless chicken breasts
1 teaspoon instant chicken bouillon granules	Seasoned salt

Combine apple juice, juice of 1/2 lime, cornstarch and bouillon. Cook and stir over medium heat until bubbly. Continue cooking and stirring for 2 more minutes. Stir in mint. Remove skin and fat from chicken breasts and place on grill. Sprinkle the top of breasts with seasoned salt. After about 8 minutes turn over chicken and squeeze the remaining lime juice on breasts. Brush with lime glaze and continue cooking until done. Any remaining glaze may be added at the table. May be served atop Rice Pilaf. Serves 4. *Chicken breasts may be also cooked in the oven. If you choose this method, cook chicken in a glass dish with 2 tablespoons of heated oil until browned. Bake covered 25 to 30 minutes or until done. Remove and add lime glaze. This is a low calorie recipe. Enjoy.*

Damian Priour
Glass

Ginger Lime Chicken

3 tablespoons vegetable oil
2 to 4 cloves garlic, minced
Dash of cayenne pepper
1 small onion, diced
1½ teaspoons minced ginger
   root

1 pound boneless, skinless
   chicken breast, cut in small
   pieces
½ cup dry white vermouth
Juice of 1 large lime with pulp
1 cup whipping cream
Cooked rice for 2

In a large heavy skillet heat oil and add garlic, pepper, onion and ginger root. Sauté over medium heat until onion begins to soften. Add chicken and sauté until just cooked. Remove chicken and reserve. Add vermouth and lime juice, reducing by half. Add cream and reduce until sauce is slightly thickened. Add chicken and heat through. Serve over rice. Serves 2. *Prepare the rice according to package directions, adding ½ teaspoon lime zest to rice. After rice is cooked, sprinkle with a few mint leaves.*

Tom Nichols
Metal and Stone Sculpture

Chicken Paprika

1 chicken, cut up and
   skinned
Salt and pepper
1 ounce paprika

Flour
1 cup butter
2 cups half and half cream

Sprinkle chicken with salt and pepper. Coat heavily with paprika. Dust with flour. Melt butter in a 12 inch skillet; add chicken, cover and cook over very low heat for about 1 hour, turning at least once while browning. Add a little water if necessary to keep moist. Just before the chicken is done pour in cream and stir thoroughly to coat chicken. Uncover skillet and bring to a boil until thickened. Take care not to curdle the milk. Serves 4. *This is delicious left over and reheated. It is especially good served with mashed potatoes. With green peas and cantaloupe, my family considered it "The Perfect Meal".*

Annette Morris
Pencil Drawings and Stone Lithographs

Annette Morris, Austin, who shows pencil drawings and stone lithographs at Laguna Gloria Art Museum's Fiesta, is also a connoisseur of Southern cooking. A couple of generations back, her German-Texas grandmother was influenced by recipes from a close Syrian friend; and the results were: "pass the Chicken Paprika, please."

Chicken Dijon

1 chicken, cut up	1 to 2 onions, sliced
Salt and pepper	Mushrooms, sliced
Dijon mustard	1 can beef broth

Wash chicken and pat dry. Sprinkle with salt and lots of pepper, and place in a baking pan. Then liberally spoon on dijon mustard on all the chicken that you can see. Cover with onion slices and mushrooms. Pour broth over all and cook at 350° for 45 minutes to 1 hour, basting every 20 minutes. Serve with rice and a vegetable or a salad. Serves 4 to 6.

Ellen Wallenstein
Photography

Ellen Wallenstein, Austin, photographic acquisitions coordinator for nationally-known Steck-Vaughn Publications, is sharing a "first-time-one dish" recipe because the ingredients are readily available and the recipe is easy to follow. Ellen, a New Yorker, earned her M.F.A. '78 from Pratt Institute, New York City. She was on the faculty of the Art Department at The University of Texas from 1978-1985.

Chicken With Eggplant

4 cups eggplant, cut in shoestring strips	4 tablespoons oil
	5 hot peppers, seeds removed and shredded
½ cup chicken, cut in shoestring strips	
1 tablespoon cornstarch	1 clove garlic, minced
2 tablespoons soy sauce	1 tablespoon fresh ginger, chopped
1 tablespoon sherry	1 cup soup stock

Cover eggplant with boiling water for 5 minutes, drain well. Dredge chicken with cornstarch, soy sauce and sherry. Heat oil in pan and sauté peppers until they turn in color, remove from pan. Sauté chicken until done, add eggplant, garlic, ginger and soup stock. Heat. Serves 6.

Ferne Schrier
Clay

Ferne Schrier, El Paso, is a Laguna Gloria Art Museum Fiesta exhibitor. Her works in clay continues to draw plaudits from her patrons. Ferne's Chicken with Eggplant Chinese recipe is a prepare ahead cinch and reheats without a loss of savor.

• *If chicken is cooked with NO SAUCE, (fried, baked or broiled) it is safe at room temperature up to 4 hours. If the day is warmer than 70 to 75°, it is best to wrap the cold chicken in foil or plastic, then in several layers of newspaper.*

Chicken Piccata

8	boned and skinned chicken breasts	½	cup white wine
1	cup flour	¼	cup fresh lemon juice
½	teaspoon salt	3	tablespoons capers, drained
½	teaspoon white pepper	2	beaten egg yolks
8	tablespoons butter	¼	cup chopped fresh parsley
			Lemon slices

Pound chicken breasts between two pieces of waxed paper until very thin. Dredge chicken breasts in a mixture of the flour, salt and pepper. In a skillet, melt the butter and brown chicken on all sides. Add wine, capers and lemon juice and simmer until tender, about 4 to 5 minutes. Remove chicken from skillet. Add beaten egg yolk to remaining liquid in skillet and whisk until thickened. Return chicken to skillet. Reheat quickly and garnish with parsley and sliced, twisted lemon wedges. Serves 6 to 8.

Hal Larsen
Watercolor Collage and Graphics

Quail Norman Style

4	quail, cleaned and picked		Salt to taste
1	tart green apple	⅛	teaspoon white pepper
6	cloves garlic, divided	2	tablespoons dry white wine
16	juniper berries, divided	2	tablespoons Calvados or
	Flour		Armagnac
4	tablespoons butter	1	cup whipping cream

Peel, core and chop the apple. Fill the cavity of each quail with 1 garlic clove, 2 juniper berries and pieces of the apple. Tie each quail with kitchen twine so legs are close to body. Dredge in flour. In a large skillet melt butter over medium heat. Add 2 cloves minced garlic, salt, white pepper, 8 juniper berries and remaining apple. Sauté for 3 minutes. Add quail, turning until lightly browned on all sides. Add wine, cook uncovered until alcohol is evaporated, 1 to 2 minutes. Reduce heat and cover skillet. Steam until quail are barely cooked. Remove from skillet and cover with foil tent. Place contents of skillet in food processor and purée. Strain through cheesecloth and return liquid to skillet. Over low heat add Calvados. Let alcohol evaporate and add whipping cream. Reduce until slightly thickened. Add quail and heat through. Serves 2.

Bill Dodd
Metal and Stone Sculpture

Beef Bindalu

1 tablespoon cumin	1½ teaspoons ground
½ teaspoon coriander	cinnamon
1 tablespoon dry mustard	1 tablespoon ginger
1 teaspoon turmeric	1 cup white vinegar
2 tablespoons allspice	2 to 3 pounds beef cut in 1
½ teaspoon pepper	inch cubes
½ teaspoon cardamon	2 tablespoons vegetable oil
1¼ teaspoons cayenne pepper	6 cloves garlic, minced
½ teaspoon ground cloves	2 onions, thinly sliced
½ teaspoon salt	3 bay leaves

Mix first twelve spices together in a large bowl. Add vinegar to make a thin paste. Place meat in paste and marinate for 24 hours in refrigerator. Heat oil in a large stew pot and add meat with spices and vinegar marinade. Add remaining ingredients and simmer gently for 2 hours, or until tender. Serves 6 to 8.

Malcolm Bucknall
Oils

Malcolm R. Bucknall, Austin, a recent exhibitor in the Laguna Gloria Art Museum's New Works presentation, has been named as a Fellow by the National Endowment of the Arts Association. His B.F.A. is from The University of Texas and his M.F.A. is from the University of Washington. He uses oils, watercolors and washes on works he sells to obtain funds for the choice meats his special bindalu from India requires. (Bindalu: a unique curry for marinating.) Use of curry was learned when he spent a year as a student at Santiniketan, the Ashran of Rabindranath Tagore, India.

Bologna Cups And Peas

6 slices bologna	2 cups miniature
2 tablespoons butter	marshmallows
2 cups cooked English peas	1 cup mayonnaise

Spread bologna slices with butter and place in heated broiler. As slices heat, they will curl into cup shapes. Drain oil and set aside to cool. Drain peas and toss with marshmallows. Fill each cup with mixture. Place a large dollop of mayonnaise on top. Serves 6. *This makes an attractive, unusual and very popular party food.*

Jim Tapley
Papermaker

Jim Tapley, Austin, Laguna Gloria Art Museum faculty member, has studied and has had bookbinding (handbinding) studios in the U.S., the Middle East, the Orient and Europe. His gift is making cast paper and producing wall-size paper murals. Special emphasis is placed on the archival life of his paper pieces. Jim's unique method of shaping his green-pea-marshmallow cup is a sign of "mens sana in corpore sano" (contact with reality).

Chicken Fried Rattlesnake

Drink about three fingers of Jack Daniels; and contemplate the rattle-snake and how you plan to kill and dress it. Drink about three fingers of Jack Daniels. Sever head from body of rattlesnake. Call E.M.S. or consult a physician. Drink three more fingers of Jack Daniels. After the snake has stopped squirming, 1 to 3 hours, slit him up or down, and remove internal organs. Discard. Have six fingers of Jack Daniels this time. Peel off skin. Using a hand axe or machete, chop snake into 3 inch sections as demonstrated in comic strip B.C. Dredge in flour. Fry in deep oil until golden brown. Drink three fingers of Jack Daniels. Tell your guests it is chicken backs, because there will be no legs and serve. Finish off Jack Daniels. This is a very simple recipe, but must be undertaken with due caution.

Joe McMordie
Whittlin'

Joe's second recipe has been a family favorite for unusual happenings. Such as: I.R.S. audits, divorces, bankruptcies, and pardons of loved ones. Just as fluid is an absolute requirement for truly inspired recipes—*Do Not* begin this perplexity without one-fifth, better make that one liter of Jack Daniels (per cook). Even range cooks who use only the nature-produced and seasoned "chips" do not alter directions to follow the first step.

Pasta With Shrimp And Walnuts

1	pound shrimp	4	tablespoons olive oil or
1	clove garlic, minced		butter
8	ounces shelled walnuts		Parmesan cheese, grated,
1	(8 ounce) package fresh egg		optional
	noodles		

Peel and devein shrimp. Peel and mince garlic. Quarter the walnuts. Start a large pot of water heating to a boil in preparation for cooking the pasta. Heat oil in a large skillet. Cook walnuts in hot oil 5 minutes, stirring. Add garlic, stir and cook 5 minutes more. Add shrimp, stir and cook 5 minutes or until all shrimp are cooked. As the shrimp are cooking, place pasta in boiling water and cook according to the instructions on the package, 3 minutes for fresh pasta. Drain pasta, toss with shrimp mixture and serve. Grated Parmesan cheese may be used as an accompaniment. Serves 4 to 6.

Steve Lindenbaum
Precious Metal Jewelry

Steve Lindenbaum, Austin (Steven-David Jewelry) has continued to draw favor for his artistic creations in precious jewelry. Steve's works have been shown at Laguna Gloria Fiesta and juried exhibits at Red River, Shreveport, La., El Paso and Houston. His Pasta with Shrimp and Walnuts is terrific for leftovers—even leftover pasta. One ingredient is an absolute must "start a large pot of water heating".

Elegant Stuffed Raccoon

1	raccoon, 3½ pounds	Dry sherry
2	tablespoons butter	1 tablespoon bacon drippings
2	green onions, chopped	1 cup dry ginger ale
¾	pound ground pork	2 tablespoons flour
2	slices white bread, diced	Raisins
1	egg	Parsley
⅓	cup milk	Preserved kumquats for garnish
¾	teaspoon salt	

Rinse raccoon and refrigerate. Remove head, tail and feet. In a 3 quart saucepan, in hot butter, cook onions. Remove from heat and stir in pork, bread, egg, milk, salt and ¼ cup sherry; refrigerate. Filet raccoon, leaving filets attached along spinal ridge. Spread stuffing mixture over raccoon meat. Tie legs to carcass and wrap with a string to create a compact raccoon tube. Insert meat thermometer into center of stuffing. Brush with bacon dripppings. Roast in a 325° oven about 2 hours or until meat thermometer reaches 180°. During last of roasting time, brush raccoon with pan drippings. When raccoon is done, place on a warm platter and keep warm. For gravy, remove raccoon from pan. Spoon off all but 2 tablespoons of fat, leaving drippings and brown bits. Add water, ginger ale and heat to boiling. Add flour and raisins and cook until thickened. Garnish with parsley and kumquats, Serve with gravy. Serves 6.

Doug Whitfield
Oils

Douglas Whitfied, Penfield, New York, is an artist of rare skills in selecting correct oil colors for his images. However, one may place tongue-in-cheek when preparing his "elegant stuffed racoon". Our Cookbook Tasting Committee talked to several racoon fanciers and their comment: "sounds just right." Doug has his feet on higher ground, he wrote: "When I first tried this recipe, I thought I was in heaven. Not only is it delicious, it is absolutely unique; a real conversation piece."

• *Although food items may come and go at Fiesta (tamales, macho taco, carnitas) our nachos have from the beginning have been a big hit! A wonderful concoction of crisp tortilla chips, hot beans, freshly grated cheese and sliced jalapeños.*

Potter's Guild Pizza

8 tablespoons yeast	Green bell pepper, chopped
5 cups hot water	Mushrooms, sliced
8 tablespoons honey	Pepperoni, sliced
1 cup vegetable oil	Sausage, sliced
9¼ cups whole wheat flour	Onions, chopped
5 cups soy flour	Pineapple, chopped
Mozzarella cheese, sliced	Almonds, sliced
Ragu traditional sauce	Mozzarella cheese, grated

Pour yeast into hot water and let sit until yeast floats, then combine with honey and oil. Add flours and knead until uniform and let rise 1 hour. Spread into well greased pans. Pre-cook at 475° for 3 to 5 minutes until light brown. Place slices of cheese directly on dough, then add sauce and other ingredients. Bake at 475° for 17 to 20 minutes or until crust is brown. Pour sauce over top. Each guild member brings their favorite topping ingredient. We have all the standards: bell peppers, mushroooms, pepperoni, sausage, onions, and the exotic toppings such as pineapple, almonds, and okra. Then cover the top with grated cheese. Cook. After the pizza is removed from the oven let it stand for 5 minutes or until you just can not take it anymore, then cut and serve. Serves 20. *We cook the pizzas in the main kiln at Laguna Gloria Art Museum. Since we use the large pans, the pies are usually about 3 inches thick and one piece is a good sized meal. Due to variety in tastes we usually make one veggie only and one meat and veggie. We have to make "maps" of the pizza as it is constructed, to remember which toppings are placed where. I have people who sign up for my pottery classes just to eat this pizza.*

Bill Mangham
Potter

Bill Mangham, an Austin potter who earned his M.F.A. at Stephen F. Austin University, Nacogdoches, Texas, is not only a Laguna Gloria Art Museum faculty member, but also teaches credit ceramics at Austin Community College. Bill strengthened the area interest in clay works by founding the Laguna Gloria Potters Guild. His art may be seen at Austin's Arts Warehouse. The Potter's Guild Pizza recipe with Ron Jandrasi's dough, makes two 18"x24" feasts. The Ragu sauces are very good!

- *When a recipe calls for just 2 tablespoons of tomato paste, what do you do with the rest of the can? Just clean the rim, seal the can in freezer wrap or foil and freeze it. The next time you need paste, use an electric opener to remove the botton of the can. Push the contents up, forcing the paste out the top.*

"Impasto" Barbecued Brisket

8 pounds brisket with ⅛ inch fat on top
1½ teaspoons salt
1½ teaspoons garlic powder
1 teaspoon marjoram
Pepper to taste

1 large onion, thinly sliced
1 large green bell pepper, thinly sliced
3 small bay leaves
2¼ cups chili sauce
2 cups water

Season brisket on both sides with a mixture of salt, garlic powder, marjoram and pepper. Line a large, shallow baking pan with onion, green pepper and bay leaves. Place brisket, fat side up, over mixture. Using *palette knife technique* paint the brisket with the chili sauce, to thickly coat entire top, but not the sides. Add water, pouring in bottom of pan, do not pour on top of meat. Bake uncovered at 275° for 5 to 6 hours, adding liquid as needed to bottom of pan. Top of brisket will be crusty and blackened. Good served hot or cold. Serves 10 to 15. *Remove bay leaves and de-grease pan drippings. Put drippings along with onions and green pepper in a blender and process to make a thick sauce.*

Beth Eidelberg
Watercolors

Beth W. Eidelberg, San Antonio, is a master of transparent watercolor. She has been a Laguna Gloria Art Museum Fiesta junk food purist since 1972. Her "Impasto" Oven Barbecue Brisket is a must when packing for Fiesta. This brisket is a standby for freezing.

You Name It Stir Fry

Vegetable oil
½ pound sliced beef
½ to 1 teaspoon salt
2 teaspoons oyster sauce, soy sauce or hoisin sauce

Sprinkle of red hot pepper seeds
Broccoli, cauliflower, snap beans, bok choy or tofu
Sliced toasted almonds
1 teaspoon cornstarch

Heat a heavy skillet or wok until hot. Quickly toss in beef with pepper seeds and stir. Add salt and seasonings stiring once more. Do not overcook. Remove beef to large platter. Stir fry vegetables in same pan over medium heat until vegetables are slightly cooked. Add more oil if necessary. Use only one or a combination of two vegetables. Arrange vegetables around meat on platter and top with toasted almonds. If a gravy is desired, mix cornstarch with water and stir into skillet during the final part of cooking. Serves 2.

R. C. Wong
Pastels, Watercolors and Oils

R. C. Wong, Austin, has a great following at Laguna Gloria's Fiesta. Her oils, pastels and watercolors are treasured heirlooms. Pardon the pun, but one may say "this original beef, sauce and vegetable Wong is right!"

Artist Breads

Cornbread

1 (8½ ounce) package Jiffy Mix Cornbread
1 egg
⅓ cup milk
1 onion, chopped
1 (4 ounce) can green chiles
1 (16 ounce) can whole kernel corn

¾ cup Cheddar or Monterey Jack cheese, grated
Dash of oil
Dash of white vinegar
2 to 3 fresh jalapeños, seeded and chopped

Mix all ingredients together and put into an oiled cast iron skillet. Bake at 350° for 20 minutes. Serves 6 to 8.

Claudia Reese
Clay

Zucchini Bread

3 eggs
3 cups grated zucchini
1 cup vegetable oil
3 teaspoons vanilla extract
2¼ cups sugar
3 cups flour
½ teaspoon baking powder

1 teaspoon baking soda
3 teaspoons cinnamon
1 cup chopped pecans or walnuts
1 cup raisins
½ cup sunflower seeds

Beat eggs until light. Stir in zucchini and add oil and vanilla. Sift together sugar, flour, baking powder, baking soda and cinnamon. Add slowly to egg mixture. Stir in pecans, raisins and sunflower seeds. Pour into 2 greased and floured loaf pans and bake in a preheated oven at 350° for 1 hour and 15 minutes to 1 hour and 30 minutes. Yields 2 loaves. *This bread will keep at least 6 months in the freezer if well wrapped.*

T. P. Speer
Graphics

T. P. Speer, Oberlin, Ohio; artist whose graphics are in demand (a most sacred word for an artist) has shared a rare Zucchini Bread which has a great "keeping" record. Perhaps one fine day, T. P. will gain equal fame with Charles M. Hall, an Oberlin college alumnus, whose method of producing aluminum provided millions to his alma mater.

"Capirotada" Mexican Bread

1	cone Piloncillo, cane sugar	Toasted bread
2	whole cloves	Cubed Velveeta cheese
2	teaspoons cinnamon	Raisins
4	cups water	Pecans, optional

Mix together Piloncillo, which is available at Mexican groceries, cloves, cinnamon and water in a saucepan and boil. Boil until liquid is reduced about by half. In an oven proof dish arrange in layers, toasted bread, cubed Velveeta, raisins, nuts, and syrup. Repeat layers until casserole is full. Bake covered in a 350° oven until bread is soft and moist and cheese is melted. Best served warm with coffee or tea. *This Mexican bread is pudding traditionally served during Lent.*

Liese Jean Scott
Graphics, Collages

Artist Desserts

Luscious Apricot Cookies

2	cups flour	3/4	cup pecans
3/4	cup melted margarine	1/2	teaspoon baking soda
1	cup sugar	1	(18 ounce) jar apricot
1/2	cup coconut		preserves

Mix together flour, margarine, sugar, coconut, pecans and baking soda. Spread half of mixture on the bottom of a 9x13 inch ungreased pan. Spread with apricot preserves; then crumble remaining flour mixture on top and gently pat down. Bake at 400° for 5 minutes, turn oven down to 350° and continue cooking for 20 minutes. Cool. Yields 24 bar cookies.

Don Collins
Acrylics

Don Collins of Austin, acrylic artist, is deeply aware of his heritage through tales of the Irish potato famine of 1847-1848; through two grandfathers who fought each other for the North and South in the Civil War; through his loving Irish mom, Mary McGlinchey Collins; and through his own experiences as a G.I. who helped close the Fort Reno (Oklahoma) Calvary Remount Station.

Bachelor Buttons

1 cup butter	1 cup chopped pecans
½ cup powdered sugar	Powdered sugar
2 cups flour	

Cream butter and sugar. Add flour and mix well. Add pecans and roll into small balls. Place on a cookie sheet and bake at 300° for about 30 minutes. While still warm, roll in powdered sugar. Yields 3 dozen.

Ed Jordan
Graphics, Pen and Ink, Watercolors, Serigraphs

Ice Box Cookies

1 (16 ounce) box brown sugar	1 teaspoon vanilla extract
½ cup shortening	3 cups flour
2 eggs	3 teaspoons baking powder
	½ cup chopped pecans

Cream sugar and shortening together. Add eggs and vanilla, mixing well. Combine flour and baking powder and add to egg mixture. Stir in pecans, and mold into 3 rolls. Wrap in waxed paper and refrigerate. When ready to bake, remove and slice roll as wanted. Bake on cookie sheets at 350° for 10 to 15 minutes. *These cookies are great for cookie cravers. Slice and bake some today, then slice and bake some more a few days later.*

Ed Jordan
Graphics, Pen and Ink, Watercolor, Serigraphs

Rock Cookies

1½ cups brown sugar	2 rings candied pineapple
1 cup butter	1 (16 ounce) container candied cherries
4 eggs	
1 cup chopped pecans	1 teaspoon cinnamon
1 cup raisins	1 teaspoon baking soda
½ pound dates	Pinch of salt
	3½ cups flour

Cream sugar and butter. Add eggs, chopped pecans, dates, candied fruit, raisins and spices. Add soda, which has been dissolved in a little water and flour. Mix thoroughly and drop by teaspoonful on to a cookie sheet. Bake at 350° for 15 minutes. *A must for our family Christmas.*

Ed Jordan
Graphics, Pen and Ink, Watercolor, Serigraphs

Buttermilk Pie

2	eggs, separated	2	cups buttermilk
1	cup sugar	1	teaspoon vanilla extract
1/2	teaspoon salt	1	unbaked pie shell
1/3	cup flour		Cinnamon or nutmeg

Beat egg yolks, and add sugar and salt. Stir flour into part of buttermilk until free from lumps. Add to egg and sugar mixture. Stir in remaining buttermilk. Fold in stiffly beaten egg whites. Pour into unbaked pie shell. Sprinkle top with cinnamon or nutmeg. Bake at 350° until set.

Ed Jordan
Graphics, Pen and Ink, Watercolor, Serigraphs

Ed Jordan, Austin, whose pen and ink sketch of Laguna Gloria Art Museum will become a collector's treasure, has weathered 17 years of Fiestas. He is an entrepreneur, windmill man and historian of how "it" happened in the rare style of J. Frank Dobie. Ed's recipes are favorites from German-Fredericksburg lineage. Many got their start from great-great grandmother Pletz (Germany) and grandmother Caroline Pfiester Jordan, recent help from Jewell Jordan, a loving mom.

Tomato Soup Cake

3	cups flour	3/4	cup butter
3/4	teaspoon salt	1 1/2	cups sugar
3	teaspoons baking powder	1	can tomato soup
1	teaspoon baking soda	3/4	soup can water
1	teaspoon ground cloves	1 1/2	cups raisins
1 1/2	teaspoons cinnamon	1 1/2	cups chopped walnuts
1 1/2	teaspoons nutmeg		

Sift together flour, salt, baking powder, soda, cloves, cinnamon and nutmeg. Cream butter with sugar. Mix dry ingredients with the sugar and butter. Add the soup and water, raisins and walnuts. Pour into a well greased 9x13 inch pan. Bake at 350°. Serves 12 to 15. *This recipe has been handed down through our family. It is easily mixed, and since it takes no eggs, it is perfect for those individuals who wish to reduce their intake of eggs. If you enjoy a spicy cake, you will love this.*

Rose Knapp
All Original Hand Puppets

Rose and Fred Knapp, puppeteers, Fredericksburg, are veteran exhibitors at Laguna Gloria Art Museum's Fiesta. Other than picking up awards "all over", they try recipes such as an unusual Tomato Soup Cake, on their four children and five grandchildren. A fun family!

"Uninvited Guests"

Alberto Meza, San Antonio, is in his 30th year as a Texan. Although Mexico offered challenges, it was the perfection of Texas' outdoor breadth that called Alberto to his overwhelming Texas love. His watercolor and acrylic painting, "Uninvited Guests", highlights his ability to capture his chosen subjects with authenticity.

Laguna Gloria Fiesta guests and Laguna Gloria Art Museum visitors are still buying approved prints of the 1984 Fiesta Poster, "Evening Gathering", a scene of a typical central Texas ranch home. Proceeds from the sale of the original work, and approved prints have gone to Laguna Gloria Art Museum.

Many gifted artists are learned in perspective and detail; but only "the few" who have lived on the land are capable of matching his excellent treatment of color, light and shadows. Alberto's superior works are shown in his San Antonio studio, many major galleries in Texas and his works are found in several prominent collections throughout North and Central America.

Appetizers & Beverages

Antipasto Cocktail Relish

1 (12 ounce) bottle chili
   sauce
1 (12 ounce) bottle hot
   catsup
1 (6 ounce) can tomato paste
1 (4 ounce) can mushroom
   stems and pieces
2 (6 ounce) cans white chunk
   tuna, drained

1 pound boiled shrimp
1 cup sweet pickle relish
1 (4½ ounce) can ripe olives,
   sliced
1½ tablespoons Worcestershire
   sauce
½ tablespoon A-1 sauce
Assorted crackers to serve

Combine chili sauce, hot catsup, tomato paste, mushrooms, tuna, shrimp, pickle relish, olives, Worcestershire sauce and A-1 sauce. It will be chunky. This keeps several weeks refrigerated. Serves 25 to 30.

Mrs. Rowland V. Firth (Susan)

Azalea's Anchovy Dip

8 ounces cream cheese
1 can anchovy fillets,
   undrained, cut up
Juice of 1 to 2 lemons or limes

3 cloves garlic, crushed and
   minced
Melba toast or crackers to serve

Blend all ingredients until thoroughly mixed. Refrigerate several hours before serving. Best with melba toast or crackers. Yields 1½ cups.

Mrs. Edward Konop (Rita)

Ceviche

1 pound white fish, cubed
1 cup lime juice
1 tablespoon olive oil
½ teaspoon mustard seed
½ cup chopped celery
½ cup chopped onion
½ cup green bell pepper,
   chopped
2 tablespoons chopped
   cilantro

2 tablespoons chopped or
   minced parsley
½ cup ripe olives, sliced
2 jalapeño peppers, seeded
   and sliced
6 cherry tomatoes, halved
Lettuce, hot sauce, tortilla chips
   to serve

Marinate fish overnight in lime juice. Drain, cover with olive oil. Add mustard seed, celery, onion, bell pepper, cilantro, parsley, olives, jalapeño peppers, and tomatoes. Toss lightly, chill. Serve on a bed of lettuce wtih tortilla chips and hot sauce.

Mrs. Henry A. Pate (Patricia)

Leslie's Ceviche

1 pound raw fish, cubed
12 ounces fresh lime juice
1 onion, chopped
2 medium tomatoes or 10 cherry tomatoes, chopped
30 Spanish olives, sliced
1/8 teaspoon cumin
20 capers

1/4 cup olive oil
7 tablespoons chopped parsley
1 teaspoon oregano
1 1/2 teaspoons fresh cilantro
Tortilla chips to serve
Lettuce, shredded

Place fish in glass bowl, cover with lime juice and let stand at room temperature for 6 to 8 hours. Check by tasting, do not let stand too long. Drain fish and pat dry. Combine remaining ingredients. Add to fish. Cover and refrigerate. Serve with tortilla chips or on shredded lettuce. Serves 5 to 6.

Leslie Rost

Hot Crab Dip

1/2 cup butter
4 to 5 cloves garlic, minced
2 onions, finely chopped
1 green bell pepper, finely chopped
2 tablespoons flour
1 (12 ounce) can evaporated milk
1 teaspoon curry powder

1 (6 ounce) jar Old English cheese
1 pound fresh crab meat
1/4 teaspoon salt
Tabasco sauce to taste
Pepper to taste
Worcestershire sauce to taste
Chips to serve

Sauté garlic, onions and pepper in butter. Add flour and milk gradually. Cream sauce with vegetables. If too thick, add regular sweet milk. Add curry powder, cheese, crab meat, salt, pepper, Tabasco and Worcestershire sauce. Serve with chips. Serves 15.

Susan Hasslocher
Guild President 1984-1985

Yogurt Vegetable Dip

1 tablespoon grated carrot
2 tablespoons grated onion
1 teaspoon grated green bell pepper
1/2 teaspoon salt

1/8 teaspoon garlic salt
1 cup plain yogurt
Fresh vegetables or crackers to serve

Mix together carrot, onion, bell pepper, salt, garlic salt and yogurt. Cover and chill. Serve with fresh vegetables or crackers. Yields 1 1/4 cups.

Mrs. Robert Shoop (Sharon)

Hot Crab Meat Dip

1 cup of white lump crab meat	1 tablespoon chopped parsley
1 cup soft bread crumbs, soaked in milk	1 teaspoon minced onion
	1/2 teaspoon salt
4 hard cooked eggs, finely chopped	1/8 teaspoon red pepper
	1 cup dry bread crumbs, sauté in butter
1 cup whipping cream	Assorted crackers to serve
1 1/2 cups mayonnaise	

Combine crab meat, soft bread crumbs, eggs, cream, mayonnaise, parsley, onion, salt, and red pepper; blend well. Place in a greased 1 1/2 quart casserole, top with dry bread crumbs. Bake at 350° for 20 minutes. Serves 8 to 10.

Mrs. Jay A. Matthews (Babs)
Guild President 1958-1959

Shrimp Dip

3 (8 ounce) packages cream cheese, softened	1 (4 ounce) jar chopped pimientos
1 medium onion, chopped	1/4 teaspoon pepper
1/4 teaspoon salt	1/2 teaspoon garlic salt
1 medium green bell pepper, chopped	3 tablespoons mayonnaise
	1 pound frozen small shrimp
	Chips to serve

Place softened cream cheese in a large bowl. Add onion, bell pepper, pimientos, salt, pepper, garlic salt and mayonnaise. Stir well. Place frozen shrimp in boiling water and cook 4 minutes. Drain shrimp in colander and rinse with cold water. Add shrimp to cream cheese mixture and stir well. Refrigerate for at least six hours. Serve with chips. Serves 16.

Mrs. Dan Green (Susan)

Shrimp With Remoulade Sauce

1 bunch green onions	2 teaspoons anchovy paste
1/2 bunch parsley	2 cups mayonnaise
1 clove garlic	1/2 cup Jataran mustard
2 tablespoons lemon juice	3 tablespoons Mr. Mustard
1/2 teaspoon celery seed	Boiled shrimp to serve
1 egg yolk	

Purée onions, parsley, garlic, lemon juice, celery seed, egg yolk and anchovy paste in blender. Add mayonnaise and mustards. Yields 3 cups.

Mrs. Sammy Juvé (Laura)

Cottage Cheese Dip

1½ cups cottage cheese
1 tablespoon grated onion
½ teaspoon salt
¼ teaspoon pepper

2 tablespoons minced pimiento
Dash of Worcestershire sauce
Chips to serve

Mash the cottage cheese well or force through a sieve. Add onion, seasonings and blend throughly. Serve with chips. Yields 1½ cups.

Lael Byers

Devil Ham Dip

4 ounces cream cheese
1 (4½ ounce) can deviled ham
Dash of Tabasco sauce
2 tablespoons mayonnaise

1 tablespoon prepared mustard
1 teaspoon minced green onion
Cocktail crackers or raw vegetables to serve

Mix cream cheese, deviled ham, Tabasco sauce, mayonnaise, mustard and onions together. Chill for several hours. Serve with crackers or raw vegetables. Yields 1¼ cups.

Mrs. Loy White (Marsha)

Mustard Dip

1 cup mayonnaise
½ cup sour cream

3 teaspoons brown mustard
Assorted raw vegetables to serve

Combine ingredients and mix well. Serve with raw vegetables. Yields 1½ cups.

Mrs. Dan Jardine (Lisa)

Vegetable And Cheese Dip

2 cups grated Cheddar cheese
1 bunch green onions, chopped
½ cup or more salsa to taste

1 pound fresh tomatoes, coarsely chopped
¼ to ½ cup chopped ripe olives
Tortilla chips to serve

Combine cheese, green onions, salsa, tomatoes, and ripe olives. Serve with tortilla chips. Yields 3 cups.

Mrs. Gary Glover (Carol)

Vegetable Dip

1/4 cup chopped watercress
1 tablespoon chopped chives
1/2 teaspoon dried tarragon
   leaves
3 flat anchovy fillets,
   chopped
2 teaspoons drained capers
2 tablespoons vegetable oil

1 teaspoon Dijon mustard
1 tablespoon lemon juice
1/8 teaspoon salt
1 egg
1 1/4 cups vegetable oil
Assorted vegetable dippers to
   serve

In a blender or food processor combine watercress, chives, tarragon, anchovies and capers. Blend until finely minced. Add 2 tablespoons oil, Dijon mustard, lemon juice, salt and egg blending until mixture thickens, about 20 seconds. Continue processing while slowly adding 1 1/4 cups vegetable oil. Serve with an assortment of vegetable dippers. Yields 2 cups.

Mrs. Henry A. Pate (Patricia)

Nacho Dip

1 (16 ounce) can jalapeño
   refried beans
Guacamole dip, use 3 avocados
1 (8 ounce) carton sour
   cream

1 (4 1/2 ounce) can chopped
   ripe olives
2 large tomatoes, diced
1 1/2 cups grated Longhorn
   cheese
Tortilla chips to serve

In a 9x13 inch dish layer ingredients in order listed starting with beans Serve with tortilla chips.

Mrs. Paul White (Suzanne)

Guacamole Dip

2 to 3 avocados, mashed
1 medium tomato, minced
1/2 small white onion, chopped
1 (4 ounce) can chopped
   green chilies
1 to 2 teaspoons lime juice

1/2 tablespoon chopped
   cilantro, optional
Seasoning salt to taste
Pepper to taste
Tabasco to taste
Tortilla chips to serve

Mix everything together well. Chill. Serve with tortilla chips.

Mrs. Larry Hall (Jane)
Fiesta Chairman 1982-1983

Mexican Bean Dip

1 (15 ounce) can refried beans	¾ cup picante sauce
4 ounces cream cheese, softened	1 (4 ounce) can diced green chilies
1 (12 ounce) carton sour cream	Salt, pepper and garlic powder to taste
1 bunch green onions, finely chopped	1 cup grated Monterey Jack or Cheddar cheese
	Tortilla chips to serve

Combine beans, cream cheese, sour cream, onions, picante sauce, green chilies, salt, pepper and garlic powder. Place in a 1½ quart baking dish. Sprinkle top with grated cheese. Bake 1 hour at 300°. Serve with chips. Serves 15. *You may also cover with guacamole after removing from oven if you wish.*

Mrs. Allan L. Williams (Rose Betty)

Rita's Famous Salsa Especial

3 to 4 jalapeños, seeds and all	1 teaspoon salt
1 clove garlic	1 (28 ounce) can tomatoes
1 small onion, chopped	Tortilla chips to serve

Put jalapeños, garlic and onion into a blender with salt. Drain juice from tomatoes into blender. Process only slightly. Add tomatoes and blend only until mixed, try to leave tomatoes a little chunky. Best refrigerated a day or two. Serve with chips. Keeps for weeks. Yields 3½ cups.

Mrs. Edward Konop (Rita)

Spinach Dip Spread

1 (10 ounce) package frozen spinach, thawed	1 cup sour cream
1 package dry vegetable soup mix	3 tablespoons finely chopped onion
1 (8 ounce) can sliced water chestnuts	1 cup mayonnaise
	Assorted crackers to serve

Combine spinach, soup mix, water chestnuts, sour cream, onion, and mayonnaise. Chill. Serve with crackers. Yields 2 cups.

Mrs. Mark Veltri (Pam)

Picadillo Dip

1	pound ground beef	1/2	teaspoon ground cumin
1	onion, finely chopped	1	teaspoon salt
1	clove garlic, crushed	1	tablespoon parsley, basil or
1	(10 ounce) can whole		oregano
	tomatoes	1/2	cup seedless raisins,
1	(8 ounce) can tomato sauce		plumped in 1/4 cup hot
1	tablespoon vinegar		stock or water
1	teaspoon sugar	1/2	cup slivered blanched
1	teaspoon cinnamon		almonds
1/2	teaspoon ground cloves		Tortilla chips to serve

Brown meat, onion and garlic. Drain, add remaining ingredients except raisins and almonds, let simmer until all flavors are mixed, about 30 minutes. Add raisins and almonds. If you prefer crunchier almonds, add just before serving. Can be made the night before serving and refrigerated. Serves 8 to 10. *May substitute olives for raisins, lean beef or pork roast for ground beef or 2 fresh tomatoes peeled and chopped for 1 cup canned tomatoes.*

Mrs. Margaret Fries

Sombrero Dip

1/2	pound ground beef	1	(8 ounce) can kidney beans
1/2	cup chopped onion,	1/2	cup grated sharp cheese
	divided	1/4	cup chopped green olives
1/4	cup chili sauce		Tortilla or corn chips to serve
1/2	teaspoon salt		
1/2	teaspoon chili powder		

Brown meat and 1/4 cup of onion; drain. Stir in chili sauce, salt and chili powder. Mash in beans; heat and stir in cheese. Top with olives and remaining onions. Serve with chips. Freezes well. Yields 1 1/2 cups.

Mrs. Willy Scott (Janet)

Queso Dip

1	large onion, chopped	1	(4 ounce) jar pimiento,
2	pounds Velveeta cheese,		drained
	cubed		Chips to serve
4	(4 ounce) cans chopped		
	green chilies, drained		

Cook onion in microwave on HIGH until tender. Add remaining ingredients; cook, stirring often. This will thicken when served cooled.

Mrs. Edward Konop (Rita)

Hot Artichoke Seafood Dip

2 (14 ounce) cans artichoke
  hearts, drained and
  chopped
2 cups mayonnaise
2 cups grated Parmesan
  cheese

2 (16 ounce) packages frozen
  crab meat with shrimp,
  thawed, drained and flaked
1/2 cup dry seasoned bread
  crumbs
Assorted crackers to serve

Combine artichoke hearts, mayonnaise, Parmesan cheese and crab meat with shrimp; mixing well. Spoon into a lightly greased 1½ quart casserole. Top with bread crumbs. Bake at 325° for 15 to 20 minutes. Serve with assorted crackers. Serves 12 to 14.

Mrs. Willard Stout (Sugie)

Crab Spread

8 ounces cream cheese
1/4 cup mayonnaise
Juice of 1 lemon
1 (6½ ounce) can crab meat
2 tablespoons minced onion,
  more to taste

1/4 teaspoon curry powder,
  more to taste
Salt to taste
Assorted crackers, to serve

Combine cream cheese, mayonnaise and lemon juice. Add crab meat, onion, curry powder and salt. Chill several hours. Serve with crackers. This spread is better if made a day ahead.

Lynn Schaefer

Salmon Ball

2 (8 ounce) packages cream
  cheese, softened
2 tablespoons lemon juice
3 teaspoons grated onion
2 teaspoons horseradish
1/2 teaspoon salt
Dash of Worcestershire sauce

1/4 teaspoon Liquid Smoke
1/4 teaspoon cayenne pepper
1 (16 ounce) can red salmon,
  drained and flaked
1/2 cup chopped pecans
3 tablespoons minced parsley
Assorted crackers to serve

Combine cream cheese, lemon juice, onion, horseradish, salt, Worcestershire sauce, Liquid Smoke and cayenne pepper until well blended. Stir in salmon. Check seasonings, additional salt may be needed. Combine parsley and pecans, spread on waxed paper. Coat salmon mixture. Wrap in waxed paper and chill thoroughly. Yields 10 servings.

Mrs. John Stark (Kay)

Crab Mold

1	tablespoon unflavored gelatin	1	cup chopped celery
3	tablespoons water	1	cup chopped green onions
1	can cream of mushroom soup	1	cup mayonnaise
8	ounces cream cheese, softened	2	(7½ ounce) cans crab meat

Combine gelatin and water in a small saucepan. Add the mushroom soup, heat until gelatin is dissolved. Pour into blender. Add cream cheese and process until smooth. Pour into bowl and fold in celery, green onions, mayonnaise and crab meat. Pour into an oiled 5 cup mold, cover with plastic wrap and refrigerate overnight. Yields a 5-cup mold.

Mrs. Gene Reinhart (Pamela)

Oyster Roll

2 (8 ounce) packages cream cheese, softened
2 (3¾ ounce) cans smoked oysters, drained and mashed
3 to 4 green onions, chopped
1 teaspoon Worcestershire sauce
1 tablespoon mayonnaise
Dash of salt and pepper
Chopped fresh parsley, onion tops or almonds
Assorted crackers to serve

Combine cream cheese and oysters. Add onions, Worcestershire sauce, mayonnaise, salt and pepper. Mix well. Form into a round or oblong shape. Sprinkle with fresh parsley, onion tops, or almonds. Chill and serve with crackers. Serves 10 to 12.

Mrs. Sammy Juvé (Laura)

Ruzenjka's Tuna Cheese Ball

3 ounces cream cheese, softened
1 tablespoon mayonnaise
1 (7 ounce) can tuna, drained
1 teaspoon horseradish
¼ teaspoon garlic salt
¼ teaspoon onion salt
½ teaspoon soy sauce
1 tablespoon capers
Assorted crackers to serve

Combine cream cheese, mayonnaise, tuna, horseradish, garlic salt, onion salt, soy sauce, and capers. Shape into ball. Chill. Serve with assorted crackers.

Mrs. Steve Bradley (Pam)

Turkey Paté

1 cup ground smoked turkey
8 ounces cream cheese, softened
3 tablespoons mayonnaise

½ cup chopped pecans
Chopped parsley to roll
Assorted crackers to serve

Process turkey, cream cheese, mayonnaise and pecans in food processor until well blended. Shape into a ball then roll in parsley. Serve with crackers.

Mrs. Fred J. Markham (Marilyn)

Calico Mold

1 envelope unflavored gelatin
1 cup sour cream
1 cup water
2 cups grated Cheddar cheese
1 (4 ounce) can diced green chilies

2 tablespoons diced pimiento
2 tablespoons finely chopped ripe olives
1 tablespoon onion, chopped
Crackers to serve

In a small saucepan, sprinkle gelatin over cold water. Let stand 3 or 4 minutes to soften. Stir over low heat until dissolved. Combine sour cream and Cheddar cheese. Stir in chilies, pimiento, ripe olives, and onion. Blend in dissolved gelatin. Pour into a mold that has been lined with plastic wrap. Fold wrap over top and refrigerate until firm, about 3 to 4 hours. Serve with tortilla chips or crackers. *Add 1 teaspoon cumin, 1 teaspoon salt, and 1 teaspoon minced garlic for a spicier taste. Use a Texas shaped cake pan for mold if desired, then mark your favorite city with a ripe olive!*

Mrs. Jerry Don Landers (Sherri)

Judy's Jezebel

8 ounces cream cheese, softened
1 (8 ounce) jar apple jelly
1 (8 ounce) jar pineapple preserves
¼ cup prepared mustard

3 ounces cream style horseradish
1 tablespoon peppercorns, crushed
Assorted crackers to serve

Place cream cheese on serving tray to soften. Combine apple jelly, pineapple preserves, mustard, horseradish and peppercorns. Pour 1 cup Jezebel sauce over cream cheese. Refrigerate remainder for your next party. Yields 2½ cups sauce.

Mrs. Ivan Erickson (Marsha)

Cheese Ball

2   (8 ounce) packages cream
    cheese, softened
8   ounces sharp Cheddar
    cheese, grated
1   (8 ounce) can crushed
    pineapple, drained

1/4 cup finely chopped green
    bell pepper
2   tablespoons chopped onion
1   tablespoon seasoned salt
1   cup chopped pecans
Assorted crackers to serve

Combine ingredients and shape into a ball. Roll in additional pecans if desired. Chill. Serve with crackers.

Mrs. Steve Bradley (Pam)

Tasty Spread For Pumpernickel

1   pound butter, softened
2   teaspoons garlic salt
2   teaspoons salt
1   teaspoon pepper
1   teaspoon sage

1   teaspoon dry mustard
1   teaspoon thyme
1   teaspoon rosemary
2   tablespoons dry parsley
Pumpernickel bread

Mix butter, garlic salt, salt, pepper, sage, dry mustard, thyme, rosemary and parsley. Spread on both sides of Pumpernickel bread. Wrap in foil and heat at 300° for about 30 minutes. Yields 24 slices.

Bonnie Zipoy

Stuffed Mushroom Caps Florentine

1   pound large fresh
    mushrooms
2/3 cup butter, melted, divided
1   teaspoon salt
1/2 teaspoon black pepper
1/3 cup chopped onion
1   (10 ounce) package frozen
    chopped spinach, thawed
    and drained

1   large egg, slightly beaten
8   ounces cream cheese,
    softened
1/8 teaspoon nutmeg
1/3 cup bread crumbs
Pimiento rings optional

Brush mushrooms and remove stems. Sauté onion, salt and pepper in 1/3 cup butter. Remove from heat and beat in the spinach, egg, cheese, nutmeg and bread crumbs. Place mushroom caps on oiled cookie sheet. Using a small spoon, fill with the spinach filling. Brush the remaining 1/3 cup melted butter over the mushrooms and bake at 350° for 20 minutes. Serves 8 to 10. *Can be made ahead and frozen either before or after baking; appearance is better if they are frozen before baking. Decorate with small pimiento strips to serve at Christmas.*

Mary Coneway

Italian Style Stuffed Mushrooms

20 large fresh mushrooms,
   save about 10 to 12 stems
   and chop
½ pound bulk Italian sausage
3 tablespoons olive oil,
   divided

1 clove garlic, minced
2 tablespoons minced parsley
⅓ to ½ cup grated Parmesan
   cheese, divided
3 tablespoons butter

Sauté sausage with stems, garlic and 1 tablespoon oil. Add oil, parsley, ¼ cup cheese. Sauté mushrooms in butter. Fill mushrooms with stuffing, rounding tops. Top with remaining Parmesan cheese. Place in shallow pan and bake at 350° for 15 to 20 minutes. Serves 6 to 8.

Mrs. Larry Hall (Jane)
Fiesta Chairman 1982-1983

Crab Canapes

1 cup crab meat
1 cup grated sharp Cheddar
   cheese
½ cup mayonnaise

Grated onion to taste
Dash of Tabasco sauce
Salt and pepper
English muffins, halved

Combine crab meat, cheese, mayonnaise, onion, Tabasco sauce, salt and pepper. Spread on English muffins. Place under broiler for 7 to 10 minutes and serve immediately. Serves 8. *This mixture can be frozen.*

Mrs. Lester Gray (Cathy)

Oysters "Mosca"

2 or 3 cups Italian bread
   crumbs
1 cup grated Parmesan cheese
2 cloves garlic, finely
   chopped

Parsley
Lemon juice
2 pounds raw oysters
Olive oil

Combine bread crumbs, Parmesan cheese, garlic and parsley. Sprinkle oysters with lemon juice. Dip oysters one by one into bread crumb mixture. Place next to each other in pan. Dribble olive oil over all. Bake at 500° until bubbling. Serves 10 to 15.

Mrs. Steve Robirds (Gay)

• *To peel garlic, drop in boiling water for 5 minutes to loosen skins.*

Chinese Shrimp Toast

8	ounces raw shrimp, shelled and cleaned	1	teaspoon minced ginger root
1	tablespoon blanched pork or bacon fat, minced	1/4	teaspoon sugar
8	water chestnuts	1	teaspoon salt
1	egg white	1	tablespoon chopped cilantro
1	tablespoon green onions minced, white part only	15	slices day old bread, crusts trimmed, cut into 4 triangles
1	tablespoon dry sherry		
1½	tablespoons cornstarch	2	cups peanut oil

Blend shrimp with pork fat and water chestnuts in food processor and process. Beat egg white with remaining ingredients except bread and oil. Add to shrimp mixture and mix well. If time permits, cover and refrigerate overnight. Just before serving, spread shrimp paste generously on bread triangles. Heat oil in wok or deep fryer to 375°. Fry triangles, paste side down for 1 to 2 minutes. Turn and fry for a few seconds more. Remove with slotted spoon; drain on paper towels. Serve immediately. Yields 60 triangles. *Shrimp toast may be fried ahead and refrigerated or frozen, then reheated, no thawing necessary. Set on a baking sheet lined with brown paper, and place in a 350° oven for 8 to 10 minutes or until crispy.*

Mrs. Paul Groos (Honey)

Marinated Shrimp

1½	cups vegetable oil	1/2	cup red cooking wine
3/4	cup soy sauce	1½	teaspoons parsley flakes
1/4	cup Worcestershire sauce	3	cloves garlic, crushed
2	tablespoons dry mustard	1/3	cup lemon juice
4	tablespoons black pepper	2	pounds boiled shrimp, peeled and deveined
1/4	cup white vinegar		

Combine oil, soy sauce, Worcestershire sauce, dry mustard, pepper, vinegar, wine, parsley flakes, garlic and lemon juice. Add shrimp. Marinate at least overnight. Serve and enjoy. Serves 8 to 10.

Susan Hasslocher
Guild President 1984-1985

• *For garlic flavored potato chips, put a peeled garlic clove in a container with chips for several hours. Discard before serving chips.*

Calamari

12 ounces beer
2 cups flour
1 teaspoon salt
Pepper to taste

1 teaspoon paprika
3 pounds squid, cleaned and
cut into rings
Oil for deep frying

Combine beer, flour, salt, pepper and paprika. Dip squid rings into the batter and let excess run off. Drop carefully into hot oil, turn to brown on both sides. Remove as soon as brown, about 30 seconds to 1 minute. Fry only a few at a time. Serves 12 to 15.

Mrs. Edward Konop (Rita)

Baked Brie In Phyllo

1/4 cup apricot preserves
2 pounds Brie or Camembert
cheese
8 ounces frozen phyllo dough
(10 to 12, 18x11 inch,
pieces), thawed

1/2 cup butter, melted
Fresh dillweed, red or green
peppers, grapes, apples or
pears to garnish

Spread preserves on top of cheese. Wrap cheese in phyllo dough, brushing each sheet with melted butter. Keep unused dough covered with damp cloth while wrapping cheese. Turn cheese over, applying a sheet of phyllo dough for even distribution. Brush phyllo wrapped cheese with melted butter. Cover and refrigerate. Before serving, place the phyllo wrapped cheese in a shallow baking pan. Bake at 425° for 8 to 12 minutes or until golden, watch carefully. Serves 24 to 30. *Garnish with dillweed, grapes, apples and pears or other decorative fruit. Kumquats are also attractive. This is easy to take to a party. Bake before leaving, then the 10 to 15 minute ride provides perfect timing for immediate serving.*

Mrs. Gary Hansen (Jean)

Toasted Cheese Appetizer

1/2 cup mayonnaise
1/4 cup grated Parmesan cheese
Salt and pepper to taste
Dash of Worcestershire sauce

Red onion, thinly sliced
Cocktail Rye or Pumpernickel
bread

Mix mayonnaise with cheese and seasonings. Put one slice of onion on each slice of cocktail bread. Cover onion with mayonnaise mixture. Sprinkle with additional grated Parmesan cheese. Place on cookie sheet. Broil until brown. This cooks quickly, watch closely. Serves 24.

Mrs. Allan L. Williams (Rose Betty)

35 Minute Brie Baked In Bread

1   can refrigerated French bread
1   pound round of Brie cheese, with rind

⅓   cup unsalted butter, softened
1   egg yolk
1   tablespoon water

Unroll the bread dough on pastry cloth, place the cheese in the center and cut the corners off the dough rectangle to be used to decorate the top. Wrap the dough around the cheese and place seam side down on a cookie sheet spread with softened butter. Use the dough scraps to make decorative shapes and put them on the top with a little of the yolk mixed with water. Brush the bread dough with the remaining yolk mixture and bake for 30 minutes at 350°. Serves 6 to 8. *Serve on a bread board and cut with a serrated knife. Can be served hot, warm or cold. It is delicious and will disappear quickly. I always make two!*

Mary Coneway

Cheese Party Cookies

1   cup butter, melted
2   cups sharp Cheddar cheese, grated
2   cups flour

1   teaspoon salt, optional
Dash red pepper
2   cups rice cereal

Pour melted butter over cheese, flour, salt and red pepper. Work in cereal with hands. Form into 1 inch balls, drop on ungreased cookie sheet and flatten with fork. Bake at 350° for 15 minutes. Freezes well.

Mrs. Lyle Koen (Pat)

Parmesan-Garlic Artichokes

1   (9 ounce) package frozen artichokes
24   Melba toast rounds
¼   cup butter, melted

¼   teaspoon garlic salt
Dash of pepper
3   tablespoons grated Parmesan cheese

Cook artichoke hearts according to package directions. Drain well, cut side down, on paper towels. Place each heart, cut side up, on a Melba toast round and place on a baking sheet. Stir together butter, garlic salt, and pepper; drizzle evenly onto crevices of artichokes and onto toast. Evenly, sprinkle with cheese. *At this point, you may cover and let stand at room temperature for as long as 6 hours.* Bake uncovered at 350° for 10 minutes or until hot. Yields 24 servings.

Mrs. Paul Outon (Peggy)

Cocktail Cheese Balls

½	cup margarine, softened	1	package dry onion soup
8	ounces sharp cheese, grated		mix
1	cup flour	¼	cup finely chopped parsley

Blend margarine and cheese well. Add flour, soup mix and parsley. Shape into bite sized balls. Bake at 400° for 5 to 10 minutes or until golden brown. Yields about 90. *May be frozen before baking if desired.*

Mrs. Chris John (Anne)

Green Onion Teasers

1	pound bacon, cooked and crumbled		Dash of pepper
2	bunches green onions, sliced	¾	cup mayonnaise
		1	pound loaf sandwich bread, crusts removed

Combine bacon, onions, pepper and mayonnaise; mixing well. Cut each slice of bread into 4 triangles, and toast on both sides. Spread about 1 teaspoon green onion mixture on each triangle. Yields approximately 60 triangles.

Mrs. Paul Outon (Peggy)

Spinach Balls

10	ounces frozen chopped spinach	½	cup grated Parmesan cheese, grated
2	cups herb seasoned stuffing mix	1	teaspoon black pepper
2	medium onions, finely chopped	1½	teaspoons thyme
1	teaspoon garlic salt	¾	cup melted butter
		5	large eggs, beaten

Cook spinach, omitting salt. Drain thoroughly; pat dry with paper towels. Add stuffing mix, onions, garlic salt, Parmesan cheese, thyme and black pepper; toss with fork until thoroughly mixed. Add butter and eggs; blend with fork. Form into balls about the size of a walnut. Bake on a greased shallow pan 18 to 20 minutes at 350°. Unbaked balls may be frozen and baked as needed. Yields 7 dozen.

Sandi Aiken

• *Americans spend an average of 30 minutes a day preparing meals. British spend 1 hour and the French 3 hours.*

Ratitos

1   (7 ounce jar) jalapeños,
    whole with stems
8   ounces Cheddar cheese,
    grated
1   cup buttermilk
1/2 cup flour, divided

1/4 cup plus 2 tablespoons
    cornmeal
1/2 teaspoon salt
Dash of pepper
Vegetable oil for frying

Slit each pepper on one side and remove seeds, leaving stems in place. Stuff peppers with grated cheese. To make batter, mix buttermilk, 1/4 cup flour, salt and pepper. Mix 1/4 cup remaining flour with cornmeal to make flour mixture. Dip each stuffed pepper in batter, roll in flour mixture, dip again in batter, and again in flour mixture. Set aside on waxed paper. Heat oil in deep fryer until very hot. Deep fry peppers until golden brown. Serve hot.

Mrs. Ben Morgan (LaRee)

Almond Bacon Hors d'Oeuvres

6   slices bacon, fried and
    crumbled
2   cups grated Loon cheese
1   cup mayonnaise
1/2 cup blanched almonds,
    sliced

1/2 teaspoon dried onion flakes
1/2 teaspoon dried garlic flakes
2   teaspoons Worcestershire
    sauce
1   loaf brick oven bread, thick
    sliced

Mix together all the ingredients, except bread. Trim bread and spread mixture over each slice. Cut each slice into 4 pieces. Place on cookie sheets and freeze until hard. Wrap and stack in freezer bags. When needed, bake at 400° for 10 to 12 minutes. Do not defrost before baking. Yields 36 servings.

Mrs. Roger W. Marcum (Debbie)

Grammy's Sausage Balls

1   pound bulk pork sausage
1   beaten egg
1/3 cup Herb Stuffing Mix
1/4 teaspoon sage
1/4 cup catsup

1/4 cup chili sauce
1   tablespoon soy sauce
2   tablespoons brown sugar
1   tablespoon white vinegar
1/2 cup water

Mix sausage, egg, stuffing mix and sage. Shape into bite sized balls. Combine catsup, chili sauce, soy sauce, brown sugar, vinegar and water; mix well. Add sausage balls and simmer 30 minutes.

Mrs. Larry Hall (Jane)
Fiesta Chairman 1982-1983

Sausage Balls In Cheese Pastry

1   pound hot pork sausage
3/4 cup dry bread crumbs
1/3 cup chicken broth
1/8 teaspoon ground nutmeg
1/4 teaspoon poultry seasoning
1 1/2 cups flour

1/4 teaspoon salt
1   teaspoon paprika
8   ounces Cheddar cheese,
    grated
1/2 cup butter, softened

Combine sausage, bread crumbs, broth, nutmeg and poultry seasoning. Form into small balls and fry in a dry skillet until done. Sift flour, salt and paprika into a large bowl. Stir in cheese. Cut in butter and work with hands until smooth. Pinch off tablespoons of dough and form around cooked sausage balls. Bake at 375° for 15 minutes. Yields 50 balls.

Mrs. Robert Shoop (Sharon)

Sausage Chestnut Balls

2   pounds seasoned bulk pork
    sausage

2   (8 ounce) cans water
    chestnuts, drained and
    halved

Form sausage into bite sized balls. Put a chestnut half in the middle each ball. Bake on ungreased cookie sheet at 400° until done. Yields 2

Mrs. Robert Shoop (Sharon)

Cocktail Pizza

1   pound ground round
1   pound bulk pork sausage
1   tablespoon oregano
1   tablespoon garlic salt
1   tablespoon Worcestershire
    sauce

1   pound Velveeta cheese,
    cubed
Rye party rounds
Grated Parmesan cheese

Brown meat and sausage together; sprinkle oregano, garlic salt, and Worcestershire sauce over meat as it browns. Drain meat mixture. Add Velveeta cheese, stir until cheese is melted and well blended. Spread on rye rounds and sprinkle with Parmesan cheese. Place on cookie sheet and broil until edges of rye slices are slightly brown and crisp. May be frozen at this point. Serves 20.

Mrs. Ross Burgh (Jo Lynne)
Guild President 1980-1981

Spicy Chicken Nachos

1 cup cooked chicken, diced	6 flour tortillas
1/2 cup water	6 slices round Monterey Jack
3 ounces picante sauce	cheese
1/4 teaspoon pepper	Sliced jalapeño peppers
1/2 teaspoon poultry seasoning	Sour cream
Vegetable Oil	

Combine chicken, water, picante sauce, pepper and poultry seasoning in a saucepan, heat thoroughly. Fry tortillas lightly in oil and drain. Distribute equal portions of the chicken mixture on the tortillas and top with a slice of cheese. Place completed tortillas on a cookie sheet and place pan on high rack of oven broiler. Broil until cheese bubbles. Remove from oven and using a pizza cutter or large knife, cut each tortilla into fourths. Garnish each section with a pepper. Serve with sour cream. Serves 2 to 3.

Susan Hasslocher
Guild President 1984-1985

Beef Wrap

8 ounces cream cheese, softened	1 (16 ounce) package thin sliced luncheon meat
3/4 cup sweet pickle relish	Toothpicks

Mix cream cheese and pickle relish until well blended. Spread mixture over each slice of meat and roll. Cut each roll into bite sized pieces and secure with toothpick.

Mrs. Marcus Bone (Beverly)
Fiesta Chairman 1983-1984

Tequila Tomatoes

2 pints cherry tomatoes, washed and hulled	3 tablespoons coarse or Kosher salt
2 cups Tequila	1 tablespoon grated lemon peel
2 limes, sliced	

Using a skewer, make 3 or 4 holes in tomatoes. Place in a bowl with Tequila and limes. Cover, chill 3 hours or overnight. Remember, the longer they marinate, the more they absorb. Combine coarse or Kosher salt with lemon peel. Serve as a dipping salt with tomatoes. Serves 8 to 16.

Mrs. Bruce Blakely (Lynn)

Marinated Carrots

5	cups sliced carrots	3/4	cup white vinegar
1	medium onion, chopped	1	teaspoon perpared mustard
1	small green bell pepper, chopped	1	teaspoon Worcestershire sauce
1	can tomato soup	1	teaspoon salt
1/2	cup vegetable oil	1	teaspoon pepper
1	cup sugar		

Cook carrots 15 minutes. Drain and cool. Combine carrots, onion, and bell pepper. Add soup, oil, sugar, vinegar, mustard, Worcestershire sauce, salt and pepper; mix well. Cover and marinate for 12 hours or overnight. Drain and serve. Yields 5 cups. Keeps 2 to 3 weeks if refrigerated. Liquid may be reused.

Mrs. Tom Connolly (Pat)

Pickled Vegetables

1	cup boiling water	Assorted fresh vegetables-
1	chicken bouillon cube	mushrooms, carrots,
1/2	cup white vinegar	zucchini, cauliflower, whole
1	package Italian dressing mix	green beans, artichoke hearts

Dissolve bouillon in water. If using carrots, cut into strips and boil for 2 minutes in bouillon mixture. Remove carrots. Add vinegar to dressing mix, then add to bouillon. Add vegetables and refrigerate at least 24 hours, shaking container from time to time.

Mrs. Steve Bradley (Pam)

Texas Trash

1	pound margarine	15	ounces Wheat Chex
3	tablespoons seasoned salt	12	ounces Rice Chex
1	tablespoon garlic salt	12	ounces Corn Chex
1	ounce Tabasco sauce	15	ounces Cheerios
4	ounces Worcestershire sauce	10	ounces pretzel sticks
1 3/4	pounds peanuts	12	ounces Cheese Nips

Slowly melt margarine and add seasoned salt, garlic salt, Tabasco and Worcestershire sauce. Preheat oven to 225°. Mix all cereals, peanuts, crackers and pretzels in large bowl. Pour liquid mixture over dry ingredients and stir until well blended. Spread on two cookie sheets and bake 30 minutes or until mixture is dry and crisp.

Susan Hasslocher
Guild President 1984-1985

Beverages

Superdrink

½ cup yogurt
½ banana, frozen and cut into
   chunks
Frozen blueberries, strawberries
   or fresh peaches

⅓ cup apple juice
1 tablespoon wheat germ
1 tablespoon soy protein
   powder or dried milk

Combine all ingredients in blender until smooth. Pour over ice cubes.
Serves 1.

Mrs. Willy Scott (Janet)

Nancy's Punch

Raspberry sherbert
Pineapple sherbert

3 (64 ounce) bottles Sprite,
   chilled, no substitute

Place large chunks in equal amounts of each sherbert to fill a punch bowl
⅔ full. Pour chilled Sprite over sherbert. Serve immediately, but it will
stay cold a long time. Serves 18 to 20. *This has been well received when I
have served it at a ladies' meeting or a wedding reception. It is lovely during
the holidays, as well as during the spring. It's pink and frothy and amaz-
ingly tasty!*

Mrs. Wade Anderson (Nancy)

Grape Punch

1 (10 ounce) jar grape jelly
1 (64 ounce) bottle 7-Up,
   divided

1 lime, sliced
⅓ cup lime juice
10 whole cloves

Combine jelly, 1 cup carbonated beverage, cloves and lime slices in a
saucepan. Heat to boiling, stirring until jelly is dissolved; simmer 5
minutes. Cool; strain to remove lime slices. Stir in lime juice. Chill
thoroughly. Add remaining carbonated beverage. Yields ½ gallon or 18
(4 ounce) servings.

Mrs. Paul Groos (Honey)

• *To create a clear ice ring, use boiled and cooled water.*

Nancy's Simple Summer Cooler

1   part pineapple juice   5   parts Sprite, chilled

Mix pineapple juice and Sprite. Pour over ice.

Mrs. Kerry Merritt (Nancy)
Guild President 1969-1970

Fruit Punch

3½ cups chilled ginger ale   1   teaspoon lemon juice
1   quart chilled cranberry   1   cup chilled apple juice
     juice cocktail   Orange slices to garnish

Combine all ingredients into a punch bowl. Add ice and float orange
slices on top. Serves 16.

Mrs. Larry Hall (Jane)
Fiesta Chairman 1982-1983

Strawberry Punch

2   (6 ounce) cans frozen   2   quarts ginger ale
     limeade   Crushed ice
2   (10 ounce) packages frozen
     strawberries

Mix limeade, strawberries and ginger ale. Pour over crushed ice. Serves
25.

Mrs. David Hart (Sue)
Fiesta Chairman 1985-1986

Frosted Coffee

8   cups cold brewed coffee   1   quart soft vanilla ice cream
2   cups sweet milk   1   quart firm vanilla ice cream

Before serving, mix coffee with milk, blend in the soft ice cream. Add
firm ice cream by spoonsful. The floating scoops of firm ice cream keep
the liquid well chilled and will add to the attractiveness of individual
servings. Serves 24.

Mrs. Ron Tobin (Bonnie)

Mulled Cider

2   quarts apple cider
3/4 cup brown sugar
1   teaspoon ground cloves

1   teaspoon ground allspice
3   cinnamon sticks
1/4 teaspoon nutmeg

Combine all ingredients in a saucepan and simmer 20 minutes. Strain before serving. Serves 8 to 10. *This cider makes your house smell wonderful during the holidays and is also a good drink.*

Mrs. Henry Mayes (Kathy)

Melanie's Louisiana Breakfast Coffee

2½ cups ground coffee
1½ ounces whole anise seeds
1½ tablespoons finely grated
    dried orange peel

Sugar to serve
Half and half cream to serve

Mix coffee, anise seeds, orange peel and store tightly, covered in refrigerator or freezer until needed. Thaw and brew, using the proportions of coffee to water you prefer. Serve with sugar and cream.

Mary Coneway

Brazilian Coffee

1/3 cup unsweetened cocoa
1   teaspoon ground cinnamon
1/2 teaspoon salt
1   (14 ounce) can sweetened
    condensed milk

2   cups water
3½ cups strong coffee
Cinnamon sticks
Ground nutmeg

Combine cocoa, cinnamon and salt into a 3 quart saucepan. Add sweetened condensed milk, stirring until smooth. Place pan over medium heat; gradually stir in water and coffee. Heat thoroughly. *Do not boil.* Garnish each cup with a cinnamon stick, and sprinkle with nutmeg. Refrigerate leftovers. Yields about 7 cups. *Add 1/2 cup brandy and 1/4 cup light rum along with water and coffee, if desired.*

Mrs. Larry Hall (Jane)
Fiesta Chairman 1982-1983

• *Put dates and other sticky dried fruits in the freezer 1 to 2 hours and you'll be able to cut or chop them easily. Also, dip knife or scissors in hot water now and then while you're cutting.*

Old Fashioned Hot Chocolate

2   (1 ounce) squares
    unsweetened chocolate
1⅓ cups boiling water
1   quart milk
⅓   cup sugar

Pinch of salt
½   teaspoon vanilla extract
Marshmallows or whipped
    cream to serve

Place chocolate in top of a double boiler; bring water to a boil. Reduce heat to low; cook until chocolate melts. Gradually add 1⅓ cups boiling water, stirring constantly. Remove from heat and set aside. Combine scalded milk, sugar and salt in a saucepan. Add chocolate mixture, stirring well. Cool over low heat, stirring occasionally. Remove from heat; stir in vanilla. If desired, top with marshmallows or whipped cream. Yields 6 cups.

Mrs. David Hart (Sue)
Fiesta Chairman 1985-1986

Hot Chocolate Mix

8   quarts dry milk
1   (11 ounce) jar Coffeemate
    or powdered creamer
1   (2 pound) box Nestle's
    Quik

1   (16 ounce) box powdered
    sugar
1   tablespoon cinnamon

Mix all ingredients and store in a covered container. Four heaping teaspoons of mix in one cup boiling water yields one delicious chocolatey drink.

Marian Herbst

Kentucky Mint Juleps

1   teaspoon sugar
½   teaspoon spring water
4   sprigs mint

Shaved ice
2   jiggers of good Kentucky
    bourbon

Make a syrup with the sugar and water. Bruise 3 sprigs of mint and rub the rim of the julep glass. Discard the mint. Fill glass ¾ full with shaved ice. Add the bourbon and let set a moment before pouring the syrup mixture over it. Stir gently. Garnish with the remaining mint sprig. Yields 1 serving.

Mrs. Roger W. Marcum (Debbie)

Cayman Cooler

Tall glass filled with ice
Milk
1   jigger Kahlua

1   jigger Vodka
Cola

Fill glass with milk to within 3/4" of top; add Kahlua, and Vodka. Top with a splash of cola. Serves 1.

Mrs. David Hart (Sue)
Fiesta Chairman 1985-1986

Orange Irish

1/4   cup Grand Marnier
1/4   cup Irish Creme

1/4   cup milk

Mix together and pour into a glass. Serves 1.

Mrs. Berry Gannaway
Fiesta Chairman 1984-1985

Ramos Gin Fizz

1   egg
1   tablespoon sugar
2   tablespoons concentrated
     lemon juice
Splash of orange juice

Splash of cream
2   drops orange flower water
1   ounce Gin
Cracked ice

Pour into a blender and process until smooth. Serves 1.

Mrs. Larry Hall (Jane)
Fiesta Chairman 1982-1983

Sparkling Wine Punch

1   (46 ounce) can pineapple
     juice
1   (12 ounce) can frozen
     lemonade concentrate

1   (46 ounce) can apple juice
4   (34 ounce) bottles sparkling
     wine, champagne or ginger
     ale, chilled

Combine juices, stir. Store in freezer overnight. When ready to serve, remove from freezer 3 to 4 hours before using so juice can become slush like. Break into pieces and place in a large punch bowl. Add wine or champagne or ginger ale. Do not add ice. The slush keeps the punch cold. Yields 40 six ounce servings. *Will freeze indefinitely.*

Mrs. Henry Mayes (Kathy)

Sangria

¾ cup sugar	1 bottle dry red wine
¾ cup water	1 (28 ounce) bottle
1 seedless orange	carbonated water
1 lemon	

In a saucepan combine sugar and water; heat, stirring until boiling. Cook rapidly 3 to 4 minutes; cool. Slice orange and lemon, then half the orange slices. Place in a bowl; pour in sugar syrup and let stand 3 to 4 hours. Before serving, place fruits and syrup in pitcher and stir in wine and carbonated water. Serve in stemmed goblets. Serves 6 to 8.

Mrs. Robert Bluntzer (Jo)

Christmas Wine Punch

3 cups orange juice	½ cup brandy
1½ cups sugar	1 bottle champagne
1½ cups lemon juice	1 cup frozen whole
1 bottle Sauterne	strawberries, halved

Combine orange juice, sugar and lemon juice, stirring until sugar dissolves. Chill. Pour orange juice mixture into a punch bowl and stir in Sauterne, brandy and champagne. Float berries and oranges on top. Serves 24.

Mrs. Bill Balcezak (Sharon)

Sparkling Holiday Punch

1 (10 ounce) package frozen strawberries, thawed	2 cups light rum
	3 bottles cold duck, chilled
2 limes, thinly sliced	
2 (6 ounce) cans frozen daiquiri mix	

Pour water into a ice ring and freeze. Arrange berries and lime slices around mold and add enough water to anchor fruit to ice. Freeze. Combine daiquiri mix and rum. Add ice ring very carefully and pour in cold duck. Yields 20 five ounce servings.

Mrs. Ron Mullen (Carole)
Guild President 1981-1982

Eggnog

12 egg yolks
1 cup sugar
2 cups bourbon
1 cup brandy
1/2 teaspoon salt

12 egg whites
1 quart milk
1 pint whipping cream
Nutmeg to taste

Beat egg yolks with sugar until thick. Slowly add bourbon and brandy, then chill for several hours. Add salt to egg whites and beat until stiff. Stir milk into bourbon mixture. Fold in beaten egg whites and beaten whipped cream. Chill until ready to serve. Garnish each serving with nutmeg. Yields 30 five ounce servings.

Mrs. Jack Leo (Cindy Sherrell)
Guild President 1979-1980

Health Kick Punch

Juice of 10 oranges
Juice of 6 lemons
6 medium bananas, sliced
1/2 cup crushed pineapple
1 1/2 cups light rum

1 cup honey
1 cup banana flavored liqueur
2/3 cup grenadine syrup
6 drops bitters
Lemon slices

Combine orange juice, lemon juice, bananas, pineapple, rum, honey, banana flavored liqueur, grenadine and bitters in a large bowl, stirring well. Pour punch mixture a third at a time into a blender and blend until smooth. Pour punch into large punch bowl and float lemon slices on top. Serve over crushed ice. Yields 3 quarts.

Mrs. Bob Richardson (Susan)

Citrus Punch

1 (6 ounce) can frozen orange juice, undiluted
1 (6 ounce) can frozen lemonade, undiluted

1 (46 ounce) can pineapple juice
1 1/2 quarts ginger ale
White rum to taste

Mix orange juice, lemonade, pineapple juice and ginger ale. Add white rum to taste. Yields 1 gallon.

Mrs. Ron Tobin (Bonnie)

Boulder Sunrises

1   fifth champagne
1   fifth orange juice
16 ounces Vodka

20 ounces ginger ale
4   ounces grenadine

Pour all ingredinets into a large punch bowl. Yields approximately 3 quarts. *This punch is absolutely wonderful, but be careful! It is potent!*

Mrs. Bill Balcezak (Sharon)

Fiesta Punch

1   (6 ounce) bottle Red
    Passion Mix
1   (12 ounce) can frozen
    orange juice
1   (12 ounce) can frozen
    lemonade

1   fifth Vodka
½   fifth Tequila
1   (2 liter) bottle ginger ale

Combine all ingredients. Serve chilled. Yields ½ gallon punch.

Mrs. Marcus Bone (Beverly)
Fiesta Chairman 1983-1984

Rosy Wassail

1   pint cranberry juice
    cocktail
1   (6 ounce) can frozen orange
    juice, thawed
2   cups water

1   tablespoon sugar
¼   teaspoon allspice
1   bottle dry Sauterne
Oranges, to serve
Cloves, to serve

In a saucepan combine cranberry juice, orange juice, water, sugar and allspice and bring to a simmer. Add Sauterne and heat through. Do not boil. Stud a thick orange with whole cloves. Pour punch into a heated bowl and float oranges. Serves 12 to 14.

Mrs. Jerry Hering (Carol)
Fiesta Chairman 1979-1980

• *Fiesta is a wonderful attraction for everyone. Friends of volunteers come from all over Texas just to have the chance to work in our Nacho booths!!*

Fruited Rosé

1	fifth Rosé wine	¼	cup sugar
1	(6 ounce) can frozen limeade	1	(6 ounce) can pineapple juice

Combine all ingredients and heat until simmering. Serve hot. Serves 6.

Mrs. Berry Gannaway
Fiesta Chairman 1984-1985

Flaming Cappuccino

	Lemon slices	2	tablespoons chocolate syrup, divided
	Sugar		
¾	cup Galliano liqueur, divided	1	cup whipping cream, whipped
6	cups hot coffee	6	cinnamon sticks

Rinse glass with hot water; dry. Dip rim of glass in lemon juice, then sugar making a ½ inch band around top. Rotate glass over the flame of an Irish coffee burner or alcohol burner until the sugar crystalizes. Pour 2 tablespoons Galliano in glass. Rotate over flame until liqueur ignites. Fill with coffee to bottom of sugar rim; stir in 1 teaspoon chocolate syrup. Top with whipped cream; garnish with a cinnamon stick. Repeat for remaining servings. Serves 6.

Mrs. Don Davis (Pat)
Fiesta Chairman 1976-1977, Guild President 1983-1984

Coffee Punch

48	cups brewed coffee	3	cups whipping cream
1	cup sugar	3	cups coffee liqueur

While coffee is still hot, mix sugar and coffee in a large container. Add cream and liqueur. Beat well with a rotary beater. Before serving, bring the mixture to a boil. Yields 54 cups.

Mrs. Gary Glover (Carol)

- *Little Fiesta has seen many fun activities: the Petting Zoo, Ferris Wheel, Train Ride and Fire Truck. Children even today enjoy the Fiesta Faces, Little Artists and Balloons.*

Homemade "Bailey's" Irish Creme

1¾ cups bourbon
1 (14 ounce) can sweetened
   condensed milk
1 cup whipping cream
4 eggs

3 tablespoons chocolate syrup
1 teaspoon dry instant coffee
1 teaspoon vanilla extract
¼ teaspoon almond extract

Process all ingredients in blender until smooth. Will keep in refrigerator up to 3 weeks. Stir before serving. Serves 4.

Jamie Dicus

Kahlua

⅔ cup dry instant coffee
2 cups water
4 cups sugar

1 vanilla bean
1 fifth brandy

Mix instant coffee, water and sugar. Heat and stir until sugar is dissolved. When cool, add vanilla bean and brandy. Store in ½ gallon dark glass jug and age for at least 3 weeks. Yields ½ gallon. *The brandy makes a better Kahlua than using Vodka.*

Mrs. Felix Wolff (Rosann)

Hot Buttered Rum Mix

1 pound butter
1 teaspoon cinnamon
1 teaspoon cloves
1 teaspoon allspice

1 teaspoon nutmeg
2 pounds light brown sugar
3 eggs, beaten
Rum

Melt butter. Add all spices. Pour over sugar and blend in eggs. Pour into pint jars. Refrigerate for at least 24 hours before using. For each mug, use 2 large tablespoons mix, a jigger of rum and hot water. Yields 4½ pints.

Mrs. Edward Konop (Rita)

- *To make homemade vanilla extract: combine 2 cups vodka or brandy and 5 vanilla beans (cut into 1 inch pieces) in an airtight jar. Cover and let stand 6 to 8 weeks. After half of extract is used, add more vodka to cover the beans.*

"Listening To Night Shadows"

Daryl Howard was awarded her B.F.A. ('70) from Sam Houston State University, Huntsville; and her M.F.A. was earned at The University of Texas at Austin. Traditional woodblock printmaking was guided by private studies with internationally famed Hodaka Yoshida, of Tokyo; and by study with the Hopi on their mesas of northern Arizona. She was a member of the faculty of Laguna Gloria Art Museum School and has taught art in public schools of Austin and Bryan, Texas. A unique experience was her work as a faculty member of the Department of Defense Schools, Tokyo, Japan.

Daryl's "Listening To Night Shadows" has a 22 carat gold leaf background controlled in its brilliance by cut lines of natural mulberry paper, and watercolored clouds torn from Japanese rice paper. All of these selected pieces are made "as one" by making a pigment from ground colored earths she found while exploring deserts of Arizona, New Mexico and Texas.

Her special workshops on woodblock printing and collage are numerous, including Laguna Gloria Art Museum; Artist in Residence sponsored by the Texas Commission on the Arts; guest artist for a Santa Fe workshop sponsored by the National Endowment for the Arts; Visual Arts Review Panel, by the Texas Commission on the Arts Education Advisory Panel; and others. She is listed in Art in America, a register of American Artists.

Gallery affiliations include: Garner and Smith, Austin; El Taller, Santa Fe and Taos; Suzanne Brown, Scottsdale; Odyssey, San Antonio; Village Artistry, Carmel, California; John Szoke Graphics, New York; Bent Tree, Lubbock; and Shoshana Wayne, Los Angeles.

Daryl, since 1972, has exhibited in eleven Fiestas sponsored by Laguna Gloria Art Museum and 72 other shows in Texas, Alabama, the Philippines, Japan, Florida, Nevada, New Mexico, Nebraska, Louisiana, Arizona and Tokyo.

Soups, Salads & Sandwiches

My Favorite Raspberry Soup

1 cup raspberries	½ cup sour cream
1 cup rosé wine	½ cup brown sugar

Put all ingredients into a blender or food processor and whirl until smooth. Chill overnight. Serve cold. Yields 6 one half cup servings.

Mrs. Paul Outon (Peggy)

Chilled Peach Soup

2 cups fresh ripe peaches, pitted, sliced, not peeled	2 cups sweet white wine
2 tablespoons sugar	1 cinnamon stick, crumbled
2 tablespoons lemon juice	⅛ teaspoon almond extract

Purée the raw peaches and place in a bowl. Cover with the sugar and lemon juice and set aside. Bring wine and cinnamon to a boil and simmer for 2 minutes. Strain and add almond extract. Add to the peach mixture and stir. Chill, stir again and serve. Serves 4 to 6.

Jean Reed

Gazpacho

1 (14 ounce) can whole tomatoes and juice	½ teaspoon freshly ground pepper
½ cup chopped celery	½ teaspoon Worcestershire sauce
½ cup chopped cucumbers	
1 small green bell pepper, sliced	1 (12 ounce) can V-8 juice
⅓ cup snipped parsley	1 (10 ounce) can Snap-E-Tom
1 clove garlic, minced	Sour cream to serve
½ cup chopped onion	Chopped green onions to garnish
⅛ teaspoon cumin	Crispy cooked bacon to garnish
3 tablespoons wine vinegar	Finely chopped avocado to garnish
2 tablespoons olive oil	
1 teaspoon salt	

Place tomatoes with juice into a food processor. Add celery, cucumber, green pepper, parsley, garlic and onion. Process very slightly. Add remaining ingredients and process for 30 seconds. Mixture should be lumpy. Chill and serve with a dollop of sour cream on top with garnishes sprinkled over the sour cream. This gazpacho keeps for over a week in the refrigerator. Serves 12.

Mrs. Bruce Knierim (Pam)
Fiesta Chairman 1981-1982

Chilled Avocado Soup With Cilantro

1   medium avocado, peeled
    and pitted
1   clove garlic, minced
1   green onion, chopped
¼   cup fresh cilantro, chopped

1   cup sour cream
2   cups chilled chicken broth
½   teaspoon salt
Dash of hot pepper sauce
Minced green onions to garnish

In a blender or food processor, combine avocado, garlic, green onions, cilantro, sour cream, chicken broth, salt and hot sauce. Purée until smooth, about 3 minutes. Cover and refrigerate for at least 2 hours. Serve with garnish of green onions. Serves 4 to 6.

Mrs. Garrel Fleming (Giny Puryear)

Easy Cheese Soup

¼   cup butter
¼   cup flour
2   cans chicken broth
2   cups milk or half and half
    cream
¼   teaspoon white pepper
2   tablespoons minced
    pimiento

¼   cup dry white wine
½   teaspoon Worcestershire
    sauce
¼ to ½ teaspoon Tabasco
    sauce
8   ounces sharp Cheddar
    cheese, grated

Melt butter in a heavy saucepan over low heat; add flour and stir until smooth. Cook 1 to 2 minutes, stirring constantly. Slowly add undiluted broth and milk and cook until thickened and bubbly. Add pepper, pimiento, wine, Worcestershire sauce and hot sauce; heat until boiling. Remove from heat and add cheese. Stir until melted. Serve immediately.

Mrs. Marcus Bone (Beverly)
Fiesta Chairman 1983-1984

Potato Soup

5   large new potatoes sliced
    with skins
2 to 3 carrots, chopped
6 to 7 slices of bacon
1   onion, chopped
2   ribs celery, chopped

1½   teaspoons salt
¼   teaspoon pepper
2   cups milk
2   cups half and half cream
Grated Cheddar cheese to
    garnish

Cook potatoes and carrots in water until tender. Drain. Sauté bacon until crisp, drain and crumble. Sauté onion and celery in 2 tablespoons bacon drippings. Combine all ingredients except cheese and simmer. You may add cornstarch to thicken somewhat. Garnish with cheese.

Mrs. C. Jay Middlebrook (Linda)

Cheese And Artichoke Soup

1/4 cup butter
1/2 cup diced onions
1/2 cup diced carrots
1/2 cup shredded celery
1/4 cup flour
1 1/2 tablespoons cornstarch
1/8 teaspoon baking soda
1 quart chicken broth
1 quart milk

2 cups grated extra sharp
    Cheddar cheese
Salt and pepper to taste
Beau Monde to taste
2 (14 ounce) cans artichoke
    hearts, quartered
Cayenne pepper for garnish
Parsley for garnish

Melt butter in a heavy skillet and sauté onions, carrots and celery. Mix together flour, cornstarch and baking soda, and add to vegetables. Add chicken broth and mix well. Add milk and stir until mixture boils and thickens. Reduce heat and add cheese. Stir until melted, then add artichokes. Garnish with a dash of cayenne pepper and parsley. Serves 6 to 8.

Mrs. David Hart (Sue)
Fiesta Chairman 1985-1986

Broccoli Cheese Soup

1 cup butter
1 1/2 onions, finely chopped
2 ribs celery, finely chopped
1 green bell pepper, finely
    chopped
1 quart chicken broth
1 tablespoon basil, finely
    chopped
2 to 3 cloves garlic, minced
2 bay leaves
1 1/2 pounds American cheese,
    grated

3 cups finely chopped
    broccoli
1/4 cup white wine
Splash of Marsala wine
1/2 cup flour
1/3 cup water
1/2 cup half and half cream
1/2 teaspoon paprika
Salt and white pepper to taste
Cayenne pepper to taste

Melt butter in a large saucepan and sauté bell pepper, onion, and celery until soft. Add chicken broth, basil, garlic and bay leaves. Bring to a boil, then reduce heat and add cheese, a little at a time wisking until smooth. Add broccoil and wines. Make a paste of the flour and water; stir into soup and cook 5 minutes. Add cream and paprika. Add salt and pepper to taste. Remove bay leaves before serving. Serves 6 to 8. *This soup freezes well.*

Mrs. John Allen (Becky)

Creamy Rice Soup

2 tablespoons butter
1 tablespoon minced onion
1/4 to 1/3 cup flour
4 cups chicken broth
2 cups cooked wild rice
1/2 teaspoon salt
1/3 cup minced ham

1/3 cup grated carrots
3 tablespoons chopped slivered almonds
1 cup half and half cream
2 tablespoons dry sherry, optional

Sauté onions in butter, blend in flour and gradually add broth. Cook until thickened. Stir in rice, salt, ham, carrots and almonds. Simmer about 5 minutes. Blend in the cream and sherry. Serves 6 to 8.

Mrs. Bill Zipoy (Bonnie)

Wild Rice Soup

4 slices bacon, chopped
1 cup finely chopped celery
1 cup finely chopped carrot
1 cup chopped mushrooms
1/2 cup chopped green onion
3 cups beef broth
2 cups V-8 juice
1 (10 ounce) package frozen English peas

1 cup quick cooking wild and long grain rice mix
1/4 cup tomato paste
1 teaspoon seasoned salt
1 teaspoon dried basil, crumbled
1/4 teaspoon freshly ground pepper

In microwave cook bacon on HIGH until crisp. Pour off all but 1 tablespoon drippings. Add celery, carrot, mushrooms and onion and sauté. Cover and cook until crisp tender. Blend in remaining ingredients. Cover and cook on HIGH, stirring twice, until soup starts to boil for about 20 to 24 minutes. Let soup stand for 5 minutes before serving. Serves 8.

Mrs. Paul Groos (Honey)

- Wild rice is really not a rice but the seed of an aquatic grass that grows in the lake areas of Wisconsin, Minnesota and other states.

Onion Soup A La Market Square

2 tablespoons butter	2 quarts hot beef bouillon
1 tablespoon olive oil	1 bay leaf
4 cups thinly sliced yellow onions	1/2 teaspoon sage
1/2 teaspoon salt	Salt and pepper to taste
1/2 teaspoon sugar	Aged Swiss cheese, sliced
Few shakes of flour	Grated Parmesan cheese
	Croutons

In a 3 quart saucepan melt butter with oil. Add onions and stir to coat. Cover pan and cook over low heat for 10 to 15 minutes. Uncover and and stir in salt and sugar. Cook over moderately high heat until brown. Lower heat and stir in flour, adding a bit more butter if flour does not absorb into a paste with the onions. Pour in about a cup of hot bouillon, stirring with a wire whisk to blend. Add the rest of the bouillon, bay leaf, sage and simmer slowly for 30 to 40 minutes. Season to taste with salt and pepper. Remove bay leaf. Soup is ready to be dressed. Line bottom and sides of small bowl with aged Swiss cheese. Pour in croutons, then onion soup. Sprinkle with grated Parmesan cheese. Top with Swiss cheese and sprinkle again with Parmesan cheese. Brown under broiler to make a nice crusty top. Serves 4 to 6. *This is an important meal to a Frenchman. It is considered to be their meat and potatoes. The essential part of French onion soup is to adequately brown the onions. Do not be afraid to sprinkle with lots of cheese and topping. This is the true French tradition.*

Mrs. Tom Buckman (Ramona)

Fresh Leek Soup

1 1/2 cups minced fresh leeks and greens	2 cups diced potatoes
1 cup chopped onion	1 cup half and half cream
1 clove garlic, minced	Salt and pepper to taste
5 tablespoons butter	Parsley to garnish, optional
1 quart chicken broth	Chopped green onion tops to garnish, optional

Sauté leeks, onion, and garlic in butter. Add broth and potatoes. Simmer for 20 minutes. Add cream and season. Serve as is or purée in blender. Serve hot or cold with parsley or chopped green onion greens. Serves 6 to 8. *This soup does not freeze well.*

Mrs. Henry A. Pate (Patricia)

- *Add a little honey to the butter in which you sauté onions for an out of the ordinary dish. Add onions when mixture begins to sizzle.*

Cheese Corn Chowder

2   cups cubed potatoes
1/2 cup sliced carrots
1/2 cup chopped onion
1/2 cup chopped celery
2   cups salted water
1   cup margarine

1/4 cup flour
2   cups milk
12 ounces sharp Cheddar cheese, grated
2   (16 ounce) cans cream style corn

Cook vegetables in water until tender. Melt butter and add flour, stirring until blended. Gradually add milk, stirring continously to make a white sauce. Slowly add Cheddar cheese and stir until melted. Add sauce to boiled vegetables, then stir in cream style corn. Heat through.

Mrs. Bob Richardson (Susan)

Red Pepper Soup

3   large red bell peppers
2   tablespoons margarine
1   medium onion, finely chopped
1   (28 ounce) can Italian plum tomatoes
1   cup dry red wine

1/2 teaspoon dill weed
1/2 teaspoon salt
1/4 teaspoon pepper
1   cup V-8 juice
1/4 cup sliced green onions for garnish

Place red bell peppers in boiling water for about 1 minute. or until skins are softened. Immerse in cold water. Peel peppers, discarding veins and seeds. Rinse, pat dry and finely chop. In a large saucepan melt margarine over medium heat. Add onion and cook until tender. In a blender, purée tomatoes and chopped peppers. Add to onion. Blend in wine, dill weed, salt and pepper. Bring to a boil; reduce heat stirring occasionally. Stir in V-8 juice and simmer 5 minutes. Garnish with sliced green onions.

Sandy Aitken

"Tocado" Soup

1   can cream of tomato soup
Milk or cream
1   avocado, halved and peeled

Lime juice
Parsley to garnish
2   lime slices to garnish

Prepare cream of tomato soup acording to directions on can, using milk or cream to dilute soup. Brush each avocado half with lime juice and warm in a 300° oven for 10 minutes. Place one avocado half in a serving bowl. Fill with soup and garnish with a sprinkle of parsley and a lime slice. Serves 2.

Mrs. R. A. Gilbert (Kay)
Guild President 1961-1962

Ground Hog Soup

1	pound bulk pork sausage	1	quart water
1	large onion, chopped	1	bay leaf
1/2	cup green bell pepper, chopped	1	teaspoon salt
		1/2	teaspoon garlic salt
1	(16 ounce) can tomatoes	1/2	teaspoon thyme
2	(16 ounce) cans kidney beans, drained and rinsed		Ground pepper to taste
		2	cups diced potatoes

Brown sausage in large skillet. Add onion and green pepper and cook until tender. Drain. Add tomatoes, beans, water and seasonings. Cook covered for 1 hour. Add potatoes and continue cooking until potatoes are tender. Remove bay leaf. Serves 8. *This soup is great on February 2nd, Ground Hog Day, or anytime.*

Mrs. Henry B. Mayes (Kathy)

Lentil Soup

1	(16 ounce) package lentils	1	large onion, chopped
1	pound Polish sausage, sliced	3	potatoes, chopped
			Salt and pepper to taste

Soak lentils in water overnight, drain. Put lentils, meat and onions in a large pot and add enough water to cover mixture. Add salt and pepper and bring to a boil. Add potatoes and lower heat. Cook until potatoes are done. Add more water if necessary. Serves 10 to 12.

Mrs. Tom Buckman (Ramona)

Portuguese Soup

2	cups chopped onion	16	ounces catsup
4	tablespoons oil	2	cups canned red kidney beans
1	pound garlic smoked sausage, sliced	1	head cabbage, cored and chopped into large pieces
2	teaspoons garlic powder	6	medium boiling potatoes, cubed
1	teaspoon salt		
1	teaspoon pepper	1/4	cup white vinegar
3	quarts beef stock		

Sauté onions in a large saucepan. Add sliced sausage and cook 3 to 4 minutes over low heat, stirring and adding garlic powder, salt and pepper. Add beef stock, catsup, beans, cabbage and potatoes. Raise heat and bring to a boil. Lower heat to a simmer. Add vinegar and simmer until cabbage and potatoes are cooked, about 1 to 1½ hours. Serves 10 to 12.

Mrs. Marc Knisely (Barbara)

Chicken In A Pot

1	whole chicken, about 2 pounds	6	carrots, cut into thick slices
2	tablespoons oil	1	green bell pepper, coarsely chopped
2	cloves garlic, minced	6	large fresh mushrooms, sliced
1	(16 ounce) can stewed tomatoes	1/4	teaspoon oregano
1/2	cup sherry	1/2	teaspoon basil
2	onions, coarsely chopped		Salt and pepper to taste

In a heavy cooking pan brown whole chicken on all sides in oil. Sauté garlic at the same time along with the chicken. Add tomatoes and sherry. Add vegetables, oregano, basil, salt and pepper. Cover and simmer until chicken is cooked and vegetables are tender. Remove bones to serve. Serves 6 to 8. *This soup can be frozen.*

Lynn Schaefer

Mulligatawny Soup

3	pounds chicken	1	tablespoon salt
1	medium onion, sliced	1/3	cup butter
1	large carrot, sliced	6	tablespoons flour
3	ribs celery, sliced	3 to 5	tablespoons curry powder
4	ounces fresh mushrooms, sliced	1	cup raisins
1	bunch parlsey, chopped	1	cup diced tart apples
2	bay leaves	1	cup rice, cooked
1	teaspoon peppercorns	2	cups half and half cream
4	whole cloves	2	cups whipping cream

Bring chicken, onion, carrot, celery, mushrooms, parlsey, bay leaves, peppercorns, cloves, and salt to a boil in 4 quarts of water. Simmer for 1 hour. In a separate large soup pot, melt butter and stir in flour and curry powder. Cook for 2 minutes. Strain stock, reserving vegetables and chicken. Add stock to flour and curry mixture, stirring constantly. Purée vegetables and add to soup. Debone chicken, dice and add to soup. Add raisins, apple, rice and half and half cream. Simmer for 15 minutes before serving. Add whipping cream and simmer another 5 minutes. Serves 8.

Mrs. Bruce Blakely (Lynn)

• *Chop carrot tops finely and add to soups, stews or braising liquid for pot roast.*

Texas Clam Chowder

1/2	cup diced bacon or salt pork	1	green bell pepper, chopped
1	cup chopped onion	2	tablespoons butter
4	cups clam juice	3	tablespoons flour
1	cup chicken broth	2	cups milk
1 1/2	cups raw potatoes	2	cups half and half cream
1	cup chopped celery	3	cups chopped clams
1	cup chopped carrots	1	teaspoon white pepper
		Salt to taste	

Cook bacon until soft, add onion and cook until transparent. Add clam juice and broth and remaining vegetables. Cook until partly done. In another saucepan, melt butter and add flour to make a roux. Gradually add milk and cream. Combine all ingredients and simmer until done. Do not boil. Serves 8 to 10.

Mrs. Henry A. Pate (Patricia)

Shrimp Gumbo

2	cups fresh okra, sliced	1	pound raw shrimp, peeled and cleaned
1/3	cup butter	2	cups hot water
2/3	cup chopped green onions, including tops	1	cup canned tomatoes
3	cloves garlic, minced	2	bay leaves
1 1/2	teaspoons salt	6	drops Tabasco sauce
1/2	teaspoon pepper	1 1/2	cups cooked rice

Sauté okra in butter for 10 minutes or until okra appears dry, stirring constantly. Add onion, garlic, salt, pepper and shrimp. Cook for 5 minutes. Add water, tomatoes and bay leaves. Cover and simmer for 20 minutes. Remove bay leaves and add hot pepper sauce. Serve over rice in bowls. Serves 6.

Mrs. Paul White (Suzanne)

Quick Gumbo

1	tablespoon butter	1/2	cup water
1/2	cup chopped onion	1/2	cup frozen sliced okra
1	can chicken gumbo soup	1/2	cup frozen shrimp
1	(6 ounce) can V-8 juice	3 to 6	drops hot red pepper sauce

Melt butter in a saucepan; add onion and cook slowly until onions turn translucent. Add remaining ingredients and bring to a boil. Reduce heat and cook for 3 to 5 minutes. Serves 4.

Mrs. Jeff Stewart (Anna)

Bouillabaisse

½	cup good quality olive oil	3	cups fish broth, consomme or clam juice
1	cup thinly sliced onion		
1	clove garlic, minced	2	pounds fresh fish fillets
2½	cups canned tomatoes	1	pound large shrimp, peeled and cleaned
¼	cup lemon juice		
3	strips lemon peel	1	dozen oysters
2	bay leaves	1	pound lobster meat
½	teaspoon freshly ground pepper	1	pound scallops or mussels, optional
8	whole cloves	½	cup sherry
1½	teaspoons salt	1	lemon, very thinly sliced

Heat oil in a large pot and sauté the onion and garlic. Add the tomatoes, lemon juice, lemon peel, seasonings and fish broth. Simmer for 30 minutes. Cut fillets into 2 inch pieces and add to soup. Simmer 8 minutes. Add the rest of the fresh seafood and simmer gently another 3 to 5 minutes or until oysters curl and shrimp and lobster are just cooked through. If scallops or mussels are added, simmer until scallops are opaque and mussels open. Garnish with the thinly sliced lemon and serve with crusty bread and plenty of big napins. Serves 6 to 8. *To make a fish stock, save fish heads, tails, fins, skin and bones, etc. from the whole fish. Cover with water and add some vegetables, such as onion, celery and parsley. Oyster juice may also be added. Season to taste and simmer for 30 minutes. Strain before using.*

Mary Coneway

Fish Chowder

3	slices bacon, diced	¼	teaspoon parsley flakes
1	medium onion, chopped		Sweet basil to taste
1	cup water		Rosemary to taste
2	medium potatoes, peeled and chopped	1	pound fillets, cut into 1 inch cubes
1¼	teaspoons salt	1½	to 2 cups half and half cream
¼	teaspoon pepper		

Cook bacon and remove. Sauté onion in drippings until tender. Add water, potatoes and seasonings. Heat to boiling, then reduce heat and simmer covered until potatoes are tender. Add fish, heat to boiling. Lower heat and cook 1 to 2 minutes. Stir in cream and bacon. Heat thoroughly, but do not boil. Serve as a soup or over rice. Serves 4 to 6.

Mrs. Robert Huffhines (Chee Chee)

Salads

Yolanda's Spinach Salad

1 (10 ounce) package fresh
  spinach
1/4 to 1/2 pound fresh
  mushrooms, sliced
1/2 pound bacon, fried crisp

3 to 4 apples, thinly sliced
1 cup mayonnaise
1/4 cup orange juice
  concentrate
1/2 onion, thinly sliced

Wash and dry spinach, tearing into bite sized pieces. Add mushrooms, bacon and apples tossing gently. Combine mayonnaise and orange juice concentrate. Pour over salad and top with sliced onion rings. Serves 6.

Yolanda Heine

Spinach Salad

1 (10 ounce) bag fresh
  spinach
1 (8 ounce) can sliced water
  chestnuts, drained
2 cups bean sprouts, washed
  and drained
1 (11 ounce) can Mandarin
  oranges, drained
4 hard cooked eggs, chopped

Sliced almonds
1 cup oil
3/4 cup sugar
1/2 teaspoon salt
1/4 cup white vinegar
1/3 cup catsup
2 tablespoons Worcestershire
  sauce
1/2 onion, chopped

Wash and dry spinach. Tear into bite sized pieces. Toss with bean sprouts, Mandarin oranges, eggs and almonds. Place remaining ingredients together in a bottle or blender and shake or blend well. Pour dressing over salad and toss. Serves 6 to 8.

Sandy Aitken

Artichoke Spinach Salad

1 1/2 pounds fresh spinach
3 green onions
1 pound fresh mushrooms,
  sliced
1 (15 ounce) can artichoke
  hearts, drained

4 tablespoons oil
1 to 2 tablespoons vinegar
Dash of grated Parmesan cheese
Salt and pepper to taste
Croutons to serve

Wash and stem spinach, drain well. Slice onions, tops and all. Add sliced mushrooms and artichokes to spinach. Combine remaining ingredients together and mix well. Pour over salad and toss. Add croutons to serve.

Mrs. Jim Trulove (Ruth Ann)

Spinach Layered Salad

1 (10 ounce) package fresh
spinach
3 hard cooked eggs, sliced
1 green bell pepper, chopped
10 slices bacon, fried and
chopped
1 head cauliflower, broken
into flowerettes

1 (16 ounce) package tiny
English peas, thawed
Chopped green onions
2 cups mayonnaise
1/2 cup sugar
2 tablespoons grated
Parmesan cheese

Wash and stem spinach and layer in a serving bowl. Next layer the eggs, bell pepper, bacon and cauliflower which has been washed and broken into small pieces. Then layer English peas and onions. Mix together mayonnaise, sugar and Parmesan cheese and spread over the top of salad. Refregerate 24 hours. Toss and serve. Serves 10 to 12.

Mrs. Paul Loftin (Liz)

Sweet and Sour Spinach Salad

1 pound fresh spinach
6 slices bacon, cooked and
crumbled
2 hard cooked eggs, chopped
1/2 cup white vinegar
1/2 cup sugar
2 tablespoons oil
1 tablespoon chopped green
onion

1 tablespoon chopped parsley
1 tablespoon chopped chives
1 teaspoon Worcestershire
sauce
1 teaspoon prepared mustard
Ground pepper to taste
1 ice cube

Wash spinach and toss with bacon and eggs. Mix all remaining ingredients in a plastic container. Shake well and chill. Pour over spinach. Season with salt and pepper if desired. Toss well. Serves 6 to 8.

Marian Herbst

Cauliflower Salad

1 head cauliflower, broken
into floweretts
2 cups chopped celery
1 bunch green onions,
chopped
1 (2 1/4 ounce) can ripe olives,
sliced

1 cup sour cream
1 cup mayonnaise
1 (.07 ounce) package Good
Seasons Italian dressing

Toss together cauliflower, celery, onions and olives. Combine sour cream, mayonnaise and Italian dressing, pour over salad. Serves 6 to 8.

Mrs. Pat Rick (Marlene)

Chicken Layered Salad

1/2 head lettuce, torn into bite sized pieces
1 (8 ounce) can sliced water chestnuts, drained
1/2 cup chopped green bell pepper
2 cups cooked chicken, cut into bite sized pieces
1 cup chopped celery
1 cup chopped red onion
1 (16 ounces) package frozen English peas, thawed
2 cups mayonnaise
3 tablespoons sugar
8 ounces Cheddar cheese, grated
8 slices cooked crisp bacon, crumbled
3 hard cooked eggs, chopped

Layer ingredients in the following order: lettuce, chicken, water chestnuts, a mixture of chopped celery, onion and green pepper and lastly peas. Mix together mayonnaise and sugar and spread over top of layered salad. Refrigerate overnight. When ready to serve, sprinkle with Cheddar cheese, bacon and eggs. Serves 8 to 10.

Mrs. Sammy Juvé (Laura)

Broccoli Salad

4 cups chopped raw broccoli
8 slices crisp fried bacon, crumbled
1/2 cup raisins
1 medium onion, finely chopped
3/4 cup mayonnaise
1/4 cup sugar
3 tablespoons white vinegar

In a large bowl toss together broccoli, bacon, raisins and onion. Combine mayonnaise, sugar and vinegar mixing well. Chill overnight. Pour over salad just before serving. Serves 4 to 6.

Mrs. Eric Van Tongerloo (Anita)

Tomato Marinade Salad

Juice of 2 lemons
1/3 cup sugar
1 red onion, chopped
1 green bell pepper, chopped
1 clove garlic, minced
2 tablespoons oil
Salt to taste
6 tomatoes, sliced

Combine all ingredients, except tomatoes and mix well. Pour over tomatoes and refrigerate overnight. Serves 6 to 8.

Mrs. Terry Hight (Gayle)

Tomato Ruff

1	cup chopped green bell pepper	1	teaspoon salt
1	cup chopped red onion		Dash of freshly ground pepper
1	cup chopped tomato	1/2	cup salad oil
1	cup chopped celery	1	cup cider vinegar
1	cup sugar	1	tablespoon sweet basil leaves

Combine vegetables in a bowl. Mix together sugar, salt, pepper, salad oil, vinegar and basil. Pour over vegetable salad and let stand several hours or overnight in the refrigerator. Spoon out with slotted spoon and serve in a bowl or in a lettuce cup. Serves 8 to 10.

Bonnie Zipoy

Make Ahead Oriental Salad

1	(17 ounce) can tiny English peas, drained	1	(4 ounce) jar pimientos
1	(16 ounce) can bean sprouts, drained	1	large onion, chopped
1	(12 ounce) can white corn, drained	1	large green bell pepper, chopped
2	(5 ounce) cans water chestnuts, drained and chopped	1	cup chopped celery
		1	cup vegetable oil
1	(6 ounce) can sliced mushrooms, drained	1	cup water
		1	cup sugar
		1/2	cup white vinegar
			Salt and pepper to taste

In a large bowl combine all vegetables together. Mix together oil, water, sugar, vinegar and seasonings, and pour over vegetables. Marinate 24 hours. Serve with slotted spoon. Serves 12.

Mrs. Eric van Tongerloo (Anita)

Marinated Mushroom Salad

2	(8 ounce) packages mushrooms, brushed and sliced	1	(14¾ ounce) jar marinated artichokes, undrained, coarsley chopped
3/4	cup vegetable oil	1	green bell pepper, chopped
1/4	cup tarragon wine vinegar	1/2	teaspoon salt
1	clove garlic, minced		Cracked black pepper to taste
1/4	cup thinly sliced red onion		Lettuce

Thoroughly combine oil, vinegar, garlic, onion, undrained artichokes, salt and pepper. Add mushrooms. Toss gently. Cover, and refrigerate overnight. Serve on a bed of lettuce. Serves 8. *This mushroom mixture is also a great topping for cream cheese spread on Melba rounds.*

Mrs. Allan L. Williams (Rose Betty)

Kraut Salad

1	(16 ounce) can sauerkraut	1/4	cup vegetable oil
1	(2 ounce) can chopped	1	teaspoon celery seed
	pimiento	1/2	teaspoon garlic salt
1/2	green bell pepper, chopped	1/2	teaspoon salt
1	medium onion, chopped	1/2	teaspoon coarsely ground
1/2	cup white vinegar		pepper
1/2	cup sugar		

Rinse and drain sauerkraut. Pat dry. Mix with pimiento, bell pepper and onion, and set aside. Combine vinegar, sugar, oil, celery seed, and seasonings, pour over salad mixture. Toss well. Refrigerate 24 hours before serving. Serves 8 to 10.

Mrs. Berry Gannaway (Jackie)
Fiesta Chairman 1984-1985

German Potato Salad

8	pounds potatoes	2	white onions, finely
1½	cups white vinegar		chopped
1½	cups water	5	tablespoons corn oil
			Fresh parsley

Boil potatoes in or out of skins and slice thin. In a saucepan boil vinegar, water and onions together until the onion is tender. Pour onion mixture over potatoes and toss with corn oil. Add freshly snipped parsley. Serve warm or cold. Serves 16.

Mrs. Edward Konop (Rita)

Picnic Rice Salad

2	cups rice	1/2	green bell pepper, finely
1/4	cup olive oil		chopped
1/3	cup white wine vinegar	1/2	cup minced fresh parsley
1/3	teaspoon salt	1/2	cup sliced green onions
1/4	teaspoon pepper	1/2	cup sliced ripe olives
1/4	teaspoon dried tarragon	1/4	cup chopped pimiento

Cook rice according to package directions. While rice is hot, place in a large mixing bowl. Add oil, vinegar, salt, pepper and tarragon, tossing lightly to blend. Refrigerate. When cool, add remaining ingredients. Refrigerate for at least 3 hours. Serves 8 to 10. *This dish travels well and will last several days in the refrigerator.*

Mrs. Ben Morgan (LaRee)

Bombay Chicken Brown Rice Salad

2 to 3 cups cooked brown rice
1 (20 ounce) package frozen
English peas, thawed
1/3 cup chopped peanuts
2 cups diced chicken
1/4 cup chopped green bell
pepper
1/2 cup chopped celery

3 tablespoons chopped green
onions
1/2 cup mayonnaise
1/2 cup plain yogurt
1 tablespoon marmalade
1 teaspoon Dijon mustard
2 teaspoons salt
1 to 2 teaspoons curry powder

Combine rice, English peas, peanuts, chicken, bell pepper, celery and onions. Toss well. Combine together mayonnaise, yogurt, marmalade, Dijon mustard and seasonings. Toss with salad to coat well. Chill in a covered container. Serves 6 to 8.

Mrs. Bruce Blakely (Lynn)

Chicken Artichoke Salad

3 (6½ ounce) jars marinated
artichokes
1 green bell pepper, chopped
1/2 cup chopped celery
8 green onions, finely
chopped

2 (6 ounce) packages chicken
flavored Rice-A-Roni
1/2 cup mayonnaise
1 chicken, boiled, deboned
and diced

Drain artichokes, reserving marinade. Cook rice according to package directions. Combine bell pepper, celery, onions, chicken and artichokes. Mix marinade and mayonnaise, pour over salad and stir well. Refrigerate several hours. Serves 8 to 10.

Mrs. Carey Brennan (Shari)

Marinated Cole Slaw

3 pounds head cabbage,
shredded
1/2 medium green bell pepper,
finely diced
1 (6 ounce) jar diced
pimientos, drained

1½ tablespoons salt
2 tablespoons sugar
1½ teaspoons coarse ground
black pepper
3/4 cup cider vinegar
3/4 cup olive oil

Shred cabbage into a large bowl. Mix together remaining ingredients and pour over cabbage. Stir to coat cabbage and store in an air tight container in refrigerator, stirring occasionally. This slaw is best if made at least 4 hours ahead of serving. Drain off marinade if not used by the second day.

Mrs. Bruce Knierim (Pam)
Fiesta Chariman 1981-1982

Macaroni Salad

1	(16 ounce) package elbow macaroni	3	teaspoons grated onion
1	(9½ ounce) jar sweet pepper relish	2	teaspoons picante sauce
		2	dashes hot pepper sauce
1	(4 ounce) jar pimiento, drained and chopped	1½	teaspoons salt
		1½	cups mayonnaise, divided
½	cup diced green bell pepper	½	cup sour cream
3	tablespoons chopped parsley	½	cup milk, divided
			Pepper

Cook macaroni, drain and rinse with cold water. In a large bowl combine relish, pimiento, green pepper, parsley, onion, picante sauce, pepper sauce, salt, 1 cup mayonnaise, sour cream and ¼ cup milk, mixing well. Add macaroni, tossing lightly until well combined, then add pepper. Cover and refrigerate until well chilled. To serve combine remaining mayonnaise and milk, stir into salad. Turn into salad bowl, garnish with salad greens. Serves 12.

Mrs. Dan Jardine (Lisa)

Garden Macaroni Salad

¾	cup mayonnaise	1	cup diced celery
1	teaspoon salt	¼	cup diced green bell pepper
¼	teaspoon basil	¼	cup sliced radishes
1	(8 ounce) package elbow macaroni, cooked and drained	2	tablespoons chopped green onion
		2	tomatoes, diced
1	cup diced cucumber		

Combine mayonnaise, salt and basil. In a large bowl mix macaroni, cucumber, celery, bell pepper, radishes, onion and tomatoes. Add mayonnaise mixture to macaroni mixture and toss well. Cover and chill at least 1 hour before serving. Serves 6 to 8.

Mrs. Rowland V. Firth (Susan)

Molded Tuna Salad

1	tablespoon unflavored gelatin	¼	cup chopped onion
		1	cup chopped celery
¼	cup water	1	cup cottage cheese
1	tablespoon lemon juice	½	cup mayonnaise
1	(6½ ounce) can tuna	½	cup chopped pecans

Sprinkle gelatin into water and lemon juice to soften. Combine all other ingredients together; add gelatin and mix well. Put into a 6 cup mold and refrigerate until set. Serves 4 to 6.

Mrs. Ron Tobin (Bonnie)

Fiesta Macaroni Salad

1 (16 ounce) package macaroni, cooked and drained
2/3 cup cider vinegar
1/4 cup vegetable oil
1 cup minced celery
1/2 cup chopped green bell pepper
6 green onions, minced
1 (2 ounce) jar pimiento, chopped and drained
3 generous dashes Worcestershire sauce

3 dashes Tabasco sauce
1 tablespoon green chilies
1 teaspoon salt
1/2 teaspoon pepper
1 (15 ounce) can black eyed peas, drained
1 (12 ounce) can corn, drained
1/2 cup chopped ripe olives
1 (2 ounce) jar stuffed green olives, chopped
1/3 cup mayonnaise

Mix macaroni and vinegar; let stand while chopping. Combine all, cover and chill for 2 to 3 days. Taste to test for salt and vinegar before serving. Serves 12.

Mrs. Don Davis (Pat)
Fiesta Chairman 1976-1977, Guild President 1983-1984

Vermicelli Salad

1 (4 ounce) package vermicelli
1 (6½ ounce) can artichoke hearts
2 large tomatoes, chopped
1 (8 ounce) package fresh mushrooms, sliced
1/2 cup chopped walnuts

3 tablespoons chopped fresh parsley
1/4 to 1/2 cup oil
1/4 to 1/2 cup red wine vinegar
1 clove garlic, minced
1/4 teaspoon salt
1/2 teaspoon basil
1/4 teaspoon pepper

Cook vermicelli until al dente, drain and cool. Drain artichokes reserving marinade and chop. Combine vermicelli, artichokes, tomatoes, mushrooms, walnuts and parsley, mixing well. Combine in a jar 1/4 cup reserved marinade, 1/4 cup oil and 1/4 cup vinegar, garlic, salt, basil and pepper. Cover and shake well. Pour over vermicelli and toss. Cover and chill thoroughly. If mixture seems dry add more marinade, oil and vinegar. Serves 6.

Mrs. Marcus Bone (Beverly)
Fiesta Chairman 1983-1984

• *Cooking time for pasta will depend on whether noodles are fresh or dry. 6 to 8 minutes for fresh and 11 minutes for dry.*

Salad Nicoise

1	cup Italian Dressing	2	tomatoes, cut in wedges
2	cups sliced cooked potatoes	1	(2 ounce) can rolled
1	cup cut green beans, cooked and drained		anchovy fillets, drained
2	quarts assorted greens, torn in bite sized pieces	1/4	cup pitted ripe olives, cut in half
1	(6 ounce) can tuna, drained and flaked	1/4	cup sliced green onion
		2	hard cooked eggs, sliced

Pour dressing over potatoes and beans. Cover and marinate in refrigerator for several hours. Drain, reserving marinade. Combine potatoes, beans, greens, tuna, tomato, anchovies, olives and onion, tossing lightly. Garnish with eggs and serve with marinade. Serves 4 to 6.

Mrs. Edward Konop (Rita)

Maca Tuni Salad

1	(9 ounce) can chunk tuna, drained	1	tablespoon prepared mustard
1	cup chopped celery	1/2	cup chopped sweet pickles
2	tablespoons sweet pickle juice	1	(7 ounce) package small shell macaroni noodles cooked and drained
1/2	cup finely chopped green onions and tops		Salt and pepper to taste
1/2	cup mayonnaise		

Mix together all ingredients and stir well. Refrigerate for several hours. Serves 6 to 8.

Mrs. Bruce Knierim (Pam)
Fiesta Chairman 1981-1982

Gulf Shrimp Salad

1	pound cooked fresh shrimp	2	tablespoons French dressing
2	cups cooked rice	2	tablespoons fresh lemon juice
1	cup sliced celery		
1/2	cup chopped fresh parsley	1	teaspoon curry powder
1/4	cup sliced ripe olives		Salad greens
1/2	cup mayonnaise		

Cover shrimp with ice water. Let stand 5 minutes and drain. Peel shrimp and cut if too large. Combine rice, celery, parsley, olives and shrimp. Combine mayonnaise, French dressing, lemon juice and curry powder; mix thoroughly. Lightly toss together dressing mixture and shrimp-rice mixture. Chill. Serve on salad greens. Serves 6.

Sylvia Stevens

Ceviche Salad

1 pound scallops	3 tablespoons olive oil
1½ cups fresh lime juice	½ teaspoon salt
1 clove garlic, crushed	½ teaspoon oregano
2 large tomatoes, chopped	¼ teaspoon pepper
1 to 2 jalapeños peppers, seeds removed, minced	4 to 5 avocados, halved, peeled and seeded

Place scallops in a glass bowl; add lime juice and refrigerate overnight. Drain scallops and add garlic, tomatoes, jalapeños, olive oil, salt, oregano and pepper, mixing well. Scoop mixture into avocado halves.

Mrs. Larry Hall (Jane)
Fiesta Chairman 1982-1983

Chicken Salad Maui

6 (20 ounce) cans pineapple chunks	6 tablespoons chopped chutney, optional
2½ cups diced celery	2½ cups sliced bananas
7½ cups chicken, cooked and cubed	1 cup salted peanuts
1½ cups sliced green stuffed olives	1½ cups shredded coconut, optional to serve
2½ cups mayonnaise	Parsley and Mandarin oranges to serve
2 tablespoons curry powder	

Mix pineapple, celery, chicken, olives, mayonnaise, curry powder and chutney; chill. Just before serving, add bananas and peanuts. Serves 20.

Mrs. R. A. Gilbert (Dottie)
Guild President 1961-1962

Kiwi Chicken Salad

2 cups cooked, cubed chicken breasts	½ cup white wine vinegar
1 (4 ounce) jar diced pimiento	¼ cup sugar
½ cup chopped celery	½ teaspoon Dijon mustard
3 to 4 kiwi, peeled and sliced, divided	½ teaspoon salt
	Dash of pepper
	1 cup vegetable oil

Mix chicken, pimiento, celery and 2 to 3 kiwi in a large bowl. Combine vinegar, sugar, mustard, salt, and pepper in a blender or food processor at high speed. Gradually add oil. Add 1 kiwi and blend until smooth. Pour over chicken and toss until well mixed. Gently stir in kiwi slices.

Mrs. Glenn Johnson (Debbie)

Chilled Chicken Spaghetti Salad

1	(8 ounce) package spaghetti, broken in half
2	chicken breasts, boiled, deboned and cut into bite sized pieces.
2	cups fresh broccoli floweretts, cooked in boiling water for 2 to 5 minutes
1½	cups sliced fresh mushrooms
10	cherry tomatoes, cut in half
¼	cup chopped red onion
½	cup Italian dressing
1	tablespoon lemon juice
1	teaspoon seasoned salt
1	teaspoon basil

Cook noodles and drain. Combine all remaining ingredients. Cover and chill. Toss well before serving. Serves 6 to 8.

Mrs. Chad Snow (Frances)

Tomato Aspic Layered Salad

Tomato Aspic:

1	tablespoon unflavored gelatin
¾	cup tomato juice
⅔	cup tomato sauce
2	teaspoons lemon juice
1	teaspoon sugar
¼	teaspoon seasoned salt
1	tablespoon grated onion
½	teaspoon horsradish

In a saucepan sprinkle gelatin over tomato juice to soften. Heat slowly, stirring until gelatin is dissolved. Add remaining ingredients, mixing well. Pour into a 6 cup mold and chill until firm.

Cottage Cheese Layer:

1	tablespoon unflavored gelatin
¼	cup cold water
¾	teaspoon salt
¼	teaspoon paprika
½	cup diced cucumber
¾	cup half and half cream
2	cups small curd creamed cottage cheese
	Salad greens to serve
	Lemon wedges to serve
	Mayonnaise to serve

Soften gelatin in cold water for 5 minutes. Dissolve over hot water. Combine all remaining ingredients. Mix well. Pour over tomato aspic layer. Chill until firm. To serve, unmold on plate. Garnish with salad greens, lemon wedges and a dollop of mayonnaise. Serves 6 to 8.

Mrs. Allan L. Williams (Rose Betty)

Holiday Cranberry Salad

3   cups fresh cranberries,
    washed
2   apples, chopped
2   cups chopped celery
1/4 teaspoon salt
1 1/2 cups sugar
1   (3 ounce) package raspberry
    gelatin

1   (3 ounce) package orange
    gelatin
3/4 cup hot water
Juice and pulp of 1 orange
1   (8 ounce) can crushed
    pineapple, drained and
    reserve juice
1   cup chopped pecans

Chop cranberries, apples and celery in food processor, and mix with salt and sugar and set aside. Soften gelatin in hot water. Add juice and pulp from orange and reserved pineapple juice. Add pecans, and combine with fruit mixture. Pour into serving dish and refrigerate to gel.

Mrs. Kyle Baker (Linda)

Frosted Strawberry Salad

1   (3 ounce) box strawberry
    gelatin
1   cup hot water
3   ounces cream cheese
1   large banana

1   (8 ounce) can crushed
    pineapple
1   (10 ounce) carton frozen
    strawberries, thawed

Dissolve gelatin in hot water. Set aside in freezer to chill until partially set. Mix remaining ingredients in blender. Cube the soft-set gelatin and stir in the fruit mixture. Chill and serve in dessert cups. Serves 4 to 6.

Mrs. Robert Storey (Carolyn)

Frosted Salad

2   (3 ounce) packages lemon
    gelatin
2   cups boiling water
2   cups ginger ale
1   (20 ounce) can crushed
    pineapple, drained, reserved
    juice to yield 1 cup
2   cups miniature
    marshmallows

2   large bananas
1/2 cup sugar
2   tablespoon flour
1   cup pineapple juice,
    reserved from salad
1   tablespoon butter
1   cup whipped cream
1/4 cup grated American cheese

Mix gelatin with boiling water until dissolved. Add ginger ale and chill until partially set. Fold in fruit and marshmallows, then chill overnight. In a saucepan cook sugar, flour, 1 cup reserved pineapple juice and butter until thickened. Fold in cream. Spread mixture on top of congealed gelatin. Top with grated cheese. Serves 8.

Lael Byers

Cranberry Salad

1 (6 ounce) package cherry
   gelatin
2 cups boiling water
1 (16 ounce) can cranberry
   sauce with whole berries

2 cups sour cream
¾ cup finely chopped celery
1 cup chopped pecans
Sour cream to serve

Dissolve gelatin in boiling water. Add cranberry sauce, beating well. Chill until partially set. Thin sour cream with some of the gelatin mixture, then fold into gelatin mixture. Mix gently but thoroughly. Add remaining ingredients. Pour into mold and chill until firm. Top with a dollop of sour cream when serving. Serves 12.

Mrs. Terry Townsend (Mimi)

Old Fashioned Fruit Salad

1 (20 ounce) crushed
   pineapple
1⅔ tablespoons cornstarch
1 egg, beaten
3 teaspoons sugar
1 teaspoon sugar
1 teaspoon lemon or lime
   juice
1 tablespoon margarine
1 teaspoon vanilla extract

1 drop yellow food coloring
2 oranges, peeled and sliced
2 apples, cored and diced
2 bananas, peeled and sliced
1 (20 ounce) can pineapple
   chunks
30 miniature marshmallows,
   optional
½ cup chopped pecans
Coconut to taste, if desired

Combine crushed pineapple, cornstarch, egg, sugar and lemon or lime juice. Cook in a saucepan until thickened. Add margarine, vanilla and food coloring. Let sauce cool. Combine fruit, marshmallows, pecans and coconut. Cover with cool sauce and chill. Serves 10 to 12.

Mrs Charlie Cantwell (Winn)

Frozen Banana Salad

3 bananas, mashed
1 cup sugar
1 cup chopped pecans
10 maraschino cherries,
   chopped

1 (8 ounces) can crushed
   pineapple, drained
2 cups sour cream
2 tablespoons lemon juice

Mix all ingredients together and freeze. Serves 6 to 8.

Mrs. John M. Davis (Alice)
Fiesta Chairman 1973-1974

Grandma's Fruit Cups

1 cup water	4 to 5 cups sliced, mixed fruit;
1½ cups sugar	cantaloupe, bananas,
4 cups apricot nectar	strawberries or kiwi

Boil water and add sugar to dissolve. Cool. Add nectar and fruits. Spoon into containers for freezing. Allow to freeze overnight. Take out the amount you need and thaw for 2 hours. Dish into individual fruit cups and serve. Serves 10.

Mrs. Chris John (Anne)

Frozen Daiquiri Salad

8 ounces cream cheese, softened	1 (16 ounce) can crushed pineapple, drained
⅓ cup mayonnaise	½ cup chopped pecans
1 package egg custard mix	1 jigger light rum
1 (6 ounce) can frozen daiquiri mix, thawed	1 envelope whipped topping, prepared according to directions

Blend in a blender the cream cheese, mayonnaise, egg custard, daiquiri and rum. Fold in pineapple, pecans and whipped topping. Pour into a 9x13 inch dish which has been lined with waxed paper and freeze for 3 hours. To serve, unmold and cut into individual servings. Serves 12.

Susan Hasslocher
Guild President 1984-1985

Apricot Salad

2 (3 ounce) packages apricot gelatin	1 (20 ounce) can crushed pineapple, undrained
⅔ cup sugar	1 (14 ounce) can sweetened condensed milk, chilled
⅔ cup water	
2 (4¾ ounce) jars apricot baby food	8 ounces cream cheese, softened
	1 cup chopped pecans

Combine gelatin, sugar and water in a small saucepan; bring to a boil, stirring to dissolve sugar and gelatin. Remove from heat, and stir in fruit; set aside to cool. Combine condensed milk and cream cheese, beating until smooth; stir in gelatin mixture, then pecans. Put into a 9 cup mold and chill until firm. Serves 20.

Mrs. Paul Groos (Honey)

Salad Dressings

Honey Lime Dressing

1 cup sugar	1 tablespoon ginger
1/3 cup lime juice	1 tablespoon dry mustard
1 teaspoon salt	2 cups vegetable oil
1/3 cup white vinegar	1 tablespoon poppy seeds,
1/2 cup honey	optional

Mix sugar, lime juice, salt, vinegar, honey, ginger and dry mustard in blender until sugar dissolves. Then slowly add oil while mixing well. Mixture should be thick and creamy. Add poppy seeds if desired. Serve over fresh fruit. Yields 3 cups.

Susan Hasslocher
Guild President 1984-1985

Homemade Ranch Dressing

1 cup sour cream	1/2 teaspoon basil
1 cup mayonnaise	Cavender's Greek seasoning to
1 small clove garlic, minced	taste
1 tablespoon dried parsley	Milk

Combine all ingredients. Thin with milk until desired pouring consistency. Serve with a green salad. Best if prepared several hours before serving. Yields 2 1/2 cups.

Mrs. Bill Wilson (Cora Lynn)

Herbal Oil And Vinegar Dressing

1 tablespoon Dijon mustard	1/4 cup vinegar
1 teaspoon sugar	3 tablespoons olive oil
1 teaspoon bouquet garni	2 tablespoons ripe olive juice,
1 teaspoon dill weed	optional

Add ingredients in order given. Stir until mustard is dissolved. Add ripe olive juice if desired. Pour on green salad and toss just before serving. Yields 1/2 cup.

Mrs. Charles Herring (Anna)

• *Shallots are different from onions. They have a flavor nearer that of garlic than onion. Never let shallots brown or they will become bitter.*

Basic Vinaigrette

1/4 cup red wine vinegar	1/4 cup olive oil
1 teaspoon Dijon mustard	1/2 teaspoon salt
1 medium shallot, finely chopped	1/8 teaspoon freshly ground pepper
1/2 cup safflower oil	

In a medium bowl combine vinegar, mustard and shallot. Whisk until blended. Slowly pour both oils into bowl, whisking continually until mixture is well blended. Add seasonings. Yields 1 cup.

Mrs. Garrel Fleming (Ginny Puryear)

Tangy Salad Dressing

2 tablespoons chopped pimiento	1/2 teaspoon sugar
	1/2 teaspoon salt
1 tablespoon minced green onion	1/4 teaspoon celery seed
	1/8 teaspoon garlic powder
1 teaspoon Dijon mustard	1 cup sour cream

Combine pimiento, green onion, mustard, sugar, salt, celery seed and garlic powder in a small mixing bowl. Gently fold in sour cream. Cover and chill 2 to 3 hours before serving. Yields 1 1/4 cups.

Mrs. John Stark (Kay)

White French Dressing

1 egg	1/3 teaspoon English mustard
1 1/2 cups vegetable oil	4 teaspoons white vinegar
1 scant teaspoon salt	4 teaspoons fresh onion juice
1/3 teaspoon white pepper	

Beat egg until thick. Add oil a few drops at a time. Then add salt, pepper, mustard, vinegar and onion juice. Chill well before serving.

Mrs. Jeff Wigginton (Mandy)

Rebecca's Sauce

8 ounces sour cream or cream cheese	1 tablespoon rum
	1/2 cup raisins, optional
1/2 cup brown sugar	Fresh fruit
1 tablespoon Irish whiskey	

Whisk together all ingredients. Pour over fresh fruit. Yields 1 1/2 to 2 cups sauce.

Lael Byers

Spinach Salad Dressing

1   cup vegetable oil
5   tablespoons red wine vinear
4   tablespoons sour cream
1½ teaspoons salt
½   teaspoon dry mustard

2   tablespoon sugar
Pepper to taste
2   teaspoons chopped parsley
2   cloves garlic, minced

Mix together all ingredients and chill 6 hours before serving. Yields 1½ cups.

Mrs. Clyde Holt (Penny)

Larry's Favorite Dressing

⅓   cup chopped onion
1   cup mayonnaise
⅓   cup vegetable oil
¼   cup catsup
2   tablespoons sugar, optional
2   tablespoons vinegar
1   teaspoon prepared mustard

½   teaspoon salt
½   teaspoon paprika
¼   teaspoon celery seed
Dash of pepper
1   cup crumbled Bleu cheese, optional

Put all ingredients except Bleu cheese in a blender and blend until smooth. Stir in Bleu cheese, then cover and chill. The Bleu cheese can be sprinkled on individual salads and not put in the dressing. Toss with your favorite salad greens. Yields 2½ cups.

Mrs. Larry Hall (Jane)
Fiesta Chairman 1982-1983

Italian Salad Dressing

½   cup olive oil
2   tablespoons minced onion
1   tablespoon grated Parmesan cheese
2   teaspoons salt
¾   teaspoon Worcestershire sauce

¾   teaspoon dried basil leaves
¾   teaspoon dry mustard
¾   teaspoon dried oregano
¾   teaspoon sugar
¾   teaspoon pepper
¼   cup red wine vinegar
1   tablespoon lemon juice

Blend olive oil, onion, Parmesan cheese, salt, Worcestershire sauce, basil, mustard, oregano, sugar and pepper in a blender for 30 seconds. Add vinegar and lemon juice and blend another 30 seconds. Toss with your favorite green salad. Yields 1cup.

Mrs. Scott Chapman (Vicki)
Fiesta Chairman 1980-1981

Sandwiches

Jumbo Pizza Sandwiches

1 loaf French or Vienna bread
4 tablespoons sliced ripe olives
1/8 teaspoon pepper
1/4 teaspoon oregano
1/2 teaspoon salt
2 tablespoon chopped green onion

1/2 pound ground beef
4 tablespoons grated Parmesan cheese
6 ounces tomato paste
14 thin slices tomato
8 slices American or Swiss cheese

Cut French bread in half, horizontally. Combine olives, pepper, oregano, salt, onion, beef, Parmesan cheese and tomato paste. Spread meat mixture over cut sides of bread. Arrange tomato slices over meat and place bread on a cookie sheet. Bake at 400° for 15 minutes. Remove from oven. Cut cheese slices in half diagonally. Cover tomato slices with overlapping cheese slices. Return to oven for 5 minutes. Remove and slice. Serves 6 to 8. *The meat mixture can be frozen for future use.*

Mrs. Larry Hall (Jane)
Fiesta Chairman 1982-1983

Ham Salad Sandwiches

3 pounds cooked ham
6 hard cooked eggs
2 tablespoons chopped green onions

Mayonnaise
Mustard
Wheat bread

Grind or chop ham. Mix in chopped eggs and onions. Bind together with mayonnaise and mustard. Make a sandwich on wheat bread that has been cut in half. Serves 24.

Mrs. Paul Outen (Peggy)

Dilled Egg Salad Sandwiches

6 hard cooked eggs, grated
1/2 cup mayonnaise
1/2 teaspoon salt
2 tablespoons Dijon mustard

2 to 3 green onions, chopped
1/2 to 1 teaspoon dillweed
Bread

Mix together eggs, mayonnaise, salt, mustard, onions and dill weed and chill. When ready to serve, spread on bread. Serves 6 to 8.

Mrs. Maracus Bone (Beverly)
Fiesta Chairman 1983-1984

Sausage And Peppers In Pockets

½ pound sweet Italian sausage, cut into ½ inch slices	1 red bell pepper, cut into ½ inch strips
½ pound hot Italian sausage, cut into ½ inch slices	2 cloves garlic, minced
3 tablespoons olive oil	1 teaspoon oregano
1 green bell pepper, cut into ½ inch strips	4 tablespoons tomato paste
	¾ cup red wine
	Salt and pepper to taste
	6 pita bread

In a large covered skillet, cook sausages in ½ cup water for 5 minutes. Uncover and cook 10 to 15 minutes, shaking pan until brown. Remove sausage and wipe out pan. Heat olive oil and sauté peppers, garlic and oregano for 10 minutes, stirring frequently. Stir in tomato paste, red wine, salt and pepper. Cook 10 minutes, then return sausages to skillet and continue to cook, covered for 10 minutes, stirring occasionally. Place sausage mixture in pita halves. Yields 12 pita halves.

Mrs. Larry Hall (Jane)
Fiesta Chairman 1982-1983

Pocket Chicken Salad

3 medium ripe avocados	9 green onions, chopped
Lemon juice	½ cup alfalfa sprouts
3 medium tomatoes, chopped	3 to 4 cups cooked chicken, cut into bite sized pieces
12 slices bacon, cooked crisp and crumbled	6 pita bread

Peel and slice avocados, dip in lemon juice. Add remaining ingredients and combine. Season to taste with salt and pepper. When ready to serve, spoon into pita halves. Serves 6.

Mrs. Ben Morgan (LaRee)

Roast Beef Sandwiches

1 boneless chuck roast, 6 to 7 pounds	1 tablespoon summer savory
Water	1 beef bouillon cube
1 bay leaf	Garlic salt to taste
	Rye bread

Cover the roast halfway with water. Add bay leaf, summer savory, bouillon cube and garlic salt; cover and bake at 225° for 6 to 8 hours. Shred beef and serve on rye bread. Serves 10.

Mrs. Brian Sullivan (Cynthia)

Reuben Sandwiches

1/2	cup mayonnaise	1	(8 ounce) package sliced
1	tablespoon chili sauce		corned beef
3	tablespoons butter	1	(16 ounce) can sauerkraut,
12	slices rye bread		washed and drained
6	slices Swiss cheese		

Combine mayonnaise and chili sauce, mixing well. Spread 1/4 tablespoon butter on one side of each piece of bread; spreading other side with mayonnaise mixture. Layer cheese, corned beef and sauerkraut on mayonnaise side of 6 pieces of bread. Top with remaining bread. Place sandwiches under broiler and broil until brown on both sides. Serves 6.

Mrs. Marcus Bone (Beverly)
Fiesta Chairman 1983-1984

New Year's Eve Sandwiches

1 1/2	pounds lean ground beef	1	teaspoon garlic salt
1	pound pork sausage	1	pound Velveeta cheese,
1	teaspoon pepper		cubed
1	teaspoon oregano	2	loaves Jewish rye bread

Brown ground beef with pork sausage and drain well. Add spices and mix. Add cubed chese and heat until melted. Spread on sliced dark rye bread. Wrap well in foil and refrigerate until ready to serve. Warm in very low oven until thoroughly heated. Serves 6 to 8.

Mrs. Bill Rhoades (Dixie)

Broiled Luncheon Sandwiches

6	slices very thin bread	1	large tomato, sliced
6	slices smoked turkey breast	1	ripe avocado, sliced
	Durkee's dressing	6	slices Swiss cheese

Spread bread with Durkee's dressing. Place a slice of turkey breast on each slice of bread. Top with sliced tomato and avocado to cover. Top with a slice of cheese. Broil until cheese melts and bubbles. Serves 6.

Mrs. Ron Tobin (Bonnie)

Picnic Hot Dogs

12 (15x12 inch) phyllo dough
leaves, thawed
Melted butter

1 package hot dogs, Polish
sausage or Knockwursts
4 slices Swiss cheese

Preheat oven to 400°. Divide phyllo into 2 sections of six leaves. Cut each section into 4 strips. Brush top leaf with melted butter. Roll hot dog and cheese in strip of phyllo. Place on a cookie sheet with strip side down. Brush again with melted butter. Cut thru diagonal slits on top of each, just through the phyllo. Bake 10 minutes. Serve with mustard. Serves 12.

Mrs. Jeff Burk (Pam)

Stroganoff Steak Sandwiches

2/3 cup beer
1/3 cup vegetable oil
1 teaspoon salt
1/4 teaspoon garlic powder
1/4 teaspoon pepper
2 pounds flank steak, about 1
inch thick

2 tablespoons butter
1/2 teaspoon paprika
4 cups sliced onion
12 slices French bread, toasted
1 cup sour cream, warmed
1/2 teaspoon horseradish

In a shallow dish, combine beer, oil, salt, garlic powder, and pepper. Place flank steak in marinade; cover. Marinate overnight in refrigerator; drain. Broil or grill steak for 5 to 7 minutes on each side. In a saucepan, melt butter; blend in paprika and a dash of salt. Add onion; cook until tender but not brown. Thinly slice meat on the diagonal across grain. For each serving, arrange meat slices over 2 slices French bread. Top with onions. Combine sour cream and horseradish; spoon onto each sandwich. Sprinkle with paprika, if desired. Serves 6.

Mrs. Larry Hall (Jane)
Fiesta Chairman 1982-1983

- *Ginger root can be kept for a long time in the refrigerator if peeled and placed in a small jar of vodka. The vodka is tasteless and takes on a spicey ginger flavor that can be used for seasoning.*

Pizza

Dough:

1	package dry yeast	1	tablespoon olive oil
1	cup lukewarm water	1	tablespoon vegetable oil
1	tablespoon sugar	3	cups whole wheat or white flour
1	teaspoon salt		

Dissolve yeast in 1 cup luke warm water. Add sugar and let stand for 5 minutes until yeast activates and makes bubbles. Add salt, oils and 2 cups flour. Mix with electric mixer on medium speed for 2 to 3 minutes, or mix thoroughly by hand. Add remaining flour, ½ cup at a time. Knead 7 to 8 minutes. Place in a greased bowl and cover until doubled in size. Punch down and form into a pizza pan and let rise again for 1 hour.

Sauce:

1½	tablespoons olive oil	½	teaspoon oregano
1	onion, chopped	¼	teaspoon garlic salt
1	(28 ounce) can Italian style crushed tomatoes	¼	teaspoon pepper
1	(8 ounce) can tomato sauce	½	teaspoon salt
		1	bay leaf

Sauté onion in olive oil over medium heat. Add remaining ingredients, stirring well. Simmer uncovered 1 hour, stirring occasionally. Remove bay leaf.

1 pound Mozzarella cheese, grated	Mushrooms, sliced
Italian sausage, sliced	Romano cheese, grated
	Parmesan cheese, grated

Put pizza together starting with crust, sauce, grated Mozzarella cheese, Italian sausage, mushrooms and ending with Romano and Parmesan cheeses. Bake at 350° for 25 minutes. Let stand for 5 to 10 minutes before slicing. Serves 4.

Mrs. Linda Musci (Richard)

"Chihuahua" Supreme

2	tablespoons butter	Oil
1	large onion, chopped	½ pound mild Cheddar cheese, grated
12	large flour tortillas	Sour cream to taste
1	cup refried beans	Sliced ripe olives, for garnish
12	all beef weiners	

Sauté onions in butter. Spread refried beans on tortillas. Sprinkle 1 tablespoon sautéed onion over beans. Put weiner on tortilla and roll up. Toothpick tortilla and contents. Fry in preheated oil until tortilla is light brown, about 3 minutes. Top immediatley with grated cheese, sour cream and ripe olives. Serves 12. *This recipe comes from 4 years as a "Chihuahua" booth chairman.*

Mrs. Khier Remadna (Lynn)

"Egg For Baby"

William B. Montgomery, Austin artist, has been experimenting to give his oils and etchings a sense of space on literal surface levels. His formal art training included undergraduate work at the University of New Mexico; special studies at the Art Institute, Perugia, Italy; and the Kansas City Art Institute.

"Egg for Baby" is one of the results of Bill's studies. It is the culmination of a hand watercolored-two color zinc plate etching. The mother's unique headdress at first draws one away from the young lad waiting for his eggs, which are being cooked in a contemporary kitchen. But the mother's Pharaoh-type dress urges one more approved look.

Since this is a Texas Sesquicentennial year, Bill recalled an ancestor Thomas Battle, Marlin, Texas, who was a member of the honor guard for General Robert E. Lee, commander in chief of the Confederate Army. His great great grandfather, Nicholas W. Battle, Waco, was one of the first circuit-riding Judges in Texas.

He has been included in 23 recent selected exhibitions, such as: "New Works", Laguna Gloria Art Museum; National Print Invitational, University of Dallas; Texas Only, Texas Fine Arts Association, Laguna Gloria Art Museum; Clifford Gallery, Dallas; Four State Survey, Santa Fe Festival of the Arts, Santa Fe; Exposicion Grafica, Guadalajara, Mexico and several "invitationals", Longview Museum, Longview, Texas.

In Texas his work is shown by Clifford Gallery, Dallas and Morgan's, Austin.

Vegetables

Sautéed Artichoke Hearts

2	(10 ounce) packages frozen artichoke hearts
1	cup sliced mushrooms
1/3	cup butter
2	teaspoons Beau Monde seasoning

1	teaspoon basil
1/2	teaspoon chervil
1	tablespoon lemon juice

Thaw artichokes. Sauté mushrooms in butter until golden. Remove from pan and reserve. Add artichokes to pan and sprinkle with Beau Monde, basil and chervil. Sauté until golden. Stir in mushrooms and lemon juice and serve immediately.

Mrs. Paul Loftin (Liz)

Stir-Fry Asparagus

1	bunch asparagus
1	teaspoon sugar

1	tablespoon butter
	Salt and pepper to taste

Cut narrow, baby asparagus on the bias into one inch pieces. Put one teaspoon sugar in the middle of a hot skillet. When sugar begins to brown, add butter. Add asparagus all around outer edge of skillet. Cover and cook two minutes. After two minutes, stir and push back to sides, then cook one more minute. Add salt and pepper. Serve immediately. Serves 2.

Susan Hasslocher
Guild President 1984-1985

Asparagus With Vegetable Sauce

1	clove garlic, minced
2	tablespoons butter, melted
1 1/2	tablespoons lemon juice

3	tablespoons mayonnaise
1	pound asparagus, trimmed and cooked

Sauté garlic in butter until soft, but not brown. Cool. Add lemon juice and mayonnaise. Serve over hot cooked asparagus.

Mrs. John Stark (Kay)

Barley Casserole

½ cup butter	3 pimientos, chopped
1 onion, chopped	2 cups chicken broth
¾ pound fresh mushrooms, sliced	Salt, pepper, garlic salt, garlic juice and parsley to taste
1¼ cups uncooked barley	

Sauté onion and mushrooms in butter. Add barley and cook until brown. Transfer mixture to a casserole, and add pimientos, chicken broth and seasonings. Cover and bake at 350° for 50 to 60 minutes. Serves 6 to 8. *This wonderful casserole has become a traditional vegetable served every year at the Fiesta Beverage Captains dinner meeting. Someone always asks for this recipe which is handed down from chairman to chairman.*

Mrs. Joe Ballanfonte (B. Ann)
Fiesta Chairman 1971-1972

Barley And Vegetable Delight

¼ small green bell pepper, chopped	1 medium zucchini, chopped
1 rib celery, chopped	⅔ cup uncooked barley
1 small onion, chopped	1⅓ cups water
2 green onions and tops, chopped	1 teaspoon salt
	1 teaspoon oregano
¼ cup parsley, chopped	Pepper to taste
1 medium tomato, chopped	1½ tablespoons olive oil
	Grated cheese to serve

Mix together all ingredients except cheese and place in a greased 2 quart casserole. Bake covered in a 350° oven for 1 hour. Remove lid, return to oven and bake until most of the liquid is absorbed, about 15 minutes. Serve with grated cheese of your choice. Serves 4. *This is a good and healthy vegetarian meal. Serve with whole wheat rolls and a tossed green salad. Feel free to experiment by adding other chopped fresh vegetables and by varying the cheese.*

Sylvia Stevens

- *Use soured milk to clean your copper cookware. Pour a little into a shallow dish pan, then set the copper bottomed pan inside that. After a brief soaking, it can be washed and dried.*

Italian Style Carrots

2 pounds carrots, peeled and
   sliced into 1/4 inch thick
   slices
5 tablespoons butter
Water to cover carrots

1/2 teaspoon salt or to taste
1/4 teaspoon sugar
Pepper to taste
3 tablespoons grated
   Parmesan cheese

Melt butter in a large skillet and add carrots in a single layer. Sauté for about 1 minute, and add enough water to almost cover the single layer. Cook over medium heat until liquid has evaporated and only butter remains in the bottom. Add salt, sugar and a few more tablespoons of water. Again, cook until the water evaporates. Continue to add water and cook down until carrots are cooked to suit your taste. Add pepper and Parmesan cheese, stirring a few times. Serves 8 to 10.

Mrs. Larry Hall (Jane)
Fiesta Chairman 1982-1983

Apricot Glazed Carrots

4 cups scrapped and sliced
   carrots
3 tablespoons butter
1/3 cup apricot preserves

1/4 teaspoon salt
1 teaspoon grated orange peel
1/4 teaspoon ground nutmeg
2 teaspoons fresh lemon juice

Cook carrots in boiling salted water until just tender, about 20 minutes. Drain. Melt butter and stir in apricot preserves, salt, orange peel, nutmeg, and lemon juice. Lightly toss carrots into butter mixture and serve at once.

Mrs. Marcus Bone (Beverly)
Fiesta Chairman 1983-1984

Carrots In Cream Sauce

1 pound carrots
Salt to taste
2 tablespoons butter

Freshly ground white pepper
1/2 cup whipping cream

Remove ends from carrots and place whole in boiling salted water until cooked, but still firm, about 15 minutes. Drain and peel carrots when cool. Cut into 1/8 inch slices. Heat butter in a skillet, and sauté carrot slices for about 5 minutes. Season with salt and pepper. Add cream, 1 tablespoon at a time, stirring slowly until cream is absorbed. Continue to stir and add cream until all cream is used. Serves 4.

Mrs. Robert Bluntzer (Jo)

Cumin Green Beans

1	pound fresh green beans	1	(15 ounce) can tomato
6	slices bacon		sauce
1	medium onion, chopped	1	tablespoon cumin seeds
1	clove garlic, minced	1	teaspoon sugar

Remove strings from beans; wash and cut into 1-inch pieces. Cook beans, covered, in a small amount of boiling salted water for 15 to 20 minutes or until tender. Drain and set aside. Cook bacon in a large skillet until crisp; remove bacon, reserving drippings. Crumble bacon and set aside. Sauté onion and garlic in bacon drippings until tender. Stir in beans, bacon and remaining ingredients; reduce heat and simmer, uncovered, 10 to 15 minutes. Serves 4.

Mrs. Paul Groos (Honey)

Green Beans With Sour Cream

1½	pounds fresh green beans	¼	cup chopped parsley
1	clove garlic, minced		Pepper to taste
¼	cup butter, melted	1	cup sour cream
2	tablespoons bread crumbs		

Remove strings and cut beans into 1-inch slices. Cook, covered in a small amount of boiling salted water for 15 to 20 minutes. Drain and reserve. Sauté garlic in butter until tender; add bread crumbs and cook until browned. Combine green beans, bread crumbs, parsley, pepper and sour cream. Place in a lightly greased casserole and bake at 350° for 15 minutes or until thoroughly heated. Serves 6.

Mrs. Scott Chapman (Vicki)
Fiesta Chairman 1980-1981

Family Favorite Green Beans

2	medium onions, finely chopped	Salt to taste
		Cayenne pepper to taste
1 to 2 cloves garlic, minced		2 pounds fresh green beans,
Bacon drippings or oil		remove stings and snap
2	large tomatoes, sliced	

Brown onions and garlic in a few tablespoons bacon drippings or oil until light golden brown. Add sliced tomatoes and cook until well done. Add salt and cayenne pepper to taste. Cook green beans in boiling, salted water for 10 minutes, then drain. Pour sauce on top; cover and cook slowly over low heat for 1 hour. Uncover pan during last 15 minutes of cooking. Serves 8 to 10.

Mrs. David Hart (Sue)
Fiesta Chairman 1985-1986

Green Bean Medley

2   pounds fresh green beans
Salt to taste
6   carrots, scraped and thickly
    sliced
12 tiny onions, peeled
6 to 8 slices bacon, cut into
    strips
1/4 cup butter

1   tablespoon sugar
1 1/4 cups water
1/4 cup half and half cream
Freshly ground black pepper
1   tablespoon chopped fresh
    chervil
1   tablespoon chopped fresh
    parsley

Trim beans and cut into 2-inch pieces. Cook in boiling salted water until tender but still firm, about 10 to 15 minutes. Meanwhile cook bacon in butter until crisp, then remove. Add carrots and onions to drippings in pan and sauté until golden brown. Add water and sugar and simmer until evaporated. Continue to cook until remaining juices have caramelized. Gently toss carrots and onions to coat well. Drain beans thoroughly and add to carrots and onions along with the bacon, cream, salt and pepper. Heat gently for a few minutes, then sprinkle with chervil and parsley just before serving. Serves 4 to 6.

Mrs. Larry Hall (Jane)
Fiesta Chairman 1982-1983

Broccoli Soufflé

2   (10 ounce) packages frozen
    chopped broccoli, cooked
    and drained
1   tablespoon butter, melted
1/2 cup mayonnaise

1   tablespoon flour
3   eggs, beaten
1   cup half and half cream
1/2 teaspoon salt

Combine drained broccoli, butter, mayonnaise and flour. Fold in eggs and cream. Pour into a greased, medium size ring mold. Place mold in a pan of hot water, and bake uncovered in a preheated 375° oven for 55 minutes or until knife inserted in center comes out clean. Unmold and serve immediately. Serves 6.

Mrs. Marcus Bone (Beverly)
Fiesta Chairman 1983-1984

Sautéed Vegetable Combo

½ cup butter
1 shallot, minced
3 pounds broccoli

1 pound mushrooms, brushed and sliced
2 red bell peppers, sliced lengthwise

In a large skillet or wok, melt butter and add shallots. Trim broccoli to use flowerettes only, saving stalks for soups. Add vegetables, all at once to hot butter and stir continuously about 4 minutes, or until crisp-tender. Do not overcook as vegetables should retain color and crispness. Serve immediately. Serves 8. *Many vegetables lend themselves to this aesthetically appealing treat. Try snow peas, green beans, asparagus, zucchini, carrots. Experiment!*

Mrs. Don Davis (Pat)
Fiesta Chairman 1976-1977, Guild President 1983-1984

Easy Broccoli-Spinach Casserole

1 (10 ounce) package frozen chopped broccoli
1 (10 ounce) package frozen chopped spinach
1 cup sour cream
2 tablespoons flour

1½ ounces Parmesan cheese, grated
½ teaspoon seasoned salt
½ teaspoon lemon pepper
¼ cup finely chopped onions, optional

Defrost broccoli and spinach and mix together in a large bowl. Drain off excess spinach liquid if necessary. In a separate small bowl, combine sour cream, flour, Parmesan cheese, salt and pepper. Stir together until well blended, adding chopped onion if you prefer. Pour into a 1 quart casserole, and bake at 350° for 30 minutes.

Mrs. Dan Bullock (Gayle)

Broccoli Italian Style

¼ cup olive oil
1 teaspoon chopped garlic
6 cups fresh broccoli floweretes

1½ cups dry white wine
¼ teaspoon salt
Pepper to taste

Heat olive oil in a large skillet. Remove pan from heat and sauté garlic about 1 minute. Add broccoli and return to heat, stirring to blend. Add wine and seasonings, and simmer uncovered for about 20 minutes. Remove broccoli to a heated serving dish; boil remaining liquid over high heat to reduce and pour over broccoli. Serves 4 to 6.

Mrs. David Hart (Sue)
Fiesta Chairman 1985-1986

Broccoli-Cheese Casserole

4   (10 ounce) packages frozen
    broccoli spears
3/4 cup diced celery
3/4 cup diced onion
1/2 cup butter or less, melted
1 1/2 cans cream of mushroom
    soup

1 1/2 to 1 3/4 cups sour cream
Juice of one lemon
1/4 cup chopped parsley
Salt, pepper and garlic powder
    to taste
2   cups grated sharp Cheddar
    cheese

Cook broccoli until tender. Drain well; allow to cool and cut into 1 inch cubes. Sauté celery and onion together in butter in a small pan. Set aside. Combine soup, sour cream, lemon juice, parsley, salt, pepper, and garlic powder in large bowl. Stir in sautéed vegetables. Add cut-up broccoli; gently mix together all ingredients and pour into a buttered casserole. Top generously with grated cheese. Bake at 350° for 20 to 30 minutes or until bubbly. Serves 10.

Mrs. David Todd (Cathy)

Quick Baked Beans

4   slices bacon, cut in strips
2/3 cup finely chopped onion
2   (16 ounce) cans pork and
    beans
1/2 cup barbecue sauce

1/3 cup firmly packed brown
    sugar
1   tablespoon prepared
    mustard

Sauté bacon and onions in a large saucepan until onions are tender. Stir in remaining ingredients, and bring to a boil. Cook 15 minutes, stirring occasionlly. Yields 4 1/2 cups, or 4 to 6 servings.

Mrs. Danny Pounds (Charlotte)

Sweet And Sour Cabbage

3   slices bacon, diced
1   medium head cabbage
1/2 medium onion, diced
1   apple, diced
2   handsfull of grapes,
    optional

2   cups water
Salt and pepper to taste
1 to 2 tablespoons white
    vinegar
1   tablespoon sugar
1 1/2 tablespoons flour, optional

Cook bacon in pan, then remove and drain. Cut cabbage into very thin slices and add to drippings. Add onion, apple, grapes and water, and cook for1 hour. When done, add salt, pepper, vinegar and sugar. Juices should be cooked down. If desired, thicken with flour mixed with warm water. Serves 4.

Mrs. Tom Buckman (Ramona)

Frosted Cauliflower

1 medium head cauliflower	½ teaspoon salt
1 cup mayonnaise	½ cup shredded Cheddar
2 teaspoons prepared mustard	cheese
1 tablespoon chopped onion	

In microwave, cook cauliflower in ¼ cup water in covered dish on HIGH for 10 to 12 minutes or until tender. Combine mayonnaise, mustard, onion and salt. Spread over cauliflower and sprinkle with shredded cheese. Microwave for 2 minutes or until cheese melts. Let stand for 2 minutes before serving.

Mrs. John Johnson (Sally)

Tomato-Corn Casserole

2 (16 ounce) cans kernel corn	1 cup grated Longhorn
1 (16 ounce) can tomatoes, chopped and undrained	Cheddar cheese
½ cup chopped green bell pepper	5 crackers, crushed
	Salt and pepper to taste

Combine all ingredients and place in a greased casserole dish. Bake at 350° for 30 minutes.

Mrs. Bill von Rosenberg (Susan)

Corn Pudding

1 (16 ounce) can cream style corn	5 eggs
1 (12 ounce) can evaporated milk	¼ cup butter, melted
	¼ teaspoon pepper
	3 tablespoons sugar, optional

Combine all ingredients in a food processor or blender and process until smooth. Pour into a lightly buttered 12x8x2 inch baking dish. Bake at 350° for 30 to 40 minutes. Serves 6 to 8.

Mrs. Marcus Bone (Beverly)
Fiesta Chairman 1983-1984

• *If you bend an asparagus stalk, it will snap at the point where it becomes tender, just where you want it to. And if you peel stalks with a vegetable peeler before you snap them, you'll have less waste and more asparagus to eat.*

Baked Corn Casserole

1 large onion, chopped	2/3 cup milk
1 medium green bell pepper, chopped	1 egg, well beaten
1/4 cup butter, melted	1 cup rolled cracker crumbs
2 1/2 cups can cream corn	1 cup grated Cheddar cheese
2 1/2 cups can whole kernel corn	2 tablespoons sugar
1 (4 ounce) jar chopped pimiento	Salt and pepper (red and black) to taste

Sauté onion and green bell pepper in butter. Combine with corn and other ingredients in the order given. Mix well and pour into a greased casserole. Bake at 350° for approximately 1 hour.

Mrs. Andy Tewell (Judy)

Stuffed Eggplant

1 large eggplant	3 tablespoons butter
1 cup coarsely chopped fresh mushrooms	Salt and pepper to taste
3 tablespoons chopped onion	1/2 cup whipping cream
1 clove garlic, minced	Bread or cracker crumbs
	Bacon slices, optional

Cut a large eggplant in half, lengthwise. Remove pulp leaving a 1/2 inch shell under the skin. Cut pulp into cubes and cook in a little salted water for 10 minutes. Sauté chopped mushrooms, chopped onions, and minced garlic in butter. Add drained eggplant, salt and pepper to taste and cream. Fill eggplant shells with mixture and sprinkle bread or cracker crumbs on the top. Minced raw bacon slices are also good sprinkled over crumbs. Bake at 350° for 45 minutes. Serves 4.

Mary Coneway

Quick Baked Eggplant

1 large eggplant, sliced 1/2 inch thick	Paprika to taste
	Garlic powder to taste
Salt and pepper to taste	Mayonnaise

Place eggplant slices on a non-stick baking pan. Sprinkle with seasonings, and broil until brown and tender. Spread mayonnaise lightly on slices, and broil until mayonnaise is brown. *This vegetable is also great as an appetizer!*

Mrs. Edward Konop (Rita)

Eggplant Vegetable Pie

1 package pie crust mix (or your own pie crust)
1/2 cup grated Romano or Parmesan cheese, divided
2 medium onions, sliced
1 green bell pepper, seeded and sliced
3/4 pound zucchini, thinly sliced

Vegetable oil
1 1/2 pounds eggplant, sliced
1 pound tomatoes, sliced
1 teaspoon salt
1/4 teaspoon pepper
Celery salt to taste
Garlic salt to taste

Roll dough to fit a 10 or 11 inch pie pan or quiche dish. Sprinkle crust with 1/4 cup cheese. In a large skillet, sauté onions, green pepper and zucchini in 3 tablespoons oil until tender. Season with salt, pepper, celery salt and garlic salt. Brown eggplant slices, a few at a time, in same skillet, adding more oil, as needed. Arrange vegetables, including tomatoes, in layers in the pie shell. Sprinkle with remaining cheese. It can be baked like this, or you may add a top crust, as I prefer. Slit in a few places, then rub a little water on top crust and sprinkle with a little more cheese. Bake at 350° for 45 minutes. Serves 6 to 8. *To prepare eggplant properly, peel eggplant, slice in rounds about 1/4 inch thick, lay on several thicknesses of paper towels, and generously salt each round. Let sit for 30 to 40 minutes, then turn over and repeat salting. Blot before frying. This removes any bitterness the eggplant might have, and also removes quite a bit of the water, which makes for easier frying.*

Mrs. Terry Armstrong (Ann)

Holiday Cheese Grits

1 cup grits
4 cups boiling water
1/2 cup corn oil margarine
1 tablespoon grated onion
1 teaspoon seasoned salt
1/2 teaspoon garlic salt
1 tablespoon Worcestershire sauce

Tabasco to taste
1 cup grated sharp Cheddar cheese
1 (6 ounce) roll of garlic cheese, cut into pieces
2 eggs, well-beaten

Cook grits according to package directions in 4 cups boiling water. Add margarine, onion, seasonings and cheese. In a separate bowl, beat together the eggs. Beat a spoonful or two of hot grits into eggs; then slowly add this egg mixture to hot grits, stirring all the time. This keeps eggs from curdling when adding to hot grits. Pour into a buttered one-quart casserole dish. Bake at 350° for 50 minutes. Let set a few minutes before serving. Serves 6 to 8.

Mrs. Dan Bullock (Gayle)

Hominy And Squash Casserole

2 (16 ounce) cans hominy	1 (4 ounce) can green chilies
2 pounds yellow squash	1½ cups sour cream
1 large onion, chopped	1 teaspoon salt
¼ cup butter or margarine	Crushed Doritos to top
½ cup water	
½ pound sharp Cheddar cheese, grated, divided	

Drain hominy. Slowly cook squash and onion in butter and water until tender. Reserve 1 cup cheese for topping and add remaining to squash mixture along with the hominy, green chilies, sour cream and salt. Pour into a 3 quart casserole and top with remaining cheese and crushed Doritos. Bake at 325° for 1 hour.

Mrs. Berry Gannaway (Jackie)
Fiesta Chairman 1984-1985

Mushroom Pie

Crust:

2 cups pastry flour	¼ pound butter
¼ teaspoon salt	¾ cup cold milk

Sift flour with salt. Cut butter into flour with 2 knives. This will be lumpy. Add enough milk to blend dough together, but don't overmix. Divide dough into 2 balls and chill for 30 minutes while preparing other ingredients.

Sauce and Filling:

6 tablespoons butter, divided	1 small onion, chopped
2 tablespoons flour	½ cup unsalted cashews, chopped
1½ cups milk	Pinch of thyme, salt, and pepper
1½ pounds mushrooms, sliced	
5 celery ribs, chopped	

To make sauce melt butter; mix in flour and make a paste. Add milk and heat until thickened, stirring frequently about 20 minutes. Next, sauté mushrooms, celery, onion, and cashews in 4 tablespoons butter until tender. Add seasonings. Cover and keep warm. Combine sauce and filling, mixing well. Preheat oven to 400°. Make pie crust to fit one 10 inch pie pan and pour in filling. Cover with top crust, making a few decorative slits to let out steam. Reduce heat to 350° and bake 30 minutes or until crust is golden.

Annette Carlozzi

Baked Onion

1 large white onion	1½ tablespoons Worcestershire
1 chicken boullion cube	sauce
1½ tablespoons softened butter	

Set the onion so that it will stand up and cut a hole in the top of the onion and ¾ of the way through the middle. Scrape out enough of the inside to place bouillon cube in bottom. You will have about a 1½ inch hole across the top of a large onion. Place the bouillon cube in the bottom of the hole and fill with Worcestershire sauce. Top with softened butter. Wrap onion tightly in foil and place in a pan in case it leaks. Cook at 350° for 1 hour. Yields one onion per person. *Serve with steak, roast, or baked potatoes. The juice is great as a sauce.*

Leslie Rost

Creamed Onions

18 to 20 small onions	1 cup shredded American
⅓ cup vegetable oil	cheese
3 tablespoons flour	Peanuts, chopped
1½ cups milk	

Peel onions and cook in a large amount of boiling salted water until tender; drain. Blend oil and flour; add milk and cook slowly until thick, stirring constantly. Add cheese and stir until melted. Add onions and heat through. Place in serving bowl and sprinkle with peanuts. Serves 6 to 8.

Susan Hasslocher
Guild President 1984-1985

Sherried Fruit

1 (16 ounce) can peaches, drained	1 (16 ounce) can black cherries, drained, pitted
1 (16 ounce) can pears, drained	¾ cup brown sugar
1 (16 ounce) can pineapple, drained	⅓ cup butter, melted
1 (16 ounce) can apricots, drained	½ cup sherry
	Cinnamon to taste

Place drained fruit in a 9x13 inch casserole. Mix brown sugar and melted butter with sherry. Pour over fruit, then sprinkle with cinnamon. Bake at 350° for 1 hour. Baste with syrup as often as possible. Serves 8 to 10. *This is best if made a day in advance and reheated the second day at 350° for 30 minutes.*

Mrs. Larry Schrader (Vicki)

Jalapeño Potatoes

4 medium red potatoes
1 small green bell pepper, slivered
1 (4 ounce) jar chopped pimientos
Salt and pepper to taste
1/4 cup butter

1 tablespoon flour
1 cup milk
1/2 (6 ounce) roll garlic cheese, cubed
1/2 (6 ounce) roll of jalepeño cheese, cubed

Boil potatoes in the jackets in salted water until tender. When cool, peel, slice and layer in a buttered casserole with slivered green pepper and pimiento. Salt and pepper each layer. Melt butter in a saucepan, add flour and stir until blended. Gradually add milk, stirring constantly. Add cheese until melted. Pour over potatoes and bake at 350° for 45 minutes to 1 hour. Serves 6 to 8. *This can be made early in the day and refrigerated until ready to bake.*

Mrs. Sammy Kurio (Frances)

Sautéed New Potatoes

3 tablespoons butter, divided
1 tablespoon oil
2 pounds small new potatoes, peeled and dried

1/4 teaspoon salt
Black pepper
Minced parsley to serve

In a large heavy skillet heat 2 tablespoons butter and oil until bubbly. Add potatoes. Cook over meduim high heat until lightly browned on all sides, 8 to10 minutes. Add salt. Reduce heat to low; cover and cook 15 to 20 minutes or until potatoes are tender and well-browned, shaking pan often. With slotted spoon, remove to warm dish. Discard pan drippings. Add remaining 1 tablespoon butter to pan, and heat until bubbly. Pour over potatoes. Sprinkle with pepper and parsley.

Mrs. Charlie Cantwell (Winn)

Sesame Potato Sticks

6 to 8 medium baking potatoes, peeled
3/4 cup sesame seeds

1/2 cup butter, melted
Salt and paprika to taste

Cut potatoes into 1 inch thick strips. Sprinkle sesame seeds on a layer of waxed paper. Dip potatoes into melted butter and coat one side with sesame seeds. Place sticks on a baking sheet and sprinkle with salt and paprika. Bake at 400° for 40 minutes or until done. Serves 8.

Mrs. Alvin J. Golden (Mary Ann)
Guild President 1978-1979

Gertrude's Fried Potatoes

6 to 8 potatoes, peeled and
   sliced

Oil for frying
1   onion, sliced, optional

Coat heavy frying pan with oil. Layer potatoes and onion in pan; cover
and fry over very low heat. Turn potatoes as they brown. Remove lid
during the last 5 minutes of cooking to crisp potatoes. Serves 4 to 6.

Mrs. Paul Loftin (Liz)

Buffet Potatoes

1   (32 ounce) package frozen
   hash brown potatoes,
   thawed
1/2 cup butter, melted
1/4 cup chopped onions

1   can cream of chicken soup
2   cups sour cream
10 ounces Cheddar cheese,
   grated
Bread Crumbs

Thaw potatoes. Combine all ingredients. Sprinkle with bread crumbs.
Bake in a 9x13 inch pan at 350° for 1 hour. *This can be cooked in the
microwave on HIGH for 20 to 25 minutes, stirring several times.*

Mrs. Lester Gray (Cathy)

Microwave Parmesan Potatoes

2   medium sized baking
   potatoes, 8 to 10 ounces
   each
1   tablespoon butter, melted

1   teaspoon oregano, divided
2   tablespoons grated
   Parmesan cheese
Paprika

Scrub potatoes and cut in half lengthwise. Melt butter. Dip cut side of
potatoes into butter. Sprinkle with oregano, about 1½ teaspoons Parmesan cheese and paprika. Place cut side up on a microwave baking tray or
sheet. Microwave 3 to 4 minutes on HIGH; rotate tray, and microwave
another 4 minutes. Potatoes should be cooked 7 minutes per pound.
Serves 2 to 4. *Don't salt in advance due to microwave requirements. Taste
and add salt after cooking, if desired.*

Mrs. Ted Nagel (Harriet)
Fiesta Chairman 1974-1975

• *Friday Night Preview of Fiesta began in 1975. In 1976 the beautiful iron front gates
to the Museum were restored and hung in place.*

Sweet Potato Timbales With Herbed Cranberry Sauce

Sweet Potatoes:

1	(16 ounce) can sweet potatoes	1	tablespoon firmly packed light brown sugar
2	large eggs	1/2	teaspoon salt
1	egg yolk	1/2	teaspoon ground cinnamon
1	cup whipping cream		

Drain and purée sweet potatoes. Add eggs, egg yolk, cream, brown sugar, salt and cinnamon; blend well in a food processor. Generously butter six 1/2 cup custard cups. Fill cups evenly with sweet potato mixture. Place filled cups in a hot water bath. Cover pan loosely with aluminum foil. Bake in a 400° oven for 45 minutes or until knife inserted in the center comes out clean. Let stand 10 minutes. Run a knife around edge of each mold. Invert onto serving platter. Serves 6.

Herbed Cranberry Sauce:

1	(8 ounce) can whole berry cranberry sauce	1/4	teaspoon basil
1/4	cup port wine	1/4	teaspoon salt

Purée cranberry sauce into a small saucepan. Add wine, basil and salt. Cook over moderate heat until thoroughly heated. Serve separately or pour over timbales.

Mrs. Ralph Wayne (Marti)

Sweet Potato Casserole

4	large or 6 medium sweet potatoes	5	slices bacon
1/4	cup butter	1/2	teaspoon salt
3/4	cup sugar	1	teaspoon pepper

Wash and boil potatoes in salted water until fork tender. Do not overcook. Peel potatoes and cut into 1/4 inch thick slices. Place slices into a casserole, adding sugar to each layer. Dot butter over top layer. Place bacon slices over all and sprinkle with salt and pepper and additional sugar. Bake at 350° for 1 hour.

Gene Hudgins

Sweet Potato Divine

1 (16 ounce) can sweet
   potatoes
1 cup butter, divided
1½ cups sugar
2 eggs, beaten
¼ cup evaporated milk

2 teaspoons vanilla extract
½ cup brown sugar
⅓ cup flour
1 cup pecans
1 cup coconut

Drain and mash potatoes. Cream together ½ cup butter, sugar, and eggs, and mix with potatoes. Add milk and vanilla, mixing well. Put in a casserole dish. For topping, soften ½ cup butter and mix with the flour, brown sugar, pecans and coconut. Crumble over casserole and bake at 350° for 40 minutes. Serves 6 to 8. *Very rich!*

Mrs. Glen Johnson (Debbie)

Green Rice

1 cup uncooked rice
1 (10 ounce) package frozen
   chopped broccoli
1 onion, chopped
3 to 4 celery ribs, chopped

¼ cup butter or margarine
1 can cream of mushroom
   soup
1 (6 ounce) jar processed
   cheese

Cook rice and broccoli according to directions on packages. Sauté onion and celery in butter. Combine rice, broccoli, vegetables, mushroom soup, and processed cheese in a casserole. Bake uncovered at 350° for 40 minutes. *May be made ahead of time and refrigerated.* Serves 8 to10.

Mrs. Howell Ridout (Debbie)

Wild Rice And Almond Casserole

½ cup butter
½ pound mushrooms, sliced
1 clove garlic, minced
2 tablespoons chopped green
   bell pepper
2 tablespoons chopped green
   onions

1 cup wild rice, washed
½ cup chopped blanched
   almonds
3 cups chicken broth

In a heavy skillet, melt butter and add mushrooms, garlic, green pepper, onions, rice and almonds. Cook for 10 minutes, stirring constantly. Add broth and place in a greased casserole. Cover tightly and bake at 375° for 1 hour. Do not salt. Serves 6.

Susan Hasslocher
Guild President 1984-1985

Easy Rice Pilaf

1	cup uncooked rice	1	can beef bouillon
1	can onion or French onion soup	½	cup butter, cut into pats

Mix together rice, onion soup and beef bouillon in a pyrex casserole. Put butter pats all over the top. Cover and bake at 350° for one hour. *My kids love this easy, no fail recipe.*

Mrs. Lester Gray (Cathy)

Mushroom Rice

1	cup rice	2	cubes bouillion, either chicken or beef or vegetable
2	cups water		
1	tablespoon butter	1	(4 ounce) can chopped mushroom pieces
½	teaspoon salt		
Pepper to taste			

Combine all the ingredients in a pan, and bring to a boil. Reduce heat to low and cook covered 15 to 20 minutes.

Mrs. Chad Snow (Frances)

Syrian Rice

2	cups dried apricots	½	green bell pepper, chopped
1	cup golden raisins	½	teaspoon curry powder
2	cups raw rice	1	cup toasted almonds
½	cup butter	Salt and pepper to taste	
1	cup minced onion		

Cover apricots and raisins with water and soak for 30 minutes. Cook rice according to package directions until done. Preheat oven to 375°. In a skillet, melt butter and sauté onion, green pepper and curry. Add almonds and the drained and chopped apricots, raisins and cooked rice. Correct seasonings as desired. Put in a greased baking dish and bake at 375° for about 30 minutes. Serves 10.

Mrs. Paul Loftin (Liz)

• *To prevent nutrient loss when preparing vegetables, cut them into large chunks and cook them in already boiling water.*

Spinach And Rice Casserole

½ cup chopped onion
½ cup chopped celery
½ cup blanched almonds
2 tablespoons butter
1 chicken bouillon cube

⅓ cup water
1 can cream of mushroom soup
2 cups cooked spinach
2 cups cooked rice

Sauté onion, celery and almonds in butter. Dissolve bouillon cube in water; mix with soup and sautéed vegetables. Spread spinach in the bottom of a pyrex casserole, and cover with half of the soup mixture. Add rice to pyrex and top with remaining soup mixture. Bake at 350° for 40 minutes.

Mrs. Lester Gray (Cathy)

Spinach With Artichokes

4 (10 ounce) packages frozen chopped spinach
11 ounces cream cheese, softened
5 tablespoons butter, melted
Juice of one lemon

Seasoned salt and pepper to taste
Several dashes of nutmeg
2 (16 ounce) cans artichoke hearts, drained

Thaw spinach, then drain well. Combine cream cheese, butter and lemon juice. Add to spinach along with seasoned salt, pepper and nutmeg. Put artichokes in a 16x8 inch baking dish and spoon spinach mixture on top. Cover with foil and punch a few holes in top. Bake at 350° for 30 minutes. Serves 14 to16. *This makes a wonderful company vegetable dish which can be made in the morning and refrigerated. If so, remove from refrigerator at least 30 minutes before baking.*

Mrs. Truman Breed, Jr. (Anne)
Guild President 1973-1974

• Spinach is available year round, though it is always at its best from mid-winter until late spring. Frozen spinach is always available and suffers less from freezing and thawing than do most other vegetables.

Baked Herb Spinach

1 cup finely chopped onion	1 1/4 cups grated Parmesan
2 cloves garlic, minced	cheese, divided
1/4 cup margarine	1/2 cup bread crumbs
5 (10 ounce) packages frozen	1 teaspoon marjoram
chopped spinach, thawed	1 teaspoon salt
and well-drained	1/4 teaspoon pepper
2 cups half and half cream	

Heat oven to 350°. Sauté onions and garlic in margarine until tender. Combine with spinach, cream, 1 cup Parmesan cheese, bread crumbs, marjoram, salt and pepper. Turn into buttered 3 quart shallow casserole. Sprinkle top with remaining cheese in a diagonal pattern. Bake 30 minutes at 350° or until bubbly. Serves 12.

Mrs. Sammy Juvé (Laura)

Spinach Madeline

2 (10 ounce) packages frozen	3/4 teaspoon garlic salt
chopped spinach	1/2 teaspoon salt, optional
4 tablespoons butter	1 (6 ounce) roll jalepeño
2 tablespoons flour	cheese, cubed
2 tablespoons chopped onion	1 teaspoon Worcestershire
1/2 cup evaporated milk	sauce
1/2 cup vegetable liquid	Red pepper to taste
1/2 teaspoon black pepper	Buttered bread crumbs
3/4 teaspoon celery salt	

Cook spinach according to package directions. Drain and reserve 1/2 cup liquid. Melt butter in saucepan over low heat. Add flour, stirring until blended and smooth, but not brown. Add onion and cook until soft, but not brown. Slowly add milk and reserved liquid, stirring constantly to avoid lumps. Cook until smooth and thick; continue stirring. Add seasonings and cheese, stirring until melted. Combine with cooked spinach. Put mixture into a casserole and top with buttered bread crumbs. *The flavor is better if prepared a day ahead, and freezes well. It's very good and very different. A sure hit!*

Mrs. Emory Gose (Pat)

Mexican Spinach

4   slices bacon
¼   cup butter, melted
1½ pounds fresh spinach or
    frozen leaf spinach
1   onion, chopped

1   clove garlic, minced
½   teaspoon cumin
Salt and pepper, to taste
1   large tomato, chopped
Dash of sugar

Fry bacon until brown; drain on paper towels. Reserve drippings, and crumble bacon. Mix butter with bacon drippings in skillet. Add spinach, onion, and garlic. Sauté until wilted. Add cumin, salt, pepper, chopped tomato and sugar. Serves 4. *Even men who don't like spinach love this dish! For a different treat, try thinly sliced yellow squash instead of spinach.*

Mrs. Terry Townsend (Mimi)

Creamed Spinach Ring

2   pounds fresh spinach or 2
    (10 ounce) packages frozen
    chopped spinach
Parmesan cheese, grated
4   tablespoons butter
1   small onion, chopped
1   cup whipping cream
1   teaspoon salt

Dash of pepper and nutmeg
4   eggs
½   cup fresh bread crumbs,
    about 2 slices
⅓   cup grated Swiss or
    Gruyere cheese
Cooked carrots to serve

Thoughly wash spinach; remove and discard large stems. Place spinach in a large kettle with just the water clinging to the leaves. Cook covered, tossing with a fork once or twice for 5 minutes or until the spinach is just tender. Drain very well and chop coarsely. (If using frozen spinach, cook as directed and drain very well.) Preheat oven to 350°. Grease well a 4½ cup ring mold and dust with Parmesan cheese. Melt butter in a large saucepan and sauté onion until tender, about 5 minutes. Add spinach, cream, salt, pepper and nutmeg and heat just to boiling. Remove from heat. In a large bowl beat the eggs slightly. Add the bread crumbs and Swiss cheese. Gradually stir in the spinach mixture. Turn into the prepared mold. Set the mold in a baking pan on the oven rack and pour boiling water into the pan to a depth of 1½ inches. Place a piece of foil or waxed paper over top of mold. Bake at 350° for 30 to 35 minutes or until a knife inserted into center comes out clean. Loosen the mold around the edge with a small spatula and invert onto a heated serving plate. Fill center of ring with cooked carrots. Serves 6 to 8. *This is a beautiful vegetable for the holiday meal and one of my family's favorites!*

Mrs. Edward Konop (Rita)

Sauté Of Sweet Peppers And Squash

2 tablespoons olive oil	6 small yellow crookneck
1/2 cup butter	squash, sliced
1 mild yellow onion or 4	1/2 clove garlic, crushed
green onions	2 tablespoons raspberry
2 yellow bell peppers, seeded	vinegar
and sliced	Salt and pepper to taste
2 red bell peppers, seeded	2 tablespoons lemon juice
and sliced	1/2 cup Italian seasoned
2 green bell peppers, seeded	breadcrumbs
and sliced	1/3 cup freshly grated
3 medium zucchini, sliced on	Parmesan cheese
the diagonal	1/2 cup pitted ripe olives

Heat oil and butter with garlic in a wok or large skillet. Sauté each vegetable separately until just tender in the order given, starting with the onion. If needed, add more oil and butter in proportions given. When all vegetables have been sautéed, add vinegar, salt, pepper and lemon juice, mixing all gently. Place in a buttered casserole dish, top with a mixture of crumbs and cheese and garnish with black olives. Bake at 400° for 15 minutes. *This is very good with fish or poultry.*

Mary Coneway

Spaghetti Squash Casserole

1 small spaghetti squash	3 tablespoons olive oil
Salt and pepper	1 (16 ounce) can Italian
1 cup water	tomatoes with basil
1/2 medium onion, chopped	1/2 teaspoon crushed oregano
1 medium large zucchini,	1/2 teaspoon garlic powder
sliced	Freshly grated Parmesan cheese
2 cloves garlic, minced	

Slice spaghetti squash in half, lengthwise. Scrape out membrane and seeds. Place halves cut side up in an oblong glass dish, and sprinkle with salt and pepper; then add approximately 1/2 cup of water to insides of each half. Cover with plastic wrap and microwave on HIGH for 8 to10 minutes, rotating dish halfway through cooking. When done, drain and cool slightly, then scrape insides of squash, forming spaghetti-like strands. Put evenly in bottom of 1 1/2 quart casserole. Sauté onions, zucchini, and garlic in olive oil until crisp-tender. Add tomatoes, oregano and garlic powder. Simmer 5 to 10 minutes. Pour over spaghetti squash mixture; season with salt and pepper, and sprinkle with grated Parmesan cheese. Bake at 350° for 15 minutes or heat in microwave on HIGH for 3 minutes. Serves 4. *Can be frozen.*

Mrs Bruce Knierim (Pam)
Fiesta Chairman 1981-1982

Squash Casserole

2 cups or more cooked yellow squash	1/2 teaspoon salt
1 cup chopped onion	1/2 teaspoon pepper
6 tablespoons margarine	1 cup grated Cheddar cheese
2 eggs	2 cups Ritz cracker crumbs, divided
1 cup milk	

Combine squash and onion, mashing squash slightly. Melt margarine and combine with eggs, milk, salt, and pepper. Mix together all ingredients, reserving 1/3 cup cracker crumbs to sprinkle on top. Bake uncovered at 375° for 40 minutes. Serves 6 to 8.

Mrs. Howell Ridout (Debbie)

Sour Cream Squash Casserole

1 1/2 pounds yellow squash	1/4 teaspoon pepper
1 tablespoon butter	1 cup sour cream
1/3 cup chopped onion	1 teaspoon dill weed
1 tablespoon water	1 tablespoon flour
1 teaspoon salt	

Put butter in a casserole and melt. Add squash, onion, water, salt and pepper. Cover and bake at 350° for 40 minutes. Combine sour cream, dill weed, and flour. Remove squash from oven and add sour cream mixture. Return to oven and bake uncovered an additional 15 minutes.

Mrs. Berry Gannaway (Jackie)
Fiesta Chairman 1984-1985

Mother's Cornbread Dressing

3 to 4 cups white bread crumbs	1 can cream of mushroom soup
6 cups cornbread crumbs	Salt and pepper to taste
1 tablespoon sage or 2 teaspoons poultry seasoning	2 eggs, beaten
4 green onions, tops and all, chopped	Turkey giblet stock

Combine bread crumbs, sage, green onions, soup, salt, pepper and eggs. Add enough turkey giblet stock to make the mixture very juicy. Place in a baking or roasting pan and bake uncovered at 350° for 1 hour to 1 hour and 30 minutes. The top will be nice and brown, and mixture will "set". Serves 6 to 8. *You can make giblet stock by simmering together for 2 hours your turkey giblets, chopped celery and celery leaves, chopped onion and water to cover. Keep adding water as needed.*

Mrs. Larry Hall (Jane)
Fiesta Chairman 1982-1983

Baked Zucchini Parmesan

5 to 6 large zucchini
3 slices bacon, cooked and crumbled
1 to 2 tablespoons bacon drippings
3 tablespoons butter, divided
1 bunch green onions, finely chopped
½ medium-sized onion, finely chopped
1 green bell pepper, finely chopped
Salt and lemon-pepper to taste
Chicken broth, optional
1 cup Italian seasoned bread crumbs
½ cup finely chopped parsley
1 cup grated Parmesan cheese
Paprika to taste

Preheat oven to 375° and place rack in middle of oven. Cut zucchini in half, lengthwise. Carefully spoon out insides of squash, and place in a bowl. Do not cut skins. Heat bacon drippings in a skillet; add 1 tablespoon butter and sauté onion and green onions over medium heat. Add green pepper and cook until onions are golden in color. Season with salt and lemon-pepper. Add reserved zucchini and cook over medium heat for 5 to 7 minutes, stirring constantly. Add some chicken broth if mixture is too dry. Add crumbled bacon, and slowly stir in bread crumbs, chopped parsley and Parmesan cheese. Remove from heat. Spoon into zucchini shells and place in a large ungreased casserole dish. Top with paprika and dot with remaining 2 tablespoons butter. Bake at 375° for 1 hour. Serves 6 to 8. *This can be prepared ahead, but not frozen.*

Mrs. Allan L. Williams (Rose Betty)

Layered Italian Zucchini

2 pounds zucchini, sliced
5 tablespoons olive oil, divided
1 (8 ounce) can Italian style tomato sauce
1 clove garlic, minced
Basil to taste
½ cup red wine
¼ pound Monterey Jack cheese, sliced
3 tablespoons grated Parmesan cheese

Sauté zucchini in 3 tablespoons oil until brown. Combine 2 tablespoons oil, tomato sauce, garlic, basil and red wine; simmer over low heat for 2 to 3 minutes. Layer zucchini, sauce and Monterey Jack cheese in a 2 quart casserole. Top with Parmesan cheese. Bake at 350° for 30 to 40 minutes. Serves 6 to 8.

Mrs. Ron Mullen (Carole)
Guild President 1981-1982

Zucchini Cheese Puff

6   medium zucchini, cut into
    large chunks
1   cup cottage cheese
1   cup grated Monterey Jack
    cheese

2   eggs, beaten
3/4 teaspoon dill weed
3/4 teaspoon salt
1/2 cup soft bread crumbs
1   tablespoon butter, melted

Simmer zucchini in salted water for 5 minutes. Drain and place in a shallow 1 1/2 quart casserole. Combine cottage cheese, Monterey Jack cheese, eggs, dill weed, and salt. Spread over zucchini and bake uncovered at 350° for 15 minutes. Toss bread crumbs with melted butter and sprinkle over casserole. Bake an additional 15 minutes. Serves 6.

Mrs. John Huckabay (Peggy)

Italian Zucchini Pie

4   cups thinly sliced, unpeeled
    zucchini
1   cup coarsely chopped onion
1/2 cup butter or margarine
1/2 cup chopped parsley
1/2 teaspoon salt
1/2 teaspoon pepper

1/4 teaspoon garlic powder
1/4 teaspoon basil
1/4 teaspoon oregano
2   eggs, well beaten
8   ounces Mozzarella cheese
1   (8 count) can crescent rolls
2   teaspoons Dijon mustard

Preheat oven to 375°. Cook zucchini and onion in margarine in a large skillet until tender, about 10 minutes. Stir in parsley and seasonings. In a large bowl, blend together eggs, and grated Mozzarella cheese. Stir in vegetable mixture. Separate dough into 8 triangles, and place in an ungreased 10 inch pie pan. Press dough over bottom and up sides of pan to form a crust. Spread crust with mustard and pour vegetables into pie pan. Bake at 375° for 18 to 20 minutes. Let stand 10 minutes.

Mrs. Tom Connolly (Pat)

Broiled Tomatoes

4   medium tomatoes, cut in
    half
Dijon mustard
Salt and freshly ground pepper

Cayenne pepper
6   tablespoons butter, melted
1/2 cup grated Parmesan cheese

Spread cut sides of tomato with mustard. Sprinkle with salt, pepper and cayenne pepper. Combine butter, breadcrumbs, and Parmesan cheese. Spoon on top of tomatoes. Broil until crumbs are brown and tomatoes are tender. Serves 8.

Mrs. Don Davis (Pat)
Fiesta Chairman 1976-1977, Guild President 1983-1984

"Salmon Run"

Melissa Miller, Austin, a self dubbed amateur naturalist, "whose paintings of emotionally charged beasts in equally natural settings is one of the most important artists working in Texas", according to Charles Kaufman, critic, Austin American Statesman.

Her formal training, which began at The University of Texas and continued at the Museum of Fine Arts, Houston; was enhanced by summer school (1974) at Yale, New Haven, and a B.F.A. from the University of New Mexico. She has been given awards and grants from Yale, the National Endowment for the Arts on three occasions, and the Anne Giles Kimbrough Fund, Dallas Museum of Art.

Melissa's recent exhibitions have included: Laguna Gloria Art Museum, Texas Fine Arts Association, "Texas Images and Visions", Huntington Gallery, University of Texas; "1983 Biennal Exhibition", Whitney Museum, New York; "Southern Fictions", Contemporary Arts Museum, Houston; "New Directions for the Michner Collection," Huntington Gallery, Austin; "Paradise Lost - Paradise Regained" the Venice (Italy) Biennale (an international review of current artistic trends which began in 1895); "Biennial 3", San Francisco Museum of Modern Art; "Fresh Paint", Museum of Fine Arts, Houston and "Texas Currents", San Antonio Art Institute, San Antonio.

"Salmon Run", a vivid display of her fantastic subjects, was recently purchased by a patron "as a promised gift to the San Francisco Museum of Modern Art".

Melissa remembers her years of "learning" were not all "ladled out". While in New Mexico, she worked as a waitress in a Route 66 cafe. She remarked her first studio on Austin's 16th Street was dark and temperatures topped 100 degrees. And she also recalled "pleasant days" as a member of the Laguna Gloria Art Museum School's faculty.

In Texas, Melissa's work is shown by Texas Gallery, Houston. More words are not necessary - mark well - "Melissa Miller is on a roll".

Seafood, Pasta, Eggs & Cheese

Coconut Shrimp

1 pound large shrimp, shelled, deveined and butterflied
1/4 cup flour
1/2 teaspoon salt
1/2 teaspoon dry mustard
1 egg

2 tablespoons cream of coconut or whipping cream
3/4 cup flaked coconut
1/3 cup bread crumbs
Vegetable oil for frying
Honey for sauce
Soy sauce for sauce
Lemon or lime juice for sauce

Combine flour, salt and dry mustard in a small bowl. Beat together egg and cream of coconut in a second small bowl. In a third bowl, combine coconut and bread crumbs. Dip shrimp into flour mixture, then into egg mixture, then in coconut mixture. Refrigerate until ready to cook. Heat 2 inches of oil in a saucepan to 350°. When oil is hot, fry shrimp a few at a time, about 2 minutes each, or until golden, turning once. Remove with slotted spoon and drain on paper towel. Keep warm in oven until all are prepared. Mix together the honey, soy sauce and lemon or lime juice in proportions to suit your taste. Serve as a sauce for the shrimp. Serves 4. *Good to prepare early in the day when you have a lot of afternoon carpools — then run in at the last minute, heat oil and fry them up!*

Mrs. Ben Morgan (LaRee)

San Leon Gulf Coast Shrimp Boil

1 bag shrimp boil
2 cans stale beer, at room temperature
1/2 cup rock salt
3 pounds small new red potatoes, unpeeled and scrubbed

6 large ears corn on the cob, cut into thirds
5 pounds shrimp in the shell
Red cocktail sauce to serve
Butter, salt and pepper to serve

Put shrimp boil, beer, rock salt and 3 gallons of water in a 12 quart pot, and bring to a boil. Add new potatoes and cook at high speed for 10 minutes. Add the corn and shrimp, and cook for 5 minutes. Turn off heat and let entire mixture rest for 10 minutes. Separate shrimp from corn and potatoes; chill shrimp on ice or refrigerate for about 20 minutes. Wrap corn and potatoes in foil to keep warm. Serve shrimp with cocktail sauce; serve potatoes and corn with plenty of butter, salt and pepper and top off the meal with plenty of cold beer.

Mrs. LeRoy Nagel (Harriet)
Fiesta Chairman 1974-1975

Marinated Barbecued Shrimp

½ cup butter	1 tablespoon fresh lemon juice
½ cup chopped green onion	
½ cup catsup	1 tablespoon sugar
½ cup water	2 teaspoons dry mustard
1 tablespoon Worcestershire sauce	1 pound medium to large shrimp, peeled and deveined
2 teaspoons grated lemon peel	
	Hot cooked rice to serve

Melt butter in a 1 quart saucepan. Stir in onion, catsup, water, Worcestershire sauce, lemon peel, lemon juice, sugar and mustard. Simmer 5 minutes. Thread shrimp on skewers and place in a shallow dish. Pour over marinade and let stand at room temperature for 1 hour or refrigerate overnight. Broil 4 to 5 inches from heat source, about 5 minutes on each side, brushing occasionally with marinade. Serve with hot rice and remaining marinade. Serves 4.

Mrs. Robert Storey (Carolyn)

Garlic Shrimp Konop

½ cup butter	Salt and pepper to taste
½ cup corn oil	1 teaspoon crushed red pepper
6 large cloves garlic, crushed and minced	
4 large bay leaves, crushed	1 cup fresh lemon or lime juice
1 teaspoon dried oregano, crushed	1 pound medium shrimp, unpeeled

Melt butter in large skillet with lid. Remove from heat and add remaining ingredients except shrimp. Let sit until ready to eat, at least 1 hour. Stir occasionally. When ready to serve, put shrimp evenly on bottom of skillet. Cook briefly on one side and turn to cook other side. Cook shrimp just until pink. Overcooking makes shrimp tough. Serves 4. *Serve in bowls with lots of whole wheat rolls to dunk into the lime-butter sauce. A fun thing to cook and just put the skillet in the middle of the table and let everyone "dig in".*

Mrs. Edward Konop (Rita)

Shrimp Kabobs

1/4 cup lemon juice
1 teaspoon salt
1 teaspoon garlic powder
1/2 cup olive oil
1 teaspoon pepper
1 tablespoon cumin
1 onion, thinly sliced

2 pounds large shrimp or enough to equal 6 to 7 shrimp per person
Green bell pepper to skewer
Fresh mushrooms to skewer
Onion wedges to skewer
Hot cooked rice to serve

Mix lemon juice, salt, garlic powder, olive oil, pepper, cumin and onion in a large bowl. Peel, devein and wash shrimp. Place shrimp into a bowl; cover and let stand at room temperature for 2 hours, turning shrimp after 1 hour. Place shrimp on two skewers; one placed through the main body and the other through the tail. This prevents the shrimp from spinning on the skewer when turned. Alternate 6 or 7 shrimp per skewer with green bell pepper, onion and mushrooms as desired. Grill over a low fire for 3 to 4 minutes each side. Serves 6 to 8.

Mrs. Charles Gouge (Darlene)

Italian Shrimp

3/4 cup melted butter, divided
1/4 cup plus 2 tablespoons flour, divided
2 teaspoons lemon juice
Black pepper to taste
1 cup hot water

4 tablespoons minced parsley
2 tablespoons minced garlic
Seasoned salt to taste, optional
2 pounds fresh shrimp
Hot cooked rice or noodles to serve

Melt 1/4 cup butter and add 2 tablespoons flour, lemon juice, and pepper, stirring until smooth. Add hot water, then reduce heat and cook for 5 minutes. Add parsley, minced garlic, and optional seasoned salt. Clean shrimp and dip in 1/4 cup flour. Place 1/2 cup butter in a 9x13 inch pan; place shrimp in pan and broil for 8 minutes. Turn shrimp over and top with lemon sauce. Broil an additional 2 minutes. Serve over rice or cooked noodles. Serves 4.

Priscilla Kirkwood

Shrimp Vermouth

5   tablespoons butter, divided
3   tablespoons olive oil
1   clove garlic, minced
2   pounds shrimp, shelled
    except for tail and
    butterflied
1/4 teaspoon salt

1/4 teaspoon black pepper
3   tablespoons dry Vermouth
5   tablespoons lemon juice,
    divided
2   tablespoons A-1 sauce
Dash of garlic powder

In a large skillet place 3 tablespoons butter, olive oil and garlic. When simmering add shrimp, salt and pepper. Turn shrimp, add Vermouth and 4 tablespoons lemon juice. Cook until just done, overcooking makes shrimp tough. Melt 2 tablespoons butter, and add A-1 sauce, 1 tablespoon lemon juice and garlic powder. Serve on the side in small bowls. Serves 6 to8.

Mrs. John Stark (Kay)

Shrimp Creole

1   onion, chopped
1   green bell pepper, chopped
1 to 2 cloves garlic, minced
1   cup chopped celery
4   tablespoons butter
1   (14 1/2 ounce) can tomatoes,
    puréed
1/2 cup tomato sauce
2   bay leaves
1   teaspoon crushed parsley

1/8 teaspoon cayenne pepper
Several dashes Tabasco sauce
Salt and pepper to taste
1   (4 1/2 ounce) jar button
    mushrooms
1 1/2 pounds fresh shrimp,
    cooked, peeled and
    deveined
Steamed rice to serve

In a large skillet, sauté onion, bell pepper, garlic and celery in butter until tender. Add tomatoes, sauce, and seasonings and simmer about 30 minutes until flavors blend. Add small amount of water as needed to thin. Add mushrooms and shrimp and simmer 10 minutes. Serve over steamed rice. Serves 6.

Mrs. Kyle Baker (Linda)

Curried Shrimp In Avocado

3 to 4 avocados, halved and
    peeled
Lime juice
1   tablespoon butter, melted
1   teaspoon curry powder
1/2 teaspoon salt

1   cup chopped tomato
1/3 cup chopped onion
1/2 to 1 pound cooked, cleaned
    shrimp, well drained
1   cup sour cream

Brush avocado halves with lime juice. Cut a small amount off the bottom of the avocado and place in a shallow baking pan. Heat for 10 minutes at 300°. In a saucepan combine butter, curry and salt; stir in tomato and onion and cook until tender. Add shrimp and heat thoroughly. Blend in sour cream and heat, but do not boil. Spoon into warm avocado halves. These can not be frozen, but the shrimp filling can be prepared ahead. Serves 6 to 8.

Mrs. R. A. Gilbert (Kay)
Guild President 1961-1962

Easy Shrimp Thermidor

1/4 cup chopped onion
2   tablespoons chopped green
    bell pepper
2   teaspoons margarine
1   can cream of potato soup
3/4 cup half and half cream

1/2 cup grated sharp cheese
2   teaspoons lemon juice
11/2 cups cooked shrimp, peeled
Pastry shells, toast points or
    steamed rice to serve

Sauté onion and green pepper in butter; add soup and cream. Heat slowly, stirring constantly. Bring just to the boiling point and add cheese. Stir to melt. Add lemon juice and shrimp. Serve in pastry shells or over toast points or rice. Serves 4.

Mrs. Glenn Johnson (Debbie)

- *To get very tender cooked shrimp, pour seasoned, or just salted, boiling water over the shelled raw shrimp, mix, cover and let stand 5 minutes with no heat.*

Shrimp Imperial

1 cup chopped green onions	1/2 teaspoon paprika
3/4 cup chopped celery	Dash black pepper
1/2 cup butter	Salt to taste
3 tablespoons flour	1 pound cooked shrimp,
2 cups half and half cream	peeled
3 ounces Parmesan cheese, grated	Buttered bread crumbs

Sauté onions and celery in butter until barely tender. Add flour, stirring until well blended, and cook a few minutes. Slowly add cream, Parmesan cheese, paprika, pepper and salt, stirring constantly until thickened. Add shrimp and pour into a greased casserole. Top with bread crumbs and bake at 325° for about 20 to 30 minutes or until hot and bubbly. Serves 4 to 6.

Mrs. Terry Townsend (Mimi)

Seafood Delight

1/2 cup minced onions	1 cup milk
1/2 cup minced green bell pepper	3 cups cooked rice
4 tablespoons butter	1 pound peeled, deveined, cooked shrimp
1 can cream of mushroom soup	6 ounces crab meat
1 (4 ounce) can chopped mushrooms, undrained	3/4 cup grated sharp cheese
	1 cup soft buttered bread crumbs

Sauté onion and green pepper in butter until golden. Combine soup, mushrooms and milk. Simmer with onion and green pepper for 10 minutes. Add rice. Cut shrimp in half and add to rice mixture with the crab meat. Place in a large casserole. Sprinkle top with cheese and bread crumbs. Bake at 350° for 45 minutes. Serves 6 to 8.

Mrs. Edward Gillen (Josie)

- *Never over-cook fish or let it get dry. When cooked, the flesh should be creamy white and opaque and should flake away from the bone.*

Crab Stuffed Shrimp

24	jumbo shrimp
1	onion, minced
1	green bell pepper, chopped
6	tablespoons butter, divided
1	cup crab meat
1	teaspoon dry mustard
1	teaspoon Worcestershire sauce
½	teaspoon salt
2	tablespoons mayonnaise
2	tablespoons flour
1	cup milk
1	tablespoon sherry
	Grated Parmesan cheese
	Paprika

Clean shrimp, leaving tails. Split shrimp and open flat. Sauté onion and green pepper in 4 tablespoons butter until soft but not brown. Add crab meat, mustard, salt and mayonnaise; set aside. Melt 2 tablespoons butter, add flour, stirring to blend well. Slowly add milk and continue to stir until thickened. Add white sauce to crab mixture along with the sherry. Mix well. Stuff the shrimp with the crab mixture and dot with extra butter. Sprinkle with Parmesan cheese and paprika. Arrange in a shallow baking pan and bake at 350° for 25 to 30 minutes. Serves 6 to 8.

Mrs. Berry Gannaway (Jackie)
Fiesta Chairman 1984-1985

Rita's Mexican Fish Stew

3 to 4	cloves garlic, minced
1	medium onion, chopped
12	ounces Hot V-8 juice
1	(8 ounce) can tomato sauce
1	teaspoon chili powder
½	teaspoon ground red pepper, optional
4	lemons, cut into chunks
1	teaspoon oregano
2	tablespoons Pernod
2	tablespoons dry Vermouth
1	cup chopped parsley
½	cup clam juice
1 to 1½	pounds firm, skinless fish fillets, cubed
8	ounces fresh mushrooms, halved
4	cantaloupe halves
	Slices of Monterey Jack cheese
	Sesame seeds to garnish
	Bolillos or Mexican hard rolls to serve

Sauté garlic and onion in microwave until tender. Add V-8 juice, tomato sauce, chili powder, red pepper, lemon pulp, oregano, Pernod, Vermouth, parsley and clam juice; simmer until thick, stirring frequently. Add fish and mushrooms and cook just until fish is tender. Do not overcook because fish becomes tough or "cooks up". Set oven at 350°. Score inside of each cantaloupe with a sharp knife. Be careful not to cut through the skin. Fill each half with fish stew and top with slices of Monterey Jack cheese. Place each half on hollowed-out lemon slices on an oven-proof plate. Bake at 350° just until cheese melts. Sprinkle with sesame seeds just before serving. To make ahead, cook stew until thick and freeze or refrigerate until ready to use, then add fish and mushrooms. Serves 4.

Mrs. Edward Konop (Rita)

Sole And Shrimp En Papillote Mornay

Mornay Sauce:

4 tablespoons butter	2 drops garlic juice
4 tablespoons flour	1 or 2 drops Tabasco sauce
Dash of paprika	1 cup milk
1/2 teaspoon salt	2 egg yolks
1 teaspoon Worcestershire sauce	

Melt butter and add flour and seasonings. Cook and stir so that it bubbles for a minute or two. Slowly add milk and egg yolks and stir constantly with a wire whisk. Cook and stir over medium heat until thickened.

Sole and Shrimp:

8 fillets of sole	1/4 teaspoon pepper
1/2 pound fresh mushrooms	1 teaspoon lemon juice
Butter or vegetable oil	1/2 teaspoon paprika
24 large raw, peeled, deveined shrimp	Prepared Mornay sauce
1 teaspoon salt	1/4 cup chopped parsley

Rinse and dry fish; arrange each fillet in the center of 8 pieces of 14 inch square foil. Slice mushrooms and sauté quickly in a little butter or good quality oil. Arrange shrimp and mushrooms over the fillets. Season with salt, pepper, lemon juice and paprika. Spoon prepared Mornay sauce over all and sprinkle with parsley. Bring foil edges together and double fold to make cooking bags. Put bags on a cookie sheet and bake at 425° for 40 minutes. Arrange bags on a parsley-covered serving platter, cut a cross over the top of each and turn back edges to serve. Serves 8.

Mary Coneway

Beurre Blanc Salmon

1/2 cup white wine vinegar	1 tablespoon chopped fresh parsley
1/4 cup dry white wine	
2 shallots, minced	2 salmon steaks, grilled
1/2 cup butter, softened	

In a small non-aluminum saucepan, bring the vinegar and shallots to a boil over high heat. Allow the mixture to boil until it has been reduced to 1 1/2 tablespoons. Remove pan from heat for a few minutes, then beat in 2 tablespoons of butter . When creamed, mix in remaining butter, 1 tablespoon at a time, until all is blended. Mix in parsley. If mixture is too liquid, chill a few minutes and mix again. Yields 3/4 cup. Serve with grilled salmon.

Leslie Rost

Seafood Stuffed Flounder

1/2	cup butter	1	teaspoon garlic powder
3/4	cup chopped onion	1/2	teaspoon salt
1	cup sliced mushrooms	1	cup crab meat
1/4	cup Vermouth	1	cup cooked, chopped
1	cup bread crumbs		shrimp
2	eggs, beaten	5	flounder, whole, boned

Melt butter in a small skillet and cook onions and mushrooms until softened. Reduce with Vermouth, then remove from heat and cool for 10 minutes. Add bread crumbs, eggs, garlic powder and salt, and mix well. Add crab meat and shrimp, mixing lightly. Spoon mixture evenly into each flounder. Arrange in a shallow buttered pan. Sprinkle with paprika and bake at 425° for 8 to 10 minutes. Serves 5.

Susan Hasslocher
Guild President 1984-1985

Deviled Fish Broil

2	teaspoons grated onion	2	tablespoons prepared
1/2	teaspoon Tabasco sauce		mustard
1	teaspoon Worcestershire		Dash of dried parsley or 1/4
	sauce		teaspoon fresh
1	teaspoon soy sauce	1	pound fish fillets
			Lemon wedges to serve

Mix together onion, Tabasco, Worcestershire sauce, soy sauce mustard and parsley. Spread on top of fish and broil 6 to 8 inches from heat until fish flakes easily. Do not overcook. Serve with lemon wedges. Serves 3.

Mrs. John Stark (Kay)

Barbara's Flounder

4 flounder fillets	2 to 3 tablespoons butter
1 large or 2 medium limes	Paprika to garnish
Salt and white pepper to taste	Parsley to serve

Place fillets in a greased 9x13 inch baking dish. Slice the center part of a lime into paper thin slices and place on top of fillets. Squeeze juice from remainder of lime onto fish. Sprinkle lightly with salt and white pepper. Dot with small dabs of butter, and sprinkle with paprika to taste. Cover with foil and bake at 300° for 20 minutes. Remove foil and bake an additional 10 minutes. Sprinkle with parsley and serve at once with some of the sauce spooned on top. Serves 4.

Barbara von Merz
Guild President 1965-1966

Grilled Swordfish Steaks

½ cup or less olive oil	½ teaspoon celery salt
½ tablespoon dried oregano, crushed	½ teaspoon pepper
½ tablespoon crushed bay leaf	3 (1 inch) thick swordfish steaks, 8 to 10 ounces each
1 tablespoon dried basil, crumbled	Melted butter to serve
Juice of 1 lemon	Finely chopped parsley to garnish
3 large cloves garlic, minced	

For marinade combine all ingredients except fish, butter and parsley and mix thoroughly. Place each swordfish steak in the marinade to cover both sides and refrigerate for at least 2 to 3 hours. Turn once or twice to make certain steaks are well coated. Grill steaks about 6 inches from heat for 5 minutes, then turn and cook for 7 minutes on the opposite side. Baste with remaining marinade. Arrange steaks on a platter and top with melted butter and parsley. Serves 4 to 6.

Mrs. Edward Konop (Rita)

Marinated Salmon Steaks

4 fresh or frozen salmon steaks, about 1 inch thick	2 tablespoons vegetable oil
⅓ cup orange juice	1 clove garlic, crushed
⅓ cup soy sauce	½ teaspoon dried basil, crushed
2 tablespoons minced parsley	

Thaw fish if frozen. Place fish in a shallow baking dish. Combine orange juice, soy sauce, parsley, oil, garlic and basil. Pour over fish. Let stand at room temperature for 2 hours or chill for 4 to 6 hours, turning steaks occasionally. Drain, reserve marinade. Place fish in a well greased wire grill basket or cook directly on grill. Grill over medium coals about 8 minutes or until fish is light brown. Baste with marinade, then turn and grill an additional 8 to 10 minutes or until fish flakes easily when tested with a fork. Meanwhile heat remaining marinade to boiling. Transfer fish to serving platter and drizzle with marinade. Serves 4. *This marinade is great with other favorite fish steaks.*

Sandi Aitken

• *For extra flavor and to prevent dryness when baking fish, brush with mayonnaise.*

Fillet Of Fish Florentine

¼ cup butter	Freshly ground pepper to taste
¼ cup flour	3 (10 ounce) packages frozen
1½ cups half and half cream	spinach, thawed and well
½ cup dry white wine	drained
2 tablespoons fresh lemon	6 fish fillets, whitefish,
juice	haddock, perch, salmon or
½ teaspoon basil	any firm-fleshed fish
¼ teaspoon dill weed	1 cup fresh bread crumbs
½ cup freshly grated	3 tablespoons butter, melted
Parmesan cheese	

Melt ¼ cup butter in a large saucepan and stir in flour. Cook and stir for 2 minutes. Slowly add cream, wine, lemon juice, basil and dill. Cook over low heat, stirring constantly, until thickened. Reduce heat, and stir in cheese and pepper. Cook just until cheese melts, then remove from heat. Squeeze spinach until dry, then add ½ cup cheese sauce and stir to blend well. Place spinach mixture in the bottom of a 9x13 inch pan or 6 individual baking dishes. Arrange fish over spinach and top with remaining cheese sauce. Combine bread crumbs and melted butter, and sprinkle over sauce. Bake at 350° for 25 to 30 minutes or until fish flakes easily. Do not overbake.

Mrs. Larry Hall (Jane)
Fiesta Chairman 1982-1983

Pescado A La Veracruzana

1 large onion, chopped	1 to 2 jalapeño peppers, minced
⅛ cup olive oil	Salt and pepper to taste
6 large tomatoes, peeled and	2 pounds red snapper fillets
chopped	or any light tasting fish
1 (3 ounce) jar green olives,	
chopped	

Sauté onions in olive oil until tender. Add tomatoes, olives, jalapeño peppers, salt and pepper. Cook covered until mixture cooks down and has a sauce consistency. Put fillets in a large baking dish and spread sauce evenly on top. Cover and bake at 350° for about 15 to 20 minutes or only until fish flakes easily with a fork. Do not overcook. Serves 4 to 6. *This is a great do-ahead meal. Prepare sauce ahead, then pour over fish at the last minute. Cook in your microwave just until done.*

Mrs. Edward Konop (Rita)

Rock Salt Fish

2　bags rock salt　　　　　　　1　whole flounder or red fish

Place a layer of rock salt about 1 inch thick on the bottom of a large roasting pan. Place cleaned and scaled fish on top of salt. Cover with another layer of rock salt and cover pan tightly with a lid. Bake at 350° for approximately 20 to 25 minutes. Scrape top layer of salt loose, and lift fish onto platter. Serves 6 to 8. *Serve with new potatoes boiled in crab boil.*

Mrs. Charles Herring, Jr. (Anna)

Salmon Loaf With Dill Sauce

Salmon Loaf:

1　(15½ ounce) can salmon
　　with juice
½　teaspoon grated onion
1　teaspoon chopped green
　　bell pepper
1　tablespoon catsup

Juice of ½ lemon
2　eggs, separated, whites
　　beaten separately
6　crackers, crumbled
1　teaspoon Worcestershire
　　sauce

Remove bones from salmon and add onion, green pepper, catsup, lemon juice, egg yolks, crackers, Worcestershire sauce and beaten egg whites. Put into a casserole and bake at 350° for about 30 to 45 minutes or until it starts to brown. Serve with dill sauce. Serves 4 to 6.

Dill Sauce:

1　cup mayonnaise
¾　cup sour cream
½　teaspoon grated onion, or
　　less

½　teaspoon tarragon vinegar,
　　or more
1　teaspoon dill weed
Dash of seasoned salt

Mix together all ingredients and serve with salmon loaf.

Mrs. John Huckabay (Peggy)

　• *If you're going to dip fish in egg before frying, add a little sherry to the egg.*

Fish In Beer Batter

1 cup flour	1 cup beer, room temperature
2 eggs, separated	4 to 6 cups plus 2 tablespoons
Salt and white pepper to taste	corn or vegetable oil
1/4 cup finely chopped green	2 pounds small fish fillets
onions	Tartar or cocktail sauce to serve

Mix flour, egg yolks, salt and pepper. Add onions, then add beer and 2 tablespoons oil. Mix well with a whisk; cover and let stand until ready to cook. Beat room temperature egg whites until stiff and fold them into beer mixture. Pat fish dry and sprinkle with salt and pepper. Heat 4 to 6 cups oil in a deep skillet or fryer until very hot. Dip pieces of fish into batter and add them to hot oil. Cook about 2½ minutes, carefully turning once or twice or until golden brown and crisp all over. Place cooked pieces on paper towels to drain. Serves 4 to 6. *This makes lots of batter and may be used as a batter for fried fresh mushrooms, okra, zucchini and even doves.*

Mrs. Leroy Nagel (Harriet)
Fiesta Chairman 1974-1975

Crawfish Etouffée

5 pounds catfish, cut into	3 ribs of celery, chopped
large pieces	1 large bunch green onions
1 teaspoon salt	and tops, chopped
1 teaspoon black pepper	2 tablespoons flour, divided
1/4 teaspoon red pepper	12 ounces tomato sauce
3 tablespoons vegetable oil	1/4 teaspoon thyme
2 cloves garlic, minced	1 large bay leaf
1 bunch parsley, chopped	2 slices lemon
1 large green bell pepper,	1/4 cup water
chopped	

Rub pieces of fish with a mixture of the salt, black and red pepper. Put oil in an unheated black iron pot. Arrange half of the fish over the bottom. Mix the garlic, parsley, green pepper, celery, and green onions and arrange half over the fish. Sprinkle vegetables with 1 tablespoon of flour and cover with half of the tomato sauce. Repeat layers of fish, vegetables, flour and tomato sauce. Add thyme, bay leaf, lemon and water. Place pot over low flame and cook slowly for 1 hour or until fish are tender. Shake pot often to prevent fish from sticking. Never stir this dish as this will break the fish. When tender, taste for seasoning and serve. Serves 10 to 12.

Mrs. Robert Huffhines (Chee Chee)

Pasta
Classic Lasagne

Basic Spaghetti Sauce:

2 pounds Italian sausage, or 3
to 4 pound Boston butt
pork roast, or Italian Meat
Balls, or 3 to 4 pounds
pork sparibs, or Bracciole,
or any combination of
these meats
2 tablespoons olive oil
1 medium onion, finely
chopped
2 cloves garlic, minced

2 (28 ounce) cans crushed
Italian tomatoes
2 tablespoons chopped fresh
parsley
1 teaspoon basil
1 teaspoon salt
1/4 teaspoon ground black
pepper
2 tablespoons grated Romano
cheese

Brown the meat thoroughly in olive oil in a heavy pot. Remove meat, and lower heat. Add onions and garlic to the hot oil, stirring constantly to prevent burning. When onions start to brown, add the tomatoes, parsley, basil, salt and pepper to the pot. Add one tomato can of water and stir thoroughly. When the sauce comes to a boil, put the meat back into the pot. Adjust the heat to a slow simmer. Cook 3 hours covered, stirring occasionally. Skim the grease from the surface and add the Romano cheese. Simmer another hour and serve over your favorite pasta or use the sauce in making classic lasagne. *Tomato spaghetti sauces can have many variations depending on the meat used for flavoring. Different meats will result in different flavored sauces. We like the pork flavor the best. Try different pastas with the sauce. Ziti, rigatoni, linguini, rotella, giant shells, fettucini or whatever else you can find are all great!*

Filling and Assembly:

2 pounds Ricotta cheese,
preferably whole milk type
1 teaspoon salt
1/2 teaspoon pepper
1 egg
1/2 cup chopped fresh parsley

12 ounces Mozzarella cheese,
grated, divided
8 tablespoons grated Romano
cheese, divided
1 (16 ounce) package Lasagne
noodles

In a deep bowl, combine the Ricotta cheese, egg, salt and pepper, mixing thoroughly. Stir in parsley and 8 tablespoons Mozzarella cheese, and 4 tablespoons Romano cheese. Blend and set aside. Cook lasagne noodles as directed on the package. Drain well and place noodles in cold water for ease in handling. Assemble lasagne in a 9x13 inch dish. First, put a layer of noodles in the bottom and spread with a generous amount of Ricotta filling. Ladle some of the sauce on top the filling, covering well. Start another layer of noodles and repeat with filling and sauce until noodles are used up. You should end up with a layer of noodles with sauce only. Top this layer with the remaining Mozzarella and Romano cheese. Bake uncovered at 350° for 50 minutes. Remove from oven and let sit 10 minutes before cutting. Serve with extra sauce. If made ahead of

(continued on next page)

time, add 15 minutes to the baking time. *Small chunks of cooked Italian sausage from the sauce makes a nice addition used sparingly in the layers. In true Italian style, the meat from the Basic Spaghetti Sauce is generally served as a separate dish to the lasagne.*

Mrs. Richard Musci (Linda)

Bracciole

2 pounds sirloin tip steak	2 tablespoons grated Romano cheese
1/2 pound salt pork	
2 tablespoons chopped fresh parsley	1 clove garlic, minced
	2 tablespoons olive oil
1/2 teaspoon salt	Basic Spaghetti Sauce
1/2 teaspoon pepper	

Slice the steak into 1/4 inch slices and pound meat with a saucer or mallett to tenderize. Cut into 5x7 inch rectangles. Mince the salt pork, parsley, and garlic and combine together. Add salt and pepper, mixing in Romano cheese. Mince everything to a fine paste. Add a few drops of olive oil if mixture is too dry to work into a paste. Spread the mixture liberally over the flattened pieces of meat. Roll meat tightly from the long end and tie with a string in each end and one in the center. Sauté the bracciole in 2 tablespoons olive oil until well browned all over. Add the bracciole to the Basic Spaghetti Sauce and simmer for at least 2 hours.

Mrs. Richard Musci (Linda)

Shrimp And Feta Cheese Sauce
A La Grecque

3/4 pound medium shrimp, cooked, shelled and deveined	4 teaspoons fresh oregano
	4 tomatoes, peeled, cored, seeded and coarsely chopped
1 pound Feta cheese, rinsed, patted dry and crumbled	
	Salt and pepper to taste
6 green onions, finely chopped	1 pound pasta, freshly cooked and drained

Combine shrimp, Feta cheese, onions, oregano, tomatoes, salt and pepper. Let stand at room temperature for 1 hour. Add freshly cooked pasta to sauce and toss to mix well. Serve immediately.

Mrs. Lee F. Looney (Cindy)

Italian Meat Balls

2	pounds ground chuck	1	cup Italian seasoned bread crumbs
2	tablespoons chopped fresh parsley	4	tablespoons grated Romano cheese
1	teaspoon salt	2	eggs
½	teaspoon ground black pepper		Olive oil
½	teaspoon garlic powder		Basic Spaghetti Sauce

In a large deep bowl, add salt, pepper and garlic powder to the ground meat. Mix thoroughly with your hands. Add bread crumbs, Romano cheese and eggs. Again, mix thoroughly. When blended, select a portion of meat about the size of a lime and roll tightly between your palms. Make these as round as possible. Brown thoroughly in hot olive oil over medium heat and cook with the Basic Spaghetti Sauce for at least 2 hours. Yields about 20 meat balls. *Dick has developed wonderful Italian meals from his family and now we all enjoy his great Italian cooking.*

Mrs. Richard Musci (Linda)

Cheese Filled Lasagne Rolls

1	pound sweet Italian sausage	2	(16 ounce) cans Italian tomatoes
1	pound hot Italian sausage		
1	pound ground beef	4	(6 ounce) cans tomato paste
1	tablespoon oil	1	(16 ounce) package lasagne noodles
1	cup chopped onion		
4	cloves garlic, minced	1	(16 ounce) container Ricotta cheese
¼	cup sugar		
	Salt to taste	2	eggs
1	tablespoon basil	½	pound Mozzarella cheese, grated plus ½ cup grated Mozzarella, divided
1½	teaspoons fennel		
½	teaspoon pepper		
½	cup chopped parsley	1	teaspoon salt
		½	cup grated Parmesan cheese

Brown the sausage and beef in oil in a skillet. Remove excess drippings and add onion, garlic, sugar and salt. Mix well. Add basil, fennel, pepper, parsley, tomatoes, and tomato paste. Simmer about 30 minutes. Cook noodles according to package directions. When done; drain and lay flat on a sheet of waxed paper. Meanwhile, mix the ricotta cheese, eggs, ½ pound grated Mozzarella cheese and 1 teaspoon salt. Spread mixture evenly on the noodles. Roll up, jelly roll fashion, and place in a 9x13 inch baking dish, seam side down. Place the rolled noodles fairly close together. Pour sauce over noodles and top with ½ cup grated Mozzarella cheese and ½ cup grated Parmesan cheese. Bake at 350° for 30 to 35 minutes. Serve each noodle with a little of the meat sauce on top.

Mrs. Ralph Wayne (Martie)

Crab Manicotti

8 manicotti shells	1 teaspoon sugar
6 ounces snow crab meat, fresh or frozen	1/2 cup water
1 1/2 cups Ricotta cheese	1/2 teaspoon basil
1/4 cup chopped walnuts	1/4 teaspoon oregano
2 tablespoons minced parsley	1/4 teaspoon marjoram
1 tablespoon grated onion	1/8 teaspoon garlic powder
1 (15 ounce) can tomato sauce	1/8 teaspoon thyme

Cook manicotti shells according to package directions. Coarsely chop crab meat and combine with Ricotta cheese, walnuts, parsley and onion, mixing well. Fill manicotti with crab mixture and place in a well-buttered 11x7 inch baking dish. Combine remaining ingredients in a medium saucepan. Cook over medium heat for 5 minutes, stirring often. Pour over shells and bake at 375° for 30 minutes or until heated. Serves 4 to 6.

Mrs. Glenn Johnson (Debbie)

Spinach Lasagne

1 small onion, chopped	12 ounces low fat cottage cheese
4 to 6 cloves garlic, minced	3 ounces Monterey Jack cheese, grated
1 1/2 cups canned tomatoes, chopped	1 ounce Parmesan cheese, grated, divided
1 1/2 cups tomato purée	1/2 teaspoon nutmeg
1 teaspoon oregano, crumbled	Pepper to taste
1 teaspoon basil, crushed	8 ounces lasagne noodles, cooked and drained
2 packets instant beef broth and seasoning mix	
4 (10 ounce) packages frozen chopped spinach, thawed, and thoroughly drained	

Cook onions in microwave until tender. Add garlic and cook briefly. Stir in tomatoes, tomato purée, spices and broth mix. Cook covered over low heat until desired thickness. In a bowl combine the spinach, cottage cheese, Monterey Jack cheese, half of the Parmesan cheese, nutmeg, and pepper. Spread a small amount of sauce in the bottom of a 9x13 inch baking dish which has been sprayed with a non-stick spray. Layer half of the noodles, cheese and sauce. Repeat layers, ending with sauce. Cover with foil and bake at 350° for 40 to 45 minutes or until hot and bubbly. Sprinkle evenly with remaining Parmesan cheese. Serves 12.

Mrs. Edward Konop (Rita)

Green Fettuccine With Scallop And Parsley Sauce

Sauce:

1/4 cup firmly packed minced fresh parsley	1 cup half and half cream
1 shallot, minced	1/2 cup whipping cream
1/4 cup butter	1 cup freshly grated Parmesan cheese
1/2 cup dry white wine	
3/4 pound scallops, cut horizontally into 1/4 inch slices	1/3 cup firmly packed minced fresh parsley
	Freshly grated nutmeg to taste
	Salt and pepper to taste

To prepare sauce, cook parsley and shallots in butter over moderate heat for 5 minutes, stirring constantly. Add wine and reduce the mixture over moderately-high heat, stirring to about 6 tablespoons. Add scallops, and cook for 1 minute, stirring. Add half and half and cream, and simmer for 2 minutes. Remove skillet from heat, and stir in Parmesan cheese, parsley, nutmeg, salt and pepper. Keep sauce warm.

Pasta:

2 tablespoons salt	2 tablespoons minced fresh parsley
1 tablespoon olive oil	Freshly grated Parmesan cheese to serve
1 1/2 pounds green fettuccine	
2 tablespoons unsalted butter, softened	

In a kettle, bring 7 quarts of water to a boil with salt and olive oil. Add fettuccine and cook for 2 to 7 minutes, or until pasta is al dente. Drain and transfer to a large platter. Toss with butter. Spoon sauce over fettuccine, sprinkle with parsley and serve with freshly grated Parmesan cheese. Serves 4 to 6.

Mrs. Paul Gross (Honey)

White Clam Sauce For Pasta

1/4 cup vegetable oil	1/4 teaspoon pepper
2 tablespoons margarine	3/4 cup water
4 cloves garlic, crushed	2 (6 1/2 ounce) cans minced clams
1/4 cup chopped parsley	
1/4 teaspoon oregano	

In a medium skillet, heat oil and margarine; add garlic, parsley, oregano, and pepper. Sauté for 1 minute. Stir in water, clams and clam broth. Reduce heat to low and simmer for 10 minutes. Serve warm over freshly cooked and drained pasta. Yields about 2 cups sauce. *This is a very popular dish in New England.*

Mrs. Bill Balcezak (Sharon)

Whole Wheat Tagliatelli Primavera

2 pounds fresh whole wheat tagliatelli
2 carrots, peeled and julienned
6 small zucchini, thinly sliced
6 stalks fresh asparagus, cut into 1 inch pieces
3/4 pound green beans, cut into 1 inch pieces
1/2 large head caulifower, broken into flowerettes
1/2 bunch fresh broccoli, broken into flowerettes
2 small yellow squash, thinly sliced
1 red bell pepper, seeded and thinly sliced
1 Jerusalem artichoke, peeled and sliced
1/4 to 1/2 cup fruity olive oil
Salt and freshly ground pepper
1/2 cup freshly chopped basil
1/2 cup chopped parsley
Grated Parmesan cheese

Cook tagliatelli until al dente. Drain, rinse with cold water and drain again. Steam vegetables, except red bell pepper and Jerusalem artichoke, separately until they are crisp-tender. Cool and drain. Toss cooked tagliatelli with the vegetables. Add olive oil, salt, pepper, basil, parsley, red bell pepper and artichoke. Add grated Parmesan cheese for flavor. Serves 12.

Mrs. Garrel Fleming (Ginny Puryear)

Pasta Florentine

2 (10 ounce) packages frozen chopped spinach
1 1/2 pounds Monterey Jack cheese, shredded
2 eggs, beaten
1 cup sour cream
1/2 cup chopped onion
1/2 cup butter
1 (8 ounce) package spaghetti, cooked
Salt and pepper to taste

Thaw spinach, and drain well. Reserve 1 cup of shredded cheese for topping. Mix remaining cheese with eggs and sour cream. Sauté onion in butter and mix all ingredients together. Pour into a 9x13 inch greased baking dish and sprinkle with reserved cheese. Bake at 350° for 30 minutes. Serves 8. *This is a wonderfully versatile dish. You can add nutmeg to taste, change the cheese flavor, add sautéed mushrooms, celery or green pepper. Experiment!*

Mrs. Henry Mayes (Kathy)

Vegie Fettuccine

8 ounces egg noodles
2 zucchini, chopped
20 mushrooms, sliced
8 to 10 green onions, tops and all, thinly sliced
½ cup butter
¾ cup half and half cream
1 egg, slightly beaten
2 cups freshly grated Parmesan cheese

Cook noodles and drain. Sauté vegetables in butter until tender. Add noodles. Mix cream with egg and add to mixture. Add cheese and serve immediately. Serves 8 to 10.

Mrs. Brian Sullivan (Cynthia)

Tortellini In Pesto Sauce

1 (16 ounce) package cheese tortellini or spinach tortellini
1 cup fresh basil
½ cup pine nuts
½ cup olive oil
2 to 3 cloves garlic, peeled and minced
¾ cup freshly grated Parmesan cheese
Cherry tomatoes and parsley to garnish

Prepare tortellini according to package directions. Drain and place in a bowl to cool. For pesto sauce process in a blender or processor the basil, pine nuts, olive oil, and garlic until a paste consistency. Add Parmesan cheese and blend. Add pesto sauce to tortellini and toss. Garnish with tomatoes or parsley. *This is even better if made ahead, but is great either hot or cold.* Serves 6 to 8.

Mrs. Allan L. Williams (Rose Betty)

Fettuccine Alfredo

1 (8 ounce) package fettuccine
¾ cup butter
¾ cup whipping cream
½ teaspoon dried whole basil
½ teaspoon pepper
¾ cup grated Parmesan cheese

Cook fettuccine until al dente, and drain well. Melt butter in a large pan, adding cream, basil and pepper. Return fettuccine to pan and toss well. Add Parmesan cheese; toss gently and serve immediatley. Serves 6 to 8.

Mrs. Marcus Bone (Beverly)
Fiesta Chairman 1983-1984

Tomato And Mozzarella Sauce With Pasta

6 to 8 ripe tomatoes, peeled, seeded and coarsely chopped (reserve juice)
1/2 pound Mozzarella cheese, coarsely shredded
1/4 cup minced fresh basil
5 tablespoons olive oil
2 cloves garlic, minced
1 tablespoon minced fresh parsley
Salt and pepper to taste
1 pound pasta

Combine tomatoes, reserved juice, cheese, basil, oil, garlic, parsley, salt and pepper in a medium bowl and blend well. Let stand at room temperature for 1 hour. Cook pasta until al denté and drain. Combine hot pasta and sauce in a large shallow bowl and toss until cheese is melted. Serve immediately. Serves 4.

Mrs. Lee F. Looney (Cindy)

Mediterranean Pasta

1 (6 ounce) can pitted large ripe olives, drained and sliced
1/2 cup olive oil
1/2 cup freshly grated Parmesan cheese
1 teaspoon minced fresh oregano
1 teaspoon minced fresh basil
1 teaspoon minced fresh thyme
1 teaspoon minced fresh sage
1 teaspoon pepper
1 pound pasta
Tomato slices to garnish

Combine olives, oil, cheese and spices in a medium bowl and mix well. Let stand at room temperature for 1 hour. Cook pasta until al dente and drain. Place pasta in a large shallow bowl and pour sauce over top, toss. Surround with tomato slices.

Mrs. Lee F. Looney (Cindy)

Pennoni Al Tonno

2 tablespoons corn oil
1 small onion, chopped
3 (6½ ounce) cans oil-packed tuna
2 cans anchovy fillets, finely chopped
1 (6 ounce) can tomato paste
12 ounces tomato juice
Garlic powder to taste
1 pound pennoni or similar pasta, cooked al dente
1½ cups grated Parmesan cheese

Cook onion in oil until clear. Add tuna and anchovies and stir for 2 to 3 minutes. Add tomato paste, tomato juice and garlic powder. Stir well and simmer about 15 to 20 minutes. Combine pasta and sauce, stirring well. Add grated cheese and serve immediately. Serves 6.

Mrs. Edward Konop (Rita)

Spaghetti Alla Carbonara

4   slices bacon
2   eggs
½   cup grated Parmesan cheese
3   tablespoons butter
½   pound spaghetti

⅓   cup whipping cream
½   teaspoon red pepper,
     crushed
Salt and pepper to taste

Bring a large pot of salted water to a boil. Meanwhile, cut the bacon crosswise into strips; beat the eggs and cheese together in a bowl; and, soften the butter. Cook the spaghetti in boiling water and cook about 8 minutes. Fry bacon until crisp. Pour off most of the drippings and add cream and red pepper to the skillet. Simmer slowly. Drain spaghetti, but do not rinse, then place in a large bowl and immediatley add butter, bacon, cream and cheese. Toss well and season with salt and pepper. Serve immediately. Serves 2.

Mrs. Bruce Blakely (Lynn)

Tortellini Alla Pana

10 to 12 fresh mushrooms,
     sliced
1   clove garlic, minced
2   zucchini, sliced
½   cup plus 3 tablespoons
     butter, divided

2   (7 ounce) boxes tortellini
5   ounces Parmesan cheese,
     grated
1   cup whipping cream
1   (14 ounce) can artichoke
     hearts, quartered

Sauté mushrooms in 1 tablespoon butter with garlic for a few minutes. Sauté zucchini in 2 tablespoons butter for a few minutes. Cook tortellini according to package directions. Drain and add ½ cup butter and Parmesan cheese. Toss until cheese is melted. Add cream, mushrooms, zucchini, and artichoke hearts and serve. If reheating, use liquid from the pasta and additional cream to moisten before heating. Serves 6.

Mrs. Adon Sitra (Carolyn A.)

Straw And Hay Fettuccine

Pastas:

6	cups loosely packed watercress leaves	4	eggs, divided
3½	cups flour, divided	1	teaspoon salt, divided
		1	tablespoon curry powder

Purée watercress in food processor or blender. Add 4 eggs, and ½ teaspoon salt. Process until a ball forms. Add any additional flour if needed. Wrap dough in plastic and let rest at least 30 minutes. For straw pasta, Blend 1½ cups flour, 2 eggs, 1 tablespoon curry powder and ½ teaspoon salt in a food processor or blender. Add additional flour if needed. Wrap in plastic and let rest for 30 minutes. Using a pasta machine, cut fettuccine noodles from both pastas following manufacturer's directions. Cut pasta while dough is still moist.

Red Pepper and Mushroom Sauce:

½	cup butter	½	cup beef broth
3	cloves garlic, minced	¾	cup whipping cream
2	red bell peppers, cut into 1 inch strips		Salt to taste
1	pound mushrooms, sliced		Freshly grated Parmesan cheese

Melt butter in a large heavy skillet over medium-low heat. Add garlic and stir 1 minute. Add peppers and cook until softened, about 5 minutes. add mushrooms and cook until soft, stirring frequently, about 4 minutes. Mix in broth and simmer 20 minutes to blend flavors. Add cream to sauce and simmer until slightly thickened, about 5 minutes. Season to taste with salt. Cook ½ pound of each pasta in boiling salted water until just tender. Drain and toss with sauce. Serve immediately. Serves 8.

Mrs. Garell Fleming (Ginny Puryear)

Fresh Pasta

1½	cups semolina flour or all-purpose flour	½	teaspoon salt
2	eggs	1	tablespoon water
		1	tablespoon olive oil

Place flour in a food processor with a chopping blade. Add one egg and process until completely incorporated. Repeat with second egg. Mixture should resemble coarse cornmeal. Add salt. While processor is running, slowly drizzle in water and then oil. During this process, you will need to stop occasionally and scrape sides of bowl. Process until dough climbs up sides of bowl or forms a ball. Remove from bowl, and knead slightly. Wrap with plastic wrap and let dough rest for 30 minutes. Roll out dough and cut to desired shape. Cook in boiling water until al dente, about 5 to 10 minutes.

Mrs. William Bradley (Alicia)

Eggs & Cheese

Dutch Omelet

1 small onion, chopped	6 eggs
1/2 pound bulk pork sausage	1/4 cup milk
2 cups shredded potatoes	1/8 teaspoon pepper
3/4 teaspoon salt, divided	Dash of cayenne pepper

Place onion and sausage in a 2 quart casserole. Microwave on HIGH stirring once or twice for 3½ to 5 minutes, or until pork loses its pink color. Remove sausage and onion and drain on paper towels. Discard all but 1 tablespoon drippings from casserole. Add potatoes to casserole; cover and microwave for 4 to 6 minutes, or until tender. Sprinkle with 1/4 teaspoon salt and stir. Combine eggs, 1/2 teaspoon salt, milk, pepper and cayenne pepper. Pour over potatoes. Sprinkle sausage mixture on top and microwave uncovered for 3 minutes. Lift edges with spatula so uncooked portion spreads evenly, taking care not to disrupt potatoes. Reduce power to MEDIUM and microwave for 8 to 14 minutes, or until eggs are almost set, rotating dish twice during cooking. Let stand loosely covered with foil for 2 minutes before serving. Serves 3 to 4.

Mrs. Lee F. Looney (Cindy)

Jack Cheese Oven Omelet

8 slices bacon, diced	1/2 teaspoon salt
4 green onions, thinly sliced	2½ cups shredded Monterey
8 eggs	Jack cheese, divided
1 cup milk	

Fry bacon and drain, saving 1 tablespoon of bacon drippings. Sauté green onions in drippings until limp. Beat eggs with milk and salt. Stir in bacon, onion and 2 cups cheese. Pour into a shallow, greased baking pan and bake uncovered at 350° for 35 to 40 minutes. Sprinkle remaining cheese on top and return to oven until cheese melts. Serves 4 to 6.

Mrs. Brian Sullivan (Cynthia)

- If you need eggs at room temperature and have forgotten to remove, place them in warm water for several minutes.

"A Little Bit Of Everything" Breakfast

5　tablespoons butter
2　cups thinly sliced peeled
　　potatoes
1　green pepper, seeded and
　　chopped
1　small onion, chopped
Dash of garlic salt, salt and
　　pepper

5　slices bacon, cooked and
　　crumbled or 1 cup cooked
　　ham
1　(2 ounce) can mushrooms,
　　drained and sliced
4 to 5 eggs
¾　cup shredded Cheddar
　　cheese

Melt butter in a large non-stick skillet over medium heat. Add potatoes, green pepper, onion, salt and pepper. Sauté until potatoes are tender and golden, about 10 minutes. Stir in bacon or ham and mushrooms. Break eggs into skillet and scramble into mixture. When eggs begin to firm, sprinkle cheese over top. Season with salt and pepper and serve immediately. Serves 4 to 5.

Mrs. Steve Robirds (Gay)

Brunch Casserole

6　slices bread, torn into
　　pieces
1　(6 ounce) jar sliced
　　mushrooms, drained
1　pound hot bulk sausage,
　　crumbled, cooked, and
　　drained

½　pound shredded Cheddar
　　cheese
1　(8 ounce) can water
　　chestnuts, chopped
½　teaspoon dry mustard
6　eggs, beaten and salted
2　cups milk

Mix together all ingredients and pour into a greased 9x13 inch dish. Place in the refrigerator overnight. Bake covered the next day at 350° for 1 hour. Serves 6 to 8.

Gene Hudgins

Penny's Eggs

10 or more slices white bread to
　　fill pan
Butter
9　eggs
3½ cups milk

Salt and pepper
½　teaspoon dry mustard
2　cups grated Cheddar cheese
½　pound bacon, diced,
　　cooked and drained

Butter bread slices on one side only; place one slice on top of buttered side to make sandwiches. Remove crusts and cut into fourths. Cover the bottom of a 9x13 inch pan with buttered sandwiches. Mix together eggs, milk, salt, pepper and dry mustard. Pour over bread. Cover with grated cheese and crumbled bacon. Refirgerate overnight. The next day, bake at 350° for 1 hour or until set. Serves 6 to 8.

Mrs. Paul Outon (Peggy)

Chilaquiles

1 large onion, chopped
Oil
3 (16 ounce) cans tomatoes
3 (4½ ounce) cans chopped
green chiles
Garlic powder to taste
Oregano to taste
Ground cumin to taste

Salt to taste
½ pound bag tortilla chips,
divided
12 eggs, beaten
1½ pounds Monterey Jack
cheese, grated, divided
3 cups sour cream
6 green onions, chopped

Sauté onions in oil until clear. Add tomatoes, chiles, and seasonings. Simmer until very thick. Place a layer of half of the tortilla chips in the bottom of a 9x13 inch casserole. Add half of the sauce, half of the cheese and all of the eggs. Top with remaining tortilla chips, sauce and cheese. Top with sour cream and sprinkle with green onions. Bake at 350° for about 40 to 45 minutes or until eggs are set. Test with a knife in the center. Serves 4 to 6.

Mrs. Edward Konop (Rita)

Green Chile Enchiladas

1 (12 ounce) can evaporated
milk
1 (15 ounce) can tomato
sauce
1 bunch green onions,
chopped

18 corn tortillas
Oil
1½ pounds Monterey Jack
cheese, grated
3 small cans chopped green
chiles

Put evaporated milk, tomato sauce and green onions in a saucepan and simmer over low heat while preparing enchiladas. Fry tortillas briefly in hot oil, remove and drain. Do not cook until crisp. Fill each tortilla with grated cheese and a spoonful of green chiles. Roll and place in a 9x13 inch baking pan. Cover with sauce and remaining cheese. Bake at 350° until cheese melts, do not overcook. The whole dish may be done ahead and frozen, but the tortillas tend to get mushy, if frozen too long. Serves 6 to 8.

Mrs. Bill von Rosenberg (Susan)

- Poached eggs will keep for 2 to 3 days when set in a bowl of cold water and stored uncovered in the refrigerator. When ready to use, drain and heat for about 1 minute in hot salted water.

Zucchini Quiche With Cheese Pastry

Pastry:

1 cup flour	½ cup cold butter, cubed
2 ounces Velveeta cheese, cubed	1 tablespoon ice water
	Tabasco sauce to taste

Combine all ingredients in a processor or mixer. Blend until dough forms into a ball. Wrap in plastic wrap and chill for 10 minutes. Roll out dough on a heavily floured surface. Line a 10 inch pan with pastry and prick entire surface with a fork. Bake in a preheated 350° for 10 minutes.

Zucchini Filling:

¼ cup butter	¼ teaspoon oregano
½ cup sliced onion	¼ teaspoon basil
4 cups thinly sliced zucchini	2 eggs
1 small clove garlic, minced	1 cup half and half cream
½ cup chopped parsley	1 cup shredded Mozzarella
½ teaspoon salt	cheese
½ teaspoon pepper	

Melt butter over medium heat and sauté onion, zucchini and garlic for 10 minutes, stirring occasionally. Add parsley, salt, pepper, oregano and basil; set aside. Beat together eggs and cream, adding shredded cheese. Blend egg and cream mixture into sautéed vegetables, stirring well. Pour into prepared pastry shell and bake at 350° for 15 to 20 minutes, or until center is set. Let stand 10 minutes before serving.

Mrs. Marcus Bone (Beverly)
Fiesta Chairman 1983-1984

Swiss Fondue Strata

1 (6 ounce) loaf Italian bread, sliced	5 eggs
	1¾ teaspoons salt
8 ounces Swiss cheese, sliced	¼ teaspoon pepper
1 clove garlic, minced	Grated nutmeg to taste
1 tablespoon butter	2 tablespoons grated
3 cups milk	Parmesan cheese
¾ cup dry white wine	

Layer bread and Swiss cheese in a greased 9x13 inch baking dish, ending with cheese. Sauté garlic in butter until golden. Beat together the garlic, milk, wine, eggs, salt, pepper and nutmeg. Pour milk mixture slowly over layers in pan; top with grated Parmesan cheese. Cover and refrigerate overnight. Bake in a preheated 350° oven for 1 hour to 1 hour and 15 minutes. Let stand a few minutes before serving. Serves 4 to 6.

Mrs. David Hart (Sue)
Fiesta Chairman 1985-1986

Crabby Benedict

Muffins and Eggs:

1 pound crabmeat	4 whole English muffins, split, toasted and buttered
8 whole canned artichoke bottoms	8 poached eggs
	2 cups Hollandaise sauce

Remove any cartilage from crab. Drain artichokes and pat dry. Place crabmeat on the toasted muffin half and top with an artichoke bottom. Add a poached egg on top and keep warm in a very low oven while preparing the sauce. Top with Hollandaise and serve immediatley. Serves 4 to 8.

Hollandaise Sauce:

6 egg yolks	1 teaspoon salt
2 to 3 tablespoons lemon juice	1 teaspoon white pepper
Tabasco sauce to taste	1 cup butter, melted

Combine egg yolks, lemon juice and seasonings in a blender or food processor. With the motor running, slowly add the warm butter to the egg mixture. Yields 2 cups.

Mrs. Paul Loftin (Liz)

Cascarone Quiche

1 (9 inch) unbaked pastry shell	6 slices bacon, cooked and crumbled
Worcestershire sauce	1 cup evaporated milk
1 cup shredded Monterey Jack cheese	3 eggs
	Salt to taste
1 (4 ounce) can chopped green chiles	Several slices of a Vadalia onion
	½ cup chopped tomatoes

Prick bottom and sides of crust with fork and brush edge with a little Worcestershire sauce. Microwave, uncovered, on HIGH for 4 to 5 minutes. Sprinkle crust with cheese and chiles and top with bacon. Heat milk in microwave on HIGH for 2 minutes. Beat together eggs and 1 teaspoon Worcestershire sauce, and carefully whisk into hot milk. Pour into pastry shell and sprinkle with salt. Microwave, uncovered, at MEDIUM power for 15 to 18 minutes or at HIGH power for 9 to 11 minutes. Rotate dish every three minutes. Custard should be slightly set in the center when done. Place sliced onions on top and sprinkle with chopped tomatoes. Allow to stand about 10 minutes before serving. Serves 6.

Mrs. John Heinitsh (Marney)

"Hill Country Turkeys"

Manuel Garza, Austin, is a self-taught artist who has unabashedly strived for the masterful touches of Charles Normann, Porfirio Salinas and Robert Wood. Garza has exhibited many times at Laguna Gloria Art Museum's Fiesta. His landscapes of scenes from his sketches and uncanny memory are part and parcel of "being there in person". He spends many working hours in exploring and storing feelings and eye-to-eye encounter with the cordiality of unusual arrangements of sunlit skies on branches and rocks.

Having spent his entire life in central Texas, he is well acquainted with the hill country scenery he re-creates on canvas. His paintings have instant feeling with those who are akin to a love of Texas landscapes. "Hill County Turkeys" brings together the brilliant yellows, sparkling browns and almost impossible presentation of greens. This painting has been given to Laguna Gloria Art Museum's Fiesta to be auctioned.

Garza particularly admired the works and teachings of the late Charles Normann. Normann was the artist of the Summerfield G. Roberts collection of Texas hero portraits which may be seen in the foyer of the Texas State Library. Garza's oils have won several awards at juried exhibits sponsored by the Texas Ranger Hall of Fame, Waco. His works are being shown in major galleries of the Southwest and are steadily increasing in value.

Meats, Poultry, Pork & Game

Thin Veal Forester

1½ pounds thin veal cutlets	½ teaspoon salt
1 clove garlic, cut	Dash of pepper
Flour	⅓ cup dry Vermouth
¼ cup butter	1 teaspoon lemon juice
½ pound mushrooms, sliced	Parsley

Pound veal to flatten to one quarter inch thickness. Rub both sides with cut garlic and sprinkle veal with flour. Sauté in butter in a hot skillet until golden. Place mushrooms on top, sprinkle with salt and pepper, and add Vermouth. Cover and simmer for 20 minutes, adding water if necessary. Sprinkle with lemon juice and parsley just before serving. Serves 6.

Mrs. Howell Ridout (Debbie)

Veal Scallopini Marsala

1½ pounds veal, trimmed, boned and cut thin	¼ cup chopped fresh basil or 4 teaspoons dried
Flour	1 cup peeled and diced tomatoes
1 tablespoon butter	1 cup Marsala
1 tablespoon olive oil	4 tablespoons grated Parmesan cheese
1 pound mushrooms, thinly sliced	¼ teaspoon salt
2 cloves garlic, pressed	1 teaspoon freshly ground pepper
¼ cup chopped fresh parsley	

Pound veal to flatten and cut into 1 inch pieces. Dredge with flour and brown lightly in butter and olive oil. Add remaining ingredients. Cover and cook at 325° for about 30 to 40 minutes or until tender. Serves 4.

Mrs. John Austin Johnson (Sally)

- *What began as the brainchild of many of the U.T. Art faculty wives has grown into a giant of an art show. The Laguna Gloria Fiesta with over 200 artists annually draws 50,000 viewers for the three day weekend extravaganza.*

Veal Shanks With Tomato-Lemon Sauce

3   tablespoons olive oil,
    divided
6   tablespoons butter, divided
1/2 cup chopped onion
1   large clove garlic, minced
1/2 cup chopped celery
1/2 cup chopped carrot
1   teaspoon rosemary, crushed
1/4 teaspoon thyme
1/2 teaspoon basil
4   tablespoons chopped
    parsley

8   slices lemon peel
12 meaty veal shanks, about 2
    inches thick
Pepper to taste
Flour to coat
1 1/2 cups dry white wine
1   cup tomatoes and juices,
    chopped
Beef broth
Salt to taste

Heat 1 tablespoon olive oil and 3 tablespoons butter in a skillet. Sauté onion, garlic, celery and carrot for a few minutes until tender. Remove vegetables from skillet and place in a large baking casserole; add the rosemary, thyme, basil, parsley and lemon peel. Tie a piece of string around the shanks to keep meat from falling apart while cooking. Season with pepper and dredge in flour. In same skillet, heat remaining oil and butter; add shanks in a single layer and lightly brown over medium-high heat. Place shanks in a single layer on top of vegetables. Add wine to drippings in skillet and simmer a few minutes, scraping sides and bottom of pan, then add tomatoes. Pour over veal shanks, adding only enough broth to almost cover the shanks. Cover casserole and bring to a simmer on top of the stove. Bake in a 350° oven for 1 hour and 30 minutes or until shanks are tender. Check every 20 minutes, adding broth as necessary. Remove shanks from casserole and reduce sauce until very thick. Serve sauce over veal. Serves 6 to 8. *This is even better if made a day in advance and then reheated.*

Mrs. Larry Hall (Jane)
Fiesta Chairman 1982-1983

Tenderloin Of Beef

2 to 3 pound beef tenderloin
Lemon-pepper seasoning
Garlic salt to taste
6   tablespoons butter
6   green onions, chopped

3/4 cup red wine
3/4 cup canned consommé
1   heaping teaspoon
    cornstarch
Juice of one-half of a lemon

Season meat with lemon-pepper and garlic salt. Sauté green onions in butter until tender. Add wine and simmer until reduced by half. Add consommé. Stir cornstarch into small amount of hot liquid and then add to mixture. Simmer over low heat. Add lemon juice. Place tenderloin in pan and baste with sauce. Bake at 300° uncovered for 45 to 60 minutes for rare. Serves 6 to 8.

Mrs. Steve Caskey (Kathy)

Steak Diane

1	cup thinly sliced mushrooms	2	tablespoons chopped parsley
1/3	cup minced shallots	2	tablespoons Dijon mustard
1	clove garlic, minced	2	tablespoons brandy or
Salt to taste			1 tablespoon brandy and
1	teaspoon lemon juice		1 tablespoon Madeira
1	teaspoon Worcestershire sauce	1	pound beef tenderloin, thinly sliced and cut into 8
6	tablespoons butter, divided		pieces

Sauté the mushrooms, shallots, and garlic in 4 tablespoons butter until tender. Add salt, lemon juice, Worcestershire sauce, parsley and mustard, stirring well. Pour in brandy and heat slightly, then light and cook until flame goes out. Keep sauce warm while cooking beef. Sauté tenderloin slices in 2 tablespoons butter over medium-high heat until medium done, about 3 to 4 minutes per side. Serve with mushroom-butter sauce.

Mrs. Scott Chapman (Vicki)
Fiesta Chairman 1980-1981

Steak Laffette

1	(12 ounce) can beer	1	medium onion, chopped
1/2	cup chili sauce	2	cloves garlic, crushed
1/4	cup vegetable oil	3	pounds sirloin steak, about
2	tablespoons soy sauce		2 inches thick
1	tablespoon Dijon mustard	1	teaspoon salt
1/2	teaspoon Tabasco sauce	1/2	teaspoon pepper
1/8	teaspoon Liquid Smoke		

Mix all ingredients, except steak, salt and pepper. Simmer for 30 minutes. Brush meat with sauce. Grill steak 4 inches from medium hot coals for 15 minutes on each side. Baste frequently with sauce. Season with salt and pepper after removing from grill. Serve with remaining sauce. Serves 6 to 8.

Mrs. Tom Connolly (Pat)

• When cooking poultry or a roast, use 1 to 2 wooden spoons rather than a fork for turning so you don't pierce the flesh and lose juices.

Belva's Fajitas

¾ cup Italian dressing
½ cup soy sauce
½ cup apple cider vinegar
⅓ cup Worcestershire sauce
½ cup brown sugar

1 teaspoon garlic powder
Juice of 1 lime
2 pounds skirt steak
12 to 16 flour tortillas

For marinade combine all ingredients except skirt steak and flour tortillas, and mix well. Marinate meat for 24 hours in refrigerator. Remove
from marinade and grill over hot coals until done. Serves 6 to 8. *Fajitas
are traditionally served with a choice of fresh salsa, Pico de Gallo, sour
cream, guacamole, refried beans, cheese and pepper strips.*

Mrs. Robert Bluntzer (Jo)

Fajitas With Pepper Strips

2 medium green bell peppers
2 medium red bell peppers
1 large onion, peeled and
halved
2 serrano peppers, stemmed,
halved and seeded

3 tablespoons unsalted butter
2 pounds cooked fajita meat
Flour tortillas or pita bread to
serve

Cut green and red peppers into small slivers. Finely chop onion and
serrano peppers. Melt butter in a large skillet. Cook vegetables, stirring
constantly, until they just lose their crispness, about 6 minutes. Remove
from heat and serve warm with fajitas in flour tortillas or pita pockets.
Yields about 4 cups peppers.

Ada Smyth

Shish Kabobs

1 cup olive oil
2 to 3 cups Rosé wine
Garlic powder to taste
1 large onion, sliced
Salt and pepper to taste
¼ cup lemon juice
Dash of crushed red pepper

Dash of oregano
2 to 3 pounds sirloin steak, cut
into 1½ inch cubes
Green pepper to grill
Onion to grill
Cherry tomatoes to grill
Cooked rice to serve, optional

Combine oil, wine, garlic powder, onion, salt and pepper, lemon juice,
red pepper and oregano. Place sirloin in dish and pour marinde over top.
Cover and refrigerate at least 4 to 5 hours or overnight. Skewer meat
with a combination of green pepper, onion, cherry tomatoes or whatever
vegetables you desire. Grill and serve with rice. Serves 6.

Mrs. Leroy Wilkins (Linda)

Steak Mornay

2 tablespoons butter	1 cup whipping cream
1/2 teaspoon salt	1/3 to 1/2 cup grated Parmesan
Dash of cayenne pepper	cheese
1/2 teaspoon Dijon mustard	2 tablespoons mayonnaise
1/4 teaspoon dry mustard	2 pounds sirloin steak, grilled

Melt butter; add salt, pepper and mustards. Stir in cream over low heat just until sauce reaches a boil. Do not boil. Add Parmesan cheese and mayonnaise and simmer for 2 minutes. Serve hot with grilled steak. Serves 6.

Mrs. Bruce Blakely (Lynn)

Swiss Steak

2 pounds round steak	1 tablespoon A-1 Sauce
1/2 cup flour	1 package dry onion soup
1/4 cup vegetable oil	mix
1/2 pound mushrooms, sliced	1 (16 ounce) can tomatoes
1/2 green bell pepper, coarsely	Mashed potatoes to serve,
chopped	optional

Cut meat into serving pieces and pound each with a mallet or saucer edge to tenderize. Dredge thoroughly with flour. Brown in hot oil in a large skillet. Remove meat from skillet, and sauté mushrooms and green pepper for 5 minutes in remaining oil. Add A-1 Sauce, soup mix and tomatoes to vegetables in skillet. Return meat to skillet and spoon over sauce. Cover pan very tightly and simmer on top of stove or bake at 350° for 2 hours. Add a small amount of water during cooking if necessary. Serves 4 to 6. *Serve with lots of fluffy mashed potatoes to really enjoy the wonderful gravy.*

Mrs. Berry Gannaway (Jackie)
Fiesta Chairman 1984-1985

- *The tannin in tea is a tenderizer. Cook tough cuts of meat in strong tea instead of water when cooking stews.*

Pepper Steak

2 pounds round or sirloin
steak
1/2 cup butter
1/2 cup sliced onion
2 green bell peppers, sliced
1/8 teaspoon garlic powder
1 (16 ounce) can tomatoes

1 beef bouillon cube
1 tablespoon cornstarch
1/4 cup water
3 tablespoons soy sauce
1 teaspoon sugar
Cooked rice to serve

Pound steak with mallet to tenderize meat and cut into thin strips approximately 2 inches wide. Melt butter in skillet, then add onion and green pepper and sauté about 2 minutes. Remove vegetables and set aside. Sprinkle beef with garlic powder and sauté until it loses its red color. Add tomatoes and bouillon cube, simmer 10 minutes. Blend cornstarch, water, soy sauce and sugar, then stir into meat mixture and cook until thickened. Add reserved onions and peppers; heat thoroughly. Serve immediately with rice. Serves 6.

Mrs. Jeff Stewart (Anna)

Mexican Fiesta Stew

2 round steaks, cut into bite-
sized pieces
Salt and pepper to taste
Vegetable oil for frying
1 large onion, diced
2 (10 ounce) cans tomatoes
and green chiles
1 (4 ounce) can chopped
green chiles

1 tablespoon chili powder
1 teaspoon cumin
1 (16 ounce) can whole
kernal corn, drained
1 large potato, peeled and
diced

Salt and pepper meat to taste, then sauté in hot oil in a large stew pot to brown. Add onion, tomatoes and green chiles, canned green chiles, chili powder and cumin, and cook about 40 minutes until liquid is reduced to a small amount. Add corn and potatoes and continue to cook until potatoes are tender. Serves 6 to 8. *This stew is very good on a cold winter day served with Mexican cornbread.*

Mrs. Scott Storm (Linda)
President 1985-1986

Beef Carbonnade

3 pounds round or chuck
   steak, cut into 2 inch cubes
Salt and freshly ground black
   pepper
1/4 pound salt pork, cubed
5 tablespoons butter, divided
6 cups thinly sliced onions
1/2 pound mushrooms, thinly
   sliced, optional
1 clove garlic, minced
3 tablespoons flour

2 cups dark beer
1 cup beef broth
1 tablespoon white wine
   vinegar
1 teaspoon brown sugar
1/4 cup minced parsley
1/2 teaspoon thyme
1 bay leaf
Buttered noodles or steamed
   potatoes to serve

Season beef with salt and pepper. Simmer salt pork in water to cover for a few minutes, and drain. In a large skillet brown salt pork cubes in 1 tablespoon butter; remove from pan and drain. Brown beef cubes in pan drippings, a few at a time, and place in a heavy casserole dish. In another skillet, sauté the onions, mushrooms and garlic until light golden brown. Add flour to the skillet and cook, stirring, over very low heat until flour starts to brown. Gradually add beer and beef broth, stirring and scraping often. When mixture is thickened, add the vinegar, and sugar and return to a boil. Add the sauce, salt pork, parsley, thyme and bay leaf to the beef cubes. Cover and bake at 325° for 1 hour and 30 minutes to 2 hours or until meat is fork-tender. Remove bay leaf and serve with buttered noodles or steamed potatoes. Serves 6 to 8.

Mrs. David Hart (Sue)
Fiesta Chairman 1985-1986

Easy Filet Of Beef Wellington

3 tablespoons butter
4 pounds beef tenderloin
Flour
2 teaspoons chopped chives
Dash of Cognac

1/4 pound liver paté
Freshly ground black pepper
2 (8 count) cans refrigerator
   crescent rolls
2 egg yolks, beaten

Melt butter in a heavy skillet, large enough to hold the meat. Flour meat and brown on all sides, allowing 10 to 15 minutes. Remove meat and keep warm while you blend chives, Cognac and paté with the butter left in pan. With a sharp knife tip, make a slit 3/4 inch deep down the length of the tenderloin to form a pocket for the paté. Spread the seasoned paté in this pocket and sprinkle the meat and paté with freshly ground pepper. On pastry cloth, roll out one can of the crescent rolls, being careful not to separate it at perforations. If this rectangle is not large enough to enclose the meat, use the second can. Set meat on the dough and wrap it so that paté side is up, and seam side of dough is down. Tuck ends under and moisten to seal. Brush with egg yolks. Extra dough may be used to make decorations to pace on top. Bake at 350° for 20 minutes.

Mary Coneway

Steak And Kidney Pie

1 ounce bacon drippings
1/2 cup chopped onion
1 pound round or chuck
 steak
1/4 pound lamb kidney
1 tablespoon flour
Salt and pepper to taste

1 1/2 cups beef stock
2 teaspoons Worcestershire
 sauce
1/2 cup sliced mushrooms
Flaky pie crust dough for a
 single crust

Melt drippings and lightly brown onions. Cut beef into 1 inch cubes, and the kidney into slightly smaller cubes. Coat meats in flour, adding salt and pepper to taste. Add to pan and stir over medium-heat. Add stock and Worcestershire sauce and continue to stir until very hot. Cover and simmer for 2 hours and 30 minutes, stirring occasionally. Place meat in a pie dish and cover with gravy, then set aside to cool. Cover with mushrooms. Add pie crust to top, sealing edges as for a pie. Bake at 425° for 20 minutes or until golden. Reduce heat to 325° and cook an additional 15 minutes. Serves 6. *I like the gravy thick, so if it is not thick enough, I always add more flour.*

Mrs. Michael Frary (Peggy)
Fiesta Chairman 1956-1957 and 1959-1960

Easy Oven Pot Roast

3 to 4 pounds chuck roast
1 can cream of mushroom
 soup
1 package dry onion soup
 mix
3 tablespoons soy sauce
1 cup Burgundy wine

Salt, pepper and garlic salt to
 taste
5 new potatoes, cut in half
4 to 5 carrots, sliced lengthwise
2 tablespoons margarine
10 to 12 fresh mushrooms,
 sliced

Preheat oven to 325°. Place roast in a large casserole and cover with mushroom soup, onion soup mix, soy sauce and wine which have been mixed together. Season with salt, pepper and garlic salt. Place potatoes and carrots around roast, then add margarine in small pieces evenly on top of roast. Cover and cook in a 325° oven for 3 to 4 hours. Fresh mushrooms are added during the last 30 minutes of cooking. Roast will be tender and have lots of gravy for serving. Serves 6.

Mrs. Allan L. Williams (Rose Betty)

Chili Beef Enchiladas

Chili Sauce:

2	pounds beef stew meat
6	cups water
2	teaspoons salt, divided
1	clove garlic, halved
1	large onion, quartered
1/2	cup vegetable oil
2/3	cup flour

1/4	cup chili powder
1	teaspoon ground cumin
1	(4 ounce) can chopped green chilies, drained
1/4	cup tomato paste
1 3/4	cups canned beef broth

Place stew meat, water, 1 teaspoon salt, garlic and onion in a large stew pot. Heat to boiling, then reduce heat; cover and simmer for approximately 3 hours or until meat is tender. Remove meat and let cool. Strain broth through sieve, discarding onions and garlic. Skim fat from broth. Measure and add water if needed to make 3 1/4 cups broth. For chili sauce heat oil in a large skillet over medium heat. Gradually add flour, chili powder and cumin, stirring constantly until mixture bubbles. Add chilies and tomato paste, and gradually stir in reserved 3 1/4 cups broth, canned beef broth and 1 teaspoon salt. Heat to boiling, stirring constantly. Cover, reduce heat and simmer 10 minutes. Shred cooled meat and mix with 1 3/4 cups chili sauce to meat. Save remainder of sauce to pour over enchiladas.

Enchiladas:

1/2	cup vegetable oil
24	corn tortillas
1	pound mild Cheddar cheese, shredded, divided
2	onions, chopped

2	(4 ounce) cans chopped ripe olives
	Shredded beef with chili sauce
	Chili sauce

Heat oil. Dip tortillas in oil for a minute to soften. Place a portion of shredded beef with sauce, cheese, onions and olives on each tortilla. Fold tortillas and place seam side down, side by side, in an oblong dish. Pour sauce over top, but do not cover. Sprinkle with a small amount of cheese. Bake at 325° for about 30 minutes or until heated. Serves 10 to 12.

Mrs. Tim Cahalane (Kathy)

• *Salt should be added after the beef is browned. Adding it before cooking draws out the juices and retards browning.*

Family Favorite Brisket

Seasoning Mix and Mop Sauce:

10 to 12 pounds brisket
1/3 cup salt
1/3 cup chili powder
2 1/2 tablespoons MSG
1 1/2 tablespoons garlic powder
1 1/2 tablespoons black pepper
1 (10 1/2 ounce) can beef consommé
1 1/3 cups water

3/4 cup Worcestershire sauce
1/3 cup cider vinegar
1/3 cup vegetable oil
1 1/2 teaspoon MSG
1 teaspoon garlic powder
1 teaspoon chili powder
1 teaspoon Tabasco sauce
1 bay leaf
1/2 teaspoon paprika

Mix together the salt, 1/3 cup chili powder, 2 1/2 tablespoons MSG, 1 1/2 tablespoons garlic powder and black pepper. Store in a covered container. Combine consommé and water in a saucepan and bring to a boil. Add remaining ingredients and remove from heat. Let stand covered, overnight, at room temperature. When ready to cook brisket, rub meat with seasoned salt and grill over low heat, basting with the mop sauce.

Barbecue Sauce to Serve:

1 1/2 cups water
1 cup catsup
1/2 cup cider vinegar
1/4 cup Worcestershire sauce
4 tablespoons butter
3 ribs celery, coarsely chopped
2 tablespoons chopped onion

1 teaspoon sugar
1 teaspoon chili powder
1 teaspoon paprika
1 clove garlic
3 bay leaves
1/4 teaspoon black pepper
1/4 teaspoon salt

Combine all ingredients in a large saucepan. Bring to a boil, then turn down heat and simmer for 15 minutes. Remove from heat and strain. Serve hot with grilled meats, brisket, ribs or barbecued anything. *We have used this family favorite recipe for many years. It originally came from Walter Jetton of Fort Worth who was Lyndon Baines Johnson's famous barbecuer. For ribs, try a seasoning salt mixture of 1/3 cup salt, 1/3 cup sugar, 2 1/2 tablespoons black pepper, 2 tablespoons MSG, 1 tablespoon paprika, 1 1/2 teaspoon dried lemon peel and 1/4 ground thyme.*

Mrs. Leroy F. Nagel (Harriet)
Fiesta Chairman 1974-1975

• *In 1972 when Fiesta used metal panels for the first time, the old wooden booths were donated to the City of Austin to be used for the Santa Village scene during the Yule Fest.*

Stuffed Cabbage

1 large head cabbage	1 cup raw rice
1 pound cooked ground beef	1 teaspoon paprika
1 (16 ounce) can tomatoes, drained and chopped	Salt and pepper to taste
	1 (12 ounce) can V-8 juice
1 large onion, chopped	

Core and cook cabbage in boiling water for a few minutes, just until wilted. Separate leaves. Mix together the cooked beef, tomatoes, onion, rice, paprika and salt and pepper. Place a small portion of the mixture to each cabbage leaf. Roll up and tuck ends under, placing side by side in a 9x13 inch pan. Pour V-8 juice over the top; cover and cook at 350° for 1 hour. Serves 6. *This is a wonderful diet recipe with only 100 calories in each cabbage roll!*

Mrs. Edward Konop (Rita)

Roma Beef Roll

1½ pounds ground beef	1 teaspoon salt
1 egg	⅛ teaspoon pepper
¾ cup cracker crumbs	½ teaspoon oregano
1½ cups finely chopped onion	2 cups shredded Mozzarella cheese
2 (8 ounce) cans tomato sauce with cheese, divided	

Combine beef, egg, cracker crumbs, onion, ⅓ cup tomato sauce, salt, oregano and pepper. Mix well. On waxed paper, shape into a flat rectangle, about 10x12 inches. Sprinkle with cheese, and roll beef mixture starting with long end. Press ends together to seal. Place in shallow baking dish and bake at 350° for 1 hour. Drain off fat, then pour remainder of tomato sauce on top and bake an additional 15 minutes. Serves 4 to 6.

Mrs. Tom Buckman (Ramona)

• *Use dry heat (frying or broiling) for tender cuts of meats; moist heat (simmering stewing, braising) for less tender cuts.*

Moussaka

1	pound eggplant	1	teaspoon salt
1/2	cup chopped onion		Flour to coat eggplant
1/4	cup butter		Vegetable oil
1	pound ground beef	1	cup bread crumbs
1/4	cup dry white wine	2	tomatoes, diced
1/4	cup tomato sauce	1	cup plain yogurt
1	tablespoon parsley	2	egg yolks
1/2	teaspoon paprika	1/4	cup flour
1/4	teaspoon pepper	1/2	cup grated Parmesan cheese

Slice eggplant into one quarter inch thick slices, salt well and let stand one hour. Sauté onion in butter until golden. Add ground beef and brown, then drain. Mix wine, tomato sauce, 2 tablespoons water, parsley, paprika, pepper and salt. Pour over meat, and simmer for 15 minutes. Dredge eggplant in flour and brown in a little oil. Butter a serving dish and coat with one half of the bread crumbs. Add eggplant and meat alternately, topping with tomatoes. Beat together the yogurt, egg, and 1/4 cup flour, and pour over casserole. Sprinkle with cheese and remaining crumbs. Bake at 350° for 45 minutes. Serves 6 to 8. *This dish freezes well or can be made the day before. Great for parties and men like this if you keep the eggplant a secret!*

Mrs. Mack Stoeltje (Janet)
President 1976-1977

Creole Stuffed Peppers

4	green bell peppers	1	cup shoe peg corn
1	pound ground beef	3/4	cup water
1/2	teaspoon salt	1	(6 ounce) can tomato paste
1	package sloppy joe dry seasoning mix	1	cup grated Mozzarella cheese

Remove tops and seeds of peppers. Parboil for 5 minutes, then invert and drain. Brown beef and drain. Stir in salt, sloppy joe seasoning mix, shoe peg corn, water and tomato paste and simmer for 10 minutes. Stuff peppers with meat mixture and sprinkle with cheese. Place peppers in a large covered baking dish with a small amount of water to prevent sticking. Bake at 350° for 20 to 25 minutes. Serves 4.

Mrs. Brad Duggan (Laura)

Greek Casserole

8	ounces elbow macaroni, cooked	1	(16 ounce) can tomatoes
1/4	cup butter, melted	1/2	cup water
2	tablespoons olive oil	2	(10 ounce) packages frozen chopped spinach, thawed and squeezed dry
1	pound ground beef or lamb		
1	cup chopped onion	1/2	cup crumbled Feta cheese
1	clove garlic, minced	1/4	cup milk
1/2	teaspoon salt	2	eggs
Allspice to taste		1/2	cup grated Parmesan cheese
Pepper to taste		1/4	cup bread crumbs

Toss cooked macaroni with melted butter and layer half in the bottom of a greased 9x13 inch pan. Sauté meat, onion and garlic in olive oil until browned. Add salt, allspice, pepper, undrained tomatoes and water. Bring to a boil; reduce heat and simmer, uncovered for about 20 minutes, stirring occasionally. Spread spinach on top of macaroni layer in pan, then sprinkle with cheese. Layer with remaining macarion and top with meat sauce. Beat together the milk, eggs and Parmesan cheese. Pour over meat sauce and sprinkle top with bread crumbs. Bake at 350° for 30 minutes. Cool before cutting into squares to serve. Serves 8.

Mrs. Sammy Juvé (Laura)

Hamburger Noodle Casserole

1	pound ground beef	2 to 3 teaspoons salt	
2	tablespoons olive oil	2	bay leaves
1 1/2	cups sliced onion	1/2	teaspoon Tabasco sauce
1	clove garlic, crushed	1/8	teaspoon thyme
1	(29 ounce) can tomatoes	1/8	teaspoon marjoram
1	(6 ounce) can tomato paste	1	(8 ounce) package egg noodles, cooked
3/4	cup water		
1	teaspoon Worcestershire sauce	Parmesan cheese to grate on top	
1/2	teaspoon paprika		

Brown ground beef in olive oil until crumbly. Add remaining ingredients except egg noodles and Parmesan cheese; bring to a boil and remove from heat. Remove bay leaves and place half of mixture in a 2 1/2 quart casserole. Top with cooked noodles and place remaining meat mixture on top. Sprinkle with Parmesan cheese. Heat in a 350° oven until mixture is heated through and cheese has melted. Serves 4 to 6. *This dish is a nice change from spaghetti.*

Mrs. Tom Buckman (Ramona)

Mexican Lasagne

1 pound ground beef
1 (16 ounce) can tomatoes
1 package taco seasoning mix
1 (10 ounce) can enchilada
  sauce

1 (8 ounce) carton cream
  style cottage cheese
6 ounces Cheddar cheese,
  grated, divided
1 bag tortilla chips

Brown and drain ground beef. Add tomatoes, taco mix, and enchiliada sauce. Simmer for 20 minutes. Mix together 4 ounces Cheddar cheese and cottage cheese. Layer in a greased casserole the chips, meat and cheese mixture, ending with the meat. Sprinkle remaining Cheddar cheese on top and bake at 350° for 30 minutes. Serves 4 to 6.

Mrs. Steve Robirds (Gay)

Microwave Mexican Casserole

1 pound ground beef
4 tablespoons Worcestershire
  sauce
1 teaspoon garlic powder
1 teaspoon chili powder
1 teaspoon freshly ground
  pepper
½ to 1 medium onion,
  chopped
1 cup instant rice, cooked
5 small flour tortillas, divided

1 (16 ounce) can refried
  beans
1 (10 ounce) can tomatoes
  and chilies with cilantro or
  tomatoes with green chilies,
  drained
2 to 2½ cups grated Cheddar
  cheese
Sour cream to garnish
Ripe olives to garnish

Brown ground beef and season with Worcestershire sauce, garlic powder, chili powder and pepper. Add onion and cook until translucent. Place 4 tortillas in a microwave proof dish. Layer with beans, rice, beef, tomatoes and cheese. Top with tortilla cut into strips. Cover and cook on HIGH for 3½ minutes. Turn once and cook and additional 3½ minutes. Serve hot. Garnish with sour cream and ripe olives. Serves 6 to 8.

Mrs. Ches Blevins (Diann)

> • If you have to slice meat in very thin strips, partially freeze the meat first and you'll find it much easier to cut.

Zucchini Italienne

1	pound ground beef, cooked and crumbled		Garlic powder to taste
1	large onion, diced	1/2	teaspoon salt
1	(6 ounce) can tomato sauce		Pepper to taste
1	teaspoon basil, crushed	4	pounds zucchini
1	teaspoon oregano, crumbled	6	ounces Parmesan cheese, grated

Combine ground beef, onion, tomato sauce, basil, oregano, garlic powder, salt and pepper in a saucepan. Cover and cook over low heat, stirring occasionally until thick. Cook zucchini in boiling water for 10 minutes, then drain. Cut zucchini in half lengthwise. Place in a shallow baking dish, cut side up. Spoon meat sauce over zucchini and sprinkle evenly with Parmesan cheese. Bake at 350° for 45 minutes. *This is another one of those wonderful dishes to make ahead and bake at the last minute, and is also so low in calories.*

Mrs. Edward Konop (Rita)

Beefy Biscuit Pie

Beef Filling:

1	pound ground beef	1	egg, beaten
1/2	cup chopped celery	1	cup grated Swiss or Cheddar cheese
1/4	cup chopped onion		
2	tablespoons vegetable oil	1/2	cup sliced ripe olives
1	can cream of mushroom soup		

Cook beef, celery and onion in oil. Combine soup, egg, cheese and olives in a large bowl. Add cooked drained beef, and set aside.

Seasoned Biscuit Dough:

2	cups flour	1	teaspoon freshly ground pepper
1	tablespoon baking powder		
1	teaspoon salt	1/4	cup shortening
		3/4 to 1 cup milk	

Stir together the dry ingredients. Cut in shortening until mixture resembles coarse crumbs. Blend in enough milk to make a soft dough. Spread half of seasoned biscuit dough on bottom of a greased 8 inch square pan. Cover with beef mixture. Drop remaining biscuit dough on top in desired pattern. Bake in a preheated 400° oven for 20 to 25 minutes or until done. Serves 4 to 6.

Mrs. Steve Bradley (Pam)

Roast Lamb With Anise And Garlic

3 to 4 pound lamb rib roast
1   clove garlic, slivered

Salt and pepper to taste
1   teaspoon anise seed

Have butcher remove chine bone from roast so that carving through the rack will be easier. With the tip of a small paring knife, make shallow slits into fat side of roast, spread about 1 inch apart in a grid. Insert garlic slivers into slits. Salt and pepper the fat side and ends of rib roast; place on a roasting rack in a shallow roast pan, fat side up. Liberally sprinkle roast with anise seed and lightly pat into meat. Insert meat thermometer into thickest part of roast. Preheat oven to 550°. Place meat uncovered in center of oven and roast for 10 minutes. Lower heat to 325° and cook for approximately 1 hour and 30 minutes. Remove from oven when meat thermometer reaches 160°. Let stand for about 10 minutes before carving. Slice through the bone as individual chops.

Mrs. Richard Musci (Linda)

Poultry

Cornish Hens With Wild Rice And Grape Dressing

4   cups cooked wild and
    brown rice
1   cup whole seedless green
    grapes, halved
1/3 cup slivered almonds
8   Cornish hens

1 1/2 teaspoons salt
1/4   teaspoon white pepper
1 1/2 cups butter, melted
1/2   cup bourbon
8   tablespoons currant jelly,
      melted

Lightly mix together the cooked rice, grapes and almonds. Clean hens with a wet towel. Stuff cavities with the rice-grape mixture and fasten closed with heavy thread and skewers. Bend wings behind backs, tieing in place if necessary. Tie ends of drumsticks together. Place breast sides up in an oiled roasting pan. Mix salt, pepper and butter, and brush on hens. Roast 20 minutes in a preheated 425° oven, basting occasionally with a mixture of remaining butter and Bourbon. Reduce heat to 350° and continue to roast an additional 20 minutes, basting occasionally. Brush or pour melted currant jelly over hens and bake another 20 minutes. Serves 8.

Mary Coneway

Cornish Hens With Sour Cream

2 tart apples
6 Cornish game hens
Garlic, halved
Salt and pepper to taste
1/2 cup butter, melted
6 slices bacon
1/2 cup chicken broth or
  consommé

1/2 cup dry sherry
Mushrooms, as many as you
  like
Butter to sauté mushrooms
1/2 cup sour cream
1 teaspoon Kitchen Bouquet,
  optional
Rice to serve

Core and slice apples. Wash and dry game hens. Place apples inside cavity and rub hens with garlic, salt and pepper. Brown on all sides in butter. Place in a shallow roasting pan and wrap each breast with bacon. Add broth and sherry and cook at 450° for 40 to 60 minutes, basting as it cooks with the pan juices. Discard bacon. Sauté mushrooms in butter and add to pan juices. Stir in sour cream and Kitchen Bouquet. Serve sauce over hens and rice. Serves 6.

Mrs. Barry Gannaway (Jackie)
Fiesta Chairman 1984-1985

Chicken Magnifique

4 whole chicken breasts, split
  to make 8 pieces
1/4 cup butter
2 cups sliced mushrooms
2 cans cream of chicken soup
1 clove garlic, minced
Generous dash of crushed
  thyme

1/8 teaspoon crushed rosemary
2/3 cup half and half cream
1 package seasoned rice mix
  to serve
Parsley to garnish
Slivered almonds to garnish

Brown chicken in butter and remove from skillet. Sauté mushrooms in remaining butter. Stir in soup, garlic and seasonings. Place chicken back in pan, cover and cook slowly over low heat for 45 mintes. Stir every 15 minutes. Blend in cream and heat slowly another 2 minutes. Prepare seasoned rice mix according to package directions and spread on a platter. Layer chicken breasts on top of rice and garnish with parsley and almonds. Serve sauce on the side. Serves 8.

Mrs. Larry Deinlein (Betty)

Grilled Chicken Sinaloense

3 to 4 pounds chicken pieces
2 cups white vinegar
1 cup water
6 large cloves garlic, minced
4 tablespoons chili powder

2 tablespoons oregano, crumbled
2 teaspoons pepper
6 large bay leaves, crumbled
Salsa to serve

Remove skin and fat from chicken pieces. Combine vinegar, water, garlic, chili powder, oregano, pepper and bay leaves, and pour over chicken. Marinate for 24 hours or up to 1 week, turning twice each day. Bring to room temperature before grilling. Cook quickly over medium coals, turning often, until done but not dry. Total cooking time is about 45 minutes maximum. Serve with salsa. Serves 6 to 8. *This is a wonderful low calorie grilled chicken-Sinaloa style from the Plaza in Puerto Vallarta, Mexico.*

Mrs. Edward Konop (Rita)

Marinated Chicken Breasts Teriyaki

3 cups pineapple juice
½ cup sugar
¼ cup soy sauce
¼ cup red wine vinegar
¼ teaspoon garlic powder

2 pounds boneless chicken breasts
Pineapple rings, one per breast
Long grain and wild rice to serve

Mix together the pineapple juice, sugar, soy sauce, vinegar, and garlic powder. Wash and pat dry chicken breasts. Place chicken into marinade, making sure pieces are completely covered. Marinate in refrigerator for at least 36 hours, stirring and turning 3 or 4 times a day. Grill chicken approximately 7 minutes per side, brushing with marinade at least three times during the cooking. Grill and baste pineapple rings along with chicken. Serve each breast topped with grilled pineapple on a bed of long grain and wild rice. Serve hot marinade on the side. Serves 4 to 6.

Mrs. Ron Tobin (Bonnie)

Darlene's Chicken

6 to 8 single chicken breasts, boned
4 eggs
½ cup butter
Bread crumbs

8 ounces sliced Munster cheese
6 fresh mushrooms, sliced
¼ cup chicken broth
Lemon juice

Soak chicken breasts in eggs overnight. Roll in bread crumbs and brown in melted butter. Place in a shallow baking pan and cover with mushrooms. Top mushrooms with sliced cheese and chicken broth. Bake at 350° for 25 minutes. Sprinkle with lemon juice to serve. Serves 6 to 8.

Mrs. Wayne Basden (Darlene)

Chicken And Scampi

1	(4 pound) whole chicken, cut up	3	tablespoons snipped parsley
1	tablespoon salt	1/2	cup port wine
1/2	teaspoon pepper	8	ounces fresh mushrooms, sliced
1/4	cup butter or a combination of butter and olive oil	1	(8 ounce) can tomato sauce
		1	teaspoon dried basil
2	cloves garlic, minced	1	pound shrimp, shelled and deveined

Rub chicken well with salt and pepper. Sauté chicken in hot butter until golden. Add onions, garlic, parsley, wine, mushrooms, tomato sauce and basil; simmer, covered, about 30 minutes or until chicken is tender. Push chicken pieces to one side of skillet, then turn up heat so that tomato mixture boils; add shrimp, cooking, uncovered for 3 to 4 minutes or until shrimp turns slightly pink. To serve, first place chicken on a parsley covered platter, then pile shrimp on top. Top with some of the pan juices and serve the remaining juices in a gravy boat. Serves 4 to 6. *Nice served with parsley rice.*

Mary Coneway

Chicken Cacciatore

1	(3 pound) chicken, cut into pieces	1	teaspoon crushed oregano
Garlic salt to taste		1	teaspoon salt
2	tablespoons olive oil	1/4	teaspoon freshly ground black pepper
1	(15 ounce) can whole, peeled tomatoes	1/2	teaspoon basil
1	(28 ounce) can tomato sauce	1/2	teaspoon celery seed
		Pinch of rosemary	
1	medium onion, chopped	1/4	cup dry white wine
1	clove garlic, minced	Linguini to serve	

Season chicken lightly with garlic salt. Brown in olive oil in a heavy pot over medium heat. Remove chicken. Lower heat; Sauté onion and garlic in hot oil until light golden color. Add whole tomatoes with juice to the pan and mast with a fork. Add tomato sauce, oregano, salt, pepper, basil and celery seed, stir. When sauce comes to a boil, add browned chicken. Lower heat to a simmer and cook covered for 1 hour. Skim grease from surface, then add rosemary and wine, and simmered uncovered for 20 minutes. Serve sauce over linguini with chicken as a side dish.

Mrs. Richard Musci (Linda)

Braised Chicken With Plum Sauce

3   pounds chicken pieces
1/3 cup flour
1   teaspoon paprika
1/2 teaspoon salt
1/8 teaspoon pepper
2   tablespoons butter or margarine
2   tablespoons vegetable oil

1   cup sour cream, room temperature
1/2 cup red plum jam
1/4 cup dry white wine
2   tablespoons Dijon mustard
3/4 teaspoon dried rosemary, crushed
1/4 teaspoon salt
Dash of pepper

Combine flour, paprika, salt and pepper. Coat chicken well with flour mixture. In a large skillet fry pieces in a mixture of butter and oil until golden brown on all sides, about 10 to 12 minutes. Arrange chicken in a shallow baking pan. Combine remaining ingredients and pour over chicken. Bake at 350° for 1 hour or until chicken is tender.

Mrs. Boyd Morgan (Sherry)

Tarragon Baked Chicken

1   medium-sized whole chicken
Salt to taste
1/2 medium onion
2   tablespoons sherry
4   tablespoons margarine

1/4 cup lemon juice
1   tablespoon Worcestershire sauce
2   teaspoons tarragon
1/4 teaspoon seasoned salt
1/8 teaspoon pepper

Wash chicken and pat dry. Sprinkle inside and out with salt and place in a shallow baking dish. Cut onion into four pieces and stuff inside chicken cavity. Combine and heat the sherry, margarine, lemon juice and Worcestershire sauce. Pour over chicken, then sprinkle with tarragon, seasoned salt and pepper. Bake at 350° for 1 hour and 30 minutes to 2 hours, basting every 20 to 30 minutes. Serves 4 to 6.

Marian Herbst

Busy-Day Chicken

1   cup raw brown rice
1   whole chicken, cut into pieces
Salt and pepper to taste

1   package dry onion soup mix
4   cups boiling water

Place rice in a well greased casserole. Season chicken with salt and pepper and place on top. Sprinkle with onion soup mix and pour boiling water over the top. Bake at 350° for 1 hour or until chicken is tender. Serves 4.

Mrs. Glenn Johnson (Debbie)

Chicken Marengo

2 whole chickens, cut up	2 teaspoons minced parsley
Flour	1 (16 ounce) can tomatoes,
Salt and pepper	chopped
1/4 cup olive oil	1 cup Sauterne or dry white
4 small white onions,	wine
chopped	1 tablespoon brandy, optional
Garlic salt	1 tablespoon tomato paste
2 (4 ounce) cans sliced	1 tablespoon flour
mushrooms	

Dust chicken with flour and season with salt and pepper. Heat olive oil in a Dutch oven or large skillet and sauté chicken until brown. Remove. Add onions, garlic salt, mushrooms, parsley and cook until tender. Add tomatoes, wine, brandy, tomato paste and flour. Mix all ingredients well and simmer over medium heat about 10 minutes. Return chicken to skillet, cover and bake at 350° for about 1 hour or until chicken is done. Serve with the sauce. Serves 6 to 8.

Mrs. Fred Hansen (Gayle)
President 1968-1969

Herbed Chicken Legs

3 to 3 1/2 pounds chicken legs	Vegetable oil for browning
1/2 teaspoon thyme	1/2 teaspoon rosemary
1/2 teaspoon marjoram	2 tablespoons minced parsley
Flour	Salt and pepper to taste

Sprinkle chicken legs with marjoram and thyme and let sit 1 hour. Roll chicken in flour and cook in 1/2 inch hot oil just long enough to brown. Remove each piece as it browns and place in a shallow pan. Sprinkle with rosemary, parsley, salt and pepper. Pour off most of the oil, then add a small amount of hot water to skillet and stir thoroughly. Pour mixture over chicken and bake uncovered at 350° for 45 minutes. Serves 6 to 8. *This is a great substitute for fried chicken for picnics or lake parties. The chicken can be made ahead and even frozen before baking.*

Mrs. Mack Stoeltje (Janet)
Fiesta Chairman 1968-1969, President 1976-1977

Cheese Stuffed Chicken Breasts

4   boneless chicken breasts
½   cup cream cheese with
    herbs and spices, softened

2   tablespoons butter, softened
4   slices bacon

Pound chicken breasts to flatten. Place 1 to 2 tablespoons cream cheese and ½ tablespoon butter in center of each breast. Fold edges over so that cheese and butter are completely covered. Wrap each breast with a bacon slice and place seam side down in a baking dish. Bake at 350° for 30 minutes. Place under a broiler for 5 minutes to crisp bacon.

Mrs. Scott Chapman (Vicki)
Fiesta Chairman 1980-1981

Chicken Artichoke Bake

3   whole chicken breasts, split
1½   teaspoons salt
¼   teaspoon pepper
½   teaspoon paprika
6   tablespoons butter, divided
¼   pound fresh mushrooms,
     cleaned and halved

2   tablespoons flour
1   cup chicken broth
3   tablespoons sherry
1   (16 ounce) can artichoke
    hearts

Sprinkle chicken with salt, pepper and paprika. Brown breasts in 4 tablespoons butter in a skillet, then place in a casserole dish. Add remaining 2 tablespoons butter to skillet and sauté mushrooms. Place on top of chicken. Add flour to skillet, then add broth and sherry, stirring continuously. Cook one minute or until thickened. Arrange artichokes around chicken and pour sauce on top. Cover and bake at 375° for 40 minutes. Serves 4 to 6.

Mrs. Henry Mayes (Kathy)

Gourmet Chicken Breasts

2   whole chicken breasts, split
8   ounces fresh mushrooms,
    sliced
½   cup butter
4 to 5 green onions, chopped,
    tops and all

1   can cream of mushroom
    soup
1   cup sour cream
¼   cup white wine
Cooked rice or noodles to serve

Sauté chicken in butter until golden. Add mushrooms, onions, and cook for 2 minutes. Stir in soup, sour cream and wine. Reduce heat to a simmer. Cover and cook for 1 hour. Serve over rice or noodles.

Gene Hudgins

Party Chicken

4   whole chicken breasts, split
    to make 8 pieces
2   tablespoons butter
1   package dry Italian or Zesty
    Italian salad dressing mix
1   can cream of mushroom
    soup

1   (11 ounce) tub whipped
    cream cheese with chives
1/3 cup white wine
1/2 cup plain croutons,
    optional

Sauté chicken and butter and dry salad dressing mix. When brown, place in a 9x13 inch baking dish. Combine soup, cream cheese and wine; pour over chicken. Sprinkle croutons on top and bake at 350° for 1 hour. Serves 4 to 6.

Mrs. David Dismukes (Judy)

Zesty Skillet Chicken

2   whole chicken breasts, split
    to make 4 pieces
Paprika
1/4 cup margarine
1   package dry garlic cheese
    salad dressing mix

1   can cream of mushroom
    soup
1/2 soup can water
Rice or potatoes to serve

Wash chicken and pat dry. Sprinkle both sides with paprika. Sauté in margarine and remove from skillet. Sprinkle dry salad dressing mix into skillet, stirring constantly. Add soup and water and mix well. Return chicken to skillet. Cover and simmer on low heat for approximately 30 minutes or until chicken is tender. Serve with rice or potatoes. Serves 4.

Mrs. Chad Snow (Frances)

Easy Chicken And Beef Delight

1   package thinly sliced dried
    beef
8   slices bacon
4   whole chicken breasts, split,
    boned and skinned

1   cup sour cream
1   can cream of mushroom
    soup

Layer beef in the bottom of a greased large casserole. Wrap bacon around chicken and arrange over dried beef. Mix together the sour cream and soup, and spoon over the chicken. Bake at 275° for 3 hours, covering with foil once bacon becomes very brown. Serves 8. *This is a wonderful party dish, served with wild rice, and a green or fresh fruit salad. It can be made the day before and refrigerated.*

Sylvia Goodrich

Chicken With Wild Rice

1 package long grain and wild rice	1 can cream of mushroom soup
2 cups hot water	½ cup milk
1 whole chicken, cut up	½ cup slivered almonds
Salt and pepper	1 tablespoon butter

Place uncooked rice in bottom of a 2½ quart casserole, then sprinkle seasonings from flavor packet over rice. Add water. Sprinkle chicken with salt and pepper and arrange on top of mixture. Cover casserole and bake in a 375° oven for 1 hour and 15 minutes or until chicken is tender. Combine soup and milk and sauté almonds in butter. After chicken is done, pour soup mixture over casserole and sprinkle top with almonds. Return casserole to oven, uncovered, and bake until soup is bubbly. Serves 4 to 6.

Mrs. Felix Wolff Jr. (Rosann)

Chicken Asparagus Casserole

2 pounds boned chicken breasts	1 can cream of chicken soup
Garlic salt to taste	⅓ cup mayonnaise
⅛ teaspoon pepper	1 teaspoon lemon juice
½ cup vegetable oil	½ teaspoon curry powder
2 (10 ounce) packages frozen asparagus	¼ cup shredded Cheddar cheese

Cut chicken lengthwise into 2x4 inch strips and sprinkle with garlic salt and pepper. Brown in oil. Cook asparagus according to package directions. Drain and place in a single layer in a shallow baking dish. Stir together soup, mayonnaise, lemon juice and curry powder. Place chicken strips over asparagus, spoon sauce over chicken and sprinkle with cheese. Cover with foil and bake at 375° for 30 minutes or until bubbly. Serves 6.

Mrs. Glenn Johnson (Debbie)

Easy Chicken Enchiladas

1	(3 to 4 pound) whole chicken	1	(28 ounce) can tomatoes
½	cup butter	2	pounds Velveeta cheese, cubed
1½	cups chopped onion	30	corn tortillas
2	(10 ounce) cans tomatoes with green chiles		Vegetable oil
		2	cups sour cream

Boil and bone chicken. Cool, then tear into bite-sized pieces. Sauté onion slowly in butter until tender. Drain tomatoes, reserving liquid. Add tomatoes to onions and simmer until mixture cooks down. Add cheese, stirring until melted. Add chicken. Mixture should be thick. If too thick, add reserved tomato juice. Mixture will thicken some as it cools. Dip tortillas in hot oil over medium heat about 1 minute to soften. Drain on paper towels. Place heaping tablespoon of chicken mixture in each tortilla and roll up. Place side by side in 9x13 inch pans, and pour remaining chicken mixture on top. Spread with sour cream and bake at 350° for 30 minutes or until hot and bubbly. Serves 12 to 15. *This can be made ahead and refrigerated or frozen, but do not add sour cream until ready to bake.*

Mrs. Paul White (Suzanne)

Swiss Enchiladas

1	onion, chopped		Cumin to taste
2	tablespoons butter	12	corn tortillas
1	clove garlic, minced		Vegetable oil
2	cups tomato purée	6	chicken bouillon cubes
1	(4 ounce) can chopped green chiles	3	cups half and half cream, heated
2	cups cooked and chopped chicken	½	pound Swiss or Monterey Jack cheese, grated
	Salt and pepper to taste		

Sauté onion in butter until soft. Add garlic, tomato purée, green chiles and chicken. Season with salt, pepper and cumin to taste; simmer for 10 minutes. Dip tortillas for a few seconds in hot oil to soften. Spread a generous amount of chicken-tomato mixture on each tortilla. Roll up and place side by side in a large baking dish, seam side down. Dissolve bouillon cubes in heated cream. Pour cream over rolled enchiladas and top with grated cheese. Bake at 350° for 30 to 45 minutes.

Mrs. Larry Hall (Jane)
Fiesta Chairman 1982-1983

Almond Chicken

1/2 cup slivered almonds	2 cups diced cooked chicken
1 clove garlic, minced	or turkey
2 tablespoons margarine	1 tablespoon lemon juice
2 tablespoons flour	1/4 teaspoon almond extract
1 teaspoon dry mustard	1/4 cup chopped parsley
1/4 teaspoon salt	Cooked brown rice or pasta to
1 cup chicken broth	serve

Sauté almonds and garlic in margarine. Remove almonds and blend in flour, dry mustard and salt. Add chicken broth and heat until thickened, stirring continously. Add cooked chicken, lemon juice, almonds, almond extract and parsley. Heat and serve over rice or pasta. Serves 4.

Mrs. Willy Scott (Janet)

Chicken Portuguese

1 tablespoon Mexican red pepper, or chili powder and paprika	2 green bell peppers, finely chopped
2 tablespoons vegetable oil	1 onion, finely chopped
2 cups water	1 cup chicken broth
5 tablespoons flour	Salt to taste
3 baked and boned whole chicken breasts, split	American or Monterey Jack cheese, grated
3 tomatoes, finely chopped	Parsley to garnish
	Pimiento strips to garnish

Mix red pepper with oil, add water and bring to a boil. Stir in flour which has been mixed with a little water to form a paste and cook, stirring occasionally, for 5 minutes. Pour pepper sauce into a large, shallow greased baking dish. Lay chicken breasts over sauce. In another pan, combine tomatoes, green peppers, onion, broth and salt, and cook the mixture until the vegetables are very soft. Pour the vegetables over the chicken. Sprinkle heavily with grated cheese and bake in a 400° oven until cheese melts. Garnish with parsley and pimiento strips. Serves 6. *If milder flavor is desired, reduce amount of red pepper.*

Barbara von Merz
President 1965-1966

• *If poultry has thawed, but is still quite cold, it can be cooked and refrozen.*

Tony's Nuked Chicken

1/2 cup brown sugar	1/4 teaspoon cayenne pepper
1/3 cup soy sauce	4 half chicken breasts, boned
1/4 cup red wine	2 teaspoons cornstarch
2 tablespoons red wine vinegar	1 green bell pepper, cut into strips
2 tablespoons oil	1/4 cup chopped green onions
1 teaspoon minced ginger	1 cup shredded red cabbage
1 clove garlic, minced	2 tablespoons sesame seed
1/4 teaspoon freshly ground black pepper	2 tablespoons minced parsley
	Spinach noodles to serve

For marinade, combine in a 2 quart microwave casserole the brown sugar, soy sauce, wine, vinegar, oil, ginger, garlic, black pepper and cayenne pepper. Cut chicken into strips and add to marinade mixture. Let stand at least 30 minutes. Drain chicken, reserving 1/4 cup marinade. Combine reserved marinade and cornstarch and toss with chicken. Cover casserole with plastic wrap, turning back one edge to vent. Microwave on HIGH for 5 minutes. Uncover and stir in green pepper and onions. Re-cover, leaving one edge open, and microwave on HIGH for 2 1/2 minutes or until chicken is tender. Stir in cabbage, sesame seed and parsley, recover fully with plastic wrap and let stand 1 minute. Serve with spinach noodles. Serves 3 to 4.

Jamie Dicus

Quick And Easy Paella

3 tablspoons olive oil	1 cup frozen peas
4 cups cooked, diced chicken	1 cup frozen artichoke hearts
2 cups cubed ham	1 can chicken broth
1 (16 ounce) can peeled tomatoes, drained	1 teaspoon salt
	Dash of garlic powder
2 (7 1/2 ounce) cans minced clams, drained, reserve liquid	1/8 teaspoon saffron
	Pepper to taste
	2 cups instant rice
1 pound frozen cleaned shrimp, shelled	2 canned pimientos, sliced

Heat olive oil in a large skillet, and sauté chicken and ham. Add tomatoes, minced clams, frozen shrimp, peas and artichoke hearts. Combine chicken broth, salt, garlic powder, saffron, pepper and 1/2 cup reserved clam liquid. Pour over meat and vegetables. Boil and stir in rice until moistened, then garnish with pimientos. Cover and bake at 350° for 10 minutes. Serves 6 to 8.

Mrs. Marcus Bone (Beverly)
Fiesta Chairman 1983-1984

Mock Wienersnitzel

3   whole chicken breasts,
   skinned and boned
Salt and freshly ground pepper
Flour
2   eggs, beaten

1   cup fresh bread crumbs
1/2 cup butter
2   lemons, divided
Parsley

Cut chicken breasts in half and pound until thin. Salt and pepper each side. Dredge with flour and then dip into beaten eggs. Coat with bread crumbs, pressing lightly between waxed paper so that crumbs will adhere. Refrigerate at least 1 hour before cooking. In a heavy skillet, melt butter and sauté chicken until brown on both sides. Remove from skillet. Add juice of one lemon and parsley to drippings in pan. Cook a minute or so until blended and pour over chicken. Garnish with lemon slices and more parsley. Serves 6.

Mrs. Terry Townsend (Mimi)

Turketti

2½ cups spaghetti
3 to 4 cups diced cooked turkey
1   cup chicken broth
1   small onion, grated
1/2 cup diced green bell pepper
2   pimientos, diced

2   cans cream of mushroom
   soup
3/4 cup grated sharp Cheddar
   cheese
1/2 teaspoon pepper
Salt to taste

Cook spaghetti in boiling salted water until tender, then drain and rinse in hot water. Combine spaghetti with remaining ingredients and place in a casserole dish. Bake at 350° for 1 hour or until heated through.

Mrs. Lester Gray (Cathy)

Turkey Crunch

1   onion, chopped
2   cups celery, chopped
2   tablespoons butter
2   cans cream of celery soup
1   can cream of chicken soup
1/2 cup milk

1   (8 ounce) can sliced
   waterchestnuts
3   cups cooked turkey, diced
Chow mein noodles to top
Sliced almonds to top

Sauté onion and celery in butter until tender. Add soup and milk. Fold in waterchestnuts and turkey. Pour in a casserole dish and bake at 350° for 20 minutes. Top with noodles and almonds and bake an additional 10 minutes. Serves 8.

Susan Hasslocher
President 1984-1985

Duck With Blackberry Sauce

2 (5 pound) ducklings
2 medium onions, quartered
2 medium apples, quartered
1 teaspoon salt
1/4 teaspoon pepper
1 quart water
2 cups chopped onion
1 cup chopped celery

1 cup chopped carrots
2 (16 ounce) cans blackberries
1/4 cup Cointreau
1/4 cup blackberry jam
1 1/2 tablespoons flour
1 1/2 tablespoons butter, softened

Remove giblets and necks from ducks. Stuff each cavity with some onion and apple. Close opening with skewers. Sprinkle with salt and pepper. Place ducklings, breast side up, on a rack in a large roasting pan. Bake, uncovered at 350° for 2 hours or until done. Discard onions and apples. Set ducklings aside and keep warm. While ducks are roasting, cook giblets and necks with water, 2 cups chopped onion, celery, and carrots in a saucepan. Cover and simmer for 20 to 25 minutes. Drain well, reserving 2 cups stock. Discard giblets, necks and vegetables. Drain blackberries, reserving 2 cups juice. Combine pan scrappings, blackberry juice, reserved duck stock and Cointreau in saucepan. Boil for 15 minutes or until liquid is reduced by half. Combine jam, flour and butter and gradually add to the liquid in the pan. Heat, stirring constantly, until thickened. Stir in blackberries. Cut ducklings into quarters and place under the broiler to crisp the skins. Serve with blackberry sauce. Serves 8.

Mrs. Larry Hall (Jane)
Fiesta Chairman 1982-1983

Pork

Pork Tenderloin With Mustard Sauce

1/4 cup soy sauce
1/4 cup bourbon
2 tablespoons brown sugar
2 1/2 to 3 pounds pork tenderloin

1/3 cup sour cream
1/3 cup mayonnaise
1 tablespoon dry mustard
2 to 3 green onion, chopped

Mix together the soy sauce, bourbon and brown sugar, and marinate pork several hours, turning occasionally. Preheat oven to 325°. Remove pork from marinade and bake for 1 hour, basting with marinade. Combine sour cream, mayonnaise, dry mustard and green onions for sauce. Carve pork into thin slices and serve with sauce. Serves 8.

Mrs. C. Jay Middlebrook (Linda)

Pork Tenderloin

1 whole pork tenderloin, approximately 3 pounds, or two smaller ones	Worcestershire sauce to taste
Freshly ground salt and pepper to taste	1 onion, sliced
	2 cloves garlic, chopped
	Several sprigs parsley
	6 to 8 slices bacon

Salt, pepper and rub meat with Worcestershire sauce. Layer onion, garlic and parsley between the two pieces of the tenderloin. Wrap together with bacon. Bake at 375° approximately 1 hour or less for rare meat. Serves 8. *Serve with Baked Tomato Halves as a plate garnish.*

Mrs. Don L. Davis (Pat)
Fiesta Chairman 1976-1977, Guild President 1983-1984

Pork Tenderloin Parmigiania

1 whole pork tenderloin	1½ cups prepared spaghetti sauce
1 egg	¼ cup grated Parmesan cheese
½ teaspoon salt	2 slices Mozzarella or Provolone cheese
¼ teaspoon pepper	Fresh parsley to garnish
1 teaspoon Italian seasoning	Sliced black olives to garnish
½ cup Italian seasoned bread crumbs	
2 tablespoons olive oil	

Beat egg, then add salt and pepper. Mix Italian seasoning with crumbs. Roll tenderloin into egg mixture and then into crumbs. Brown the coated tenderloin in olive oil. Place in an oblong baking dish and cover with the spaghetti sauce. Bake covered at 350° for 45 minutes. Remove cover, sprinkle with Parmesan cheese and place cheese slices on top. Return to oven for 10 minutes more to melt the cheese. Let set on a serving patter for 10 minutes before slicing. Slice meat across the grain to serve. Garnish with sprigs of parsley and sliced black olives. Serves 5.

Mary Coneway

Baked Pork Chops

4 pork loin chops	1 tablespoon Worcestershire sauce
2 potatoes, sliced	¼ teaspoon oregano
1 onion, sliced	1 can beef consommé
2 to 3 tomatoes, sliced	

Brown pork chops in skillet. In a baking dish, arrange in a layer the chops, potatoes, onion and tomatoes. Mix Worcestershire sauce, oregano and consommé, and pour over layered ingredients. Cover and bake at 350° for 45 minutes.

Mrs. Jeff Stewart (Anna)

Cajun Pork Roast

3 to 4 pound pork loin roast	Oil for browning
2 cloves garlic, sliced very thin	1½ cups water
	1 large onion, chopped
Salt	1 green bell pepper, chopped
Cayenne pepper	Rice to serve

Remove most of the fat from pork and with a sharp knife make pockets. Insert garlic slices fairly deep into pockets and rub roast with salt and cayenne pepper. Brown on all sides in a little oil in a roasting pan or Dutch oven. Add 1½ cups water and roast at 350° for 45 minutes per pound. When done, remove roast and add onions and green pepper to the drippings. Boil until onions turn almost brown. Serve gravy over rice. Serves 10 to 12. *For a thicker gravy, you can use one can cream of celery soup and a soup can of water in place of the 1½ cups water.*

Mrs. Charles Boner (Grace)

Orange-Glazed Pork Roast With Raisin Rice

1 (3 pound) pork loin	1½ cups raw rice
1 cup orange juice	1 cup hot water
½ cup packed brown sugar	½ cup raisins
½ cup chopped onion	½ cup chopped pecans
⅓ cup chopped celery	¾ teaspoon salt
2 tablespoons butter	⅛ teaspoon pepper

Combine orange juice and sugar. Bake pork at 350° for 2 hours and 30 minutes, basting with 1 cup of orange juice mixture. Sauté onion and celery in butter. Mix with remaining ingredients, adding leftover orange juice mixture. Stir well. During the last 20 minutes of cooking time, pour rice mixture over pork; cover and bake until done. Serves 4 to 6.

Mrs. Brian Sullivan (Cynthia)

Grilled Pork Steak

1½ to 2 pounds pork steak, sliced about ¼ inch thick	¼ cup brown sugar
	¼ cup white sugar
Garlic powder or salt to taste	¼ cup sherry
½ cup soy sauce	

Sprinkle one side of each steak with garlic powder or garlic salt. Combine remaining ingredients and marinate pork at least 4 hours or overnight. Cook over charcoal. After cooking on one side, dip into sauce and continue to dip and turn pork until golden brown. Cook until done.

Mrs. John Huckabay (Peggy)

Stuffed Pork Chops

4	extra thick pork loin chops, at least 1 inch thick	2	tablespoons chopped parsley
2	tablespoons butter	1/4	teaspoon thyme
1/2	cup chopped onion	3	slices bread
1	clove garlic, minced		Salt and pepper to taste
1	(4 ounce) can chopped mushrooms, undrained	3/4	cup water, divided
		2	tablespoons flour

Cut pocket in pork chops with a sharp knife. In a heavy skillet, sauté onion and garlic in butter. Add mushrooms and juice with parsley and thyme. Cube bread and add to mixture, coating well. Remove stuffing to a bowl; salt and pepper to taste. In same skillet, brown chops on both sides. Spoon stuffing into chop pockets in pan. Add 1/2 cup water and simmer until tender, about 1 hour. When chops are done, remove from pan and add flour, stirring to loosen particles. Add 1/4 cup water and continue to cook and stir until thickened. Serves 4.

Mrs. Bob Richardson (Susan)

Barbequed Spareribs

1/2	cup margarine	1/2	cup vinegar
1/2	cup Worcestershire sauce	1/4	cup lemon juice
1	cup catsup	1	tablespoon salt
1	teaspoon pepper	3	pounds pork spareribs
1	clove garlic, minced		Salt and pepper to taste

Combine margarine, Worcestershire sauce, catsup, pepper, garlic, vinegar, lemon juice, and salt in a saucepan. Cover and simmer for 20 minutes. Grill seasoned ribs, basting with sauce during the last 15 minutes.

Mrs. Bill Rhoades (Dixie)

Pork Chops In Cream

4	pork chops, 1 inch thick	1/4	teaspoon pepper
	Apple brandy to marinate chops	1/2	pound small mushrooms
2	tablespoons butter	12	small whole pearl onions
2	tablespoons vegetable oil	1/2	cup apple brandy
1/2	teaspoon salt	1/2	cup whipping cream
			Parsley to serve

Marinate chops in brandy overnight. Brown pork in melted butter and oil. Add salt, pepper, mushrooms, onions and cook until pork is tender. Remove from skillet and keep warm. Add 1/2 cup brandy to skillet, skim grease from liquid. Gradually add cream and cook until thickened. Pour over chops and sprinkle with parsley. Serves 4.

Mrs. Carey Brennan (Shari)

Pork Chops And Vegetable Rice

4 pork loin chops	2/3 cup chopped red or green bell pepper
Salt and pepper to taste	
2/3 cup chopped celery	2/3 cup uncooked rice
2/3 cup chopped green onions with tops	1 1/3 cups chicken broth
	1 teaspoon garlic salt
	Dash of red pepper

Preheat oven to 375°. Season chops with salt and pepper. Brown on both sides in a greased skillet or one sprayed with a non-stick spray. Remove chops and set aside. Pour off all but 2 teaspoons of the drippings. Add vegetables and sauté until tender. Stir in rice, broth and seasonings. Bring to a boil. Pour all into a covered casserole. Add pork chops to mixture. Cover and bake at 375° for 25 to 30 minutes or until chops are tender. Serves 4.

Mrs. Chris John (Anne)

Stir-Fry Pork

1 pound boneless pork cutlets	6 large green bell peppers, cut into 1 inch pieces
3 teaspoons cornstarch, divided	1 1/2 teaspoons salt
1 teaspoon sugar, divided	2 slices fresh ginger root, chopped
3 tablespoons soy sauce	1 clove garlic, chopped
3 tablespoon water, divided	2 tablespoons dry sherry
5 tablespoons peanut or corn oil, divided	

Slice pork into small strips. Combine 1 1/2 teaspoons cornstarch, 1/2 teaspoon sugar, soy sauce and 1 tablespoon water. Add pork and mix well. Heat 2 tablespoons oil in a wok or skillet and add green pepper. Stir-fry for 4 to 5 minutes. Add salt and remaining sugar. Mix well and transfer to a warm platter. Clean out wok, and reheat, adding 3 tablespoons oil. Mix pork, ginger, and garlic. Add to wok and stir-fry until meat changes color and cooks until done. Sprinkle in sherry and add reserved peppers. Stir and cook until thoroughly heated. Mix 1 1/2 teaspoons cornstarch with 2 tablespoons water. Slowly pour into wok, stirring until sauce thickens and a clear glaze coats the meat and vegetables. Serve at once. Serves 6. *You can use chopped zucchini, celery, asparagus, cauliflower, broccoli, green beans, cabbage, or a combination of mushrooms with one of the vegetables instead of the green peppers.*

Mrs. Larry Hall (Jane)
Fiesta Chairman 1982-1983

Baked Ham With Mustard Sauce

1	thick ham slice, about 1½ pounds	¼	cup cold water
1	tablespoon flour	½	teaspoon Worcestershire sauce
1	teaspoon hot mustard	¼	teaspoon salt
1	cup orange juice or orange juice concentrate	¼	teaspoon paprika
2	tablespoons brown sugar	1	tablespoon raisins

Combine flour, mustard, orange juice, brown sugar, water, Worcestershire sauce, salt and paprika. Blend well and pour over ham. Bake at 350° for 40 minutes, basting 3 times. Add raisins for the last 10 minutes.

Mrs. Charles Boner (Grace)

Wild Rice Brunch Casserole

1	cup wild rice	1	teaspoon sugar
1	pound pork bulk sausage	1	teaspoon pepper
1	(4 ounce) can mushrooms, drained	2	cups canned tomatoes, drained
3	tablespoons chopped onion	1	cup grated Cheddar cheese
1	teaspoon salt		

Cook rice according to package directions. Brown sausage; remove from pan, drain well. Sauté lightly the mushrooms and onions, then add the salt, sugar, pepper, tomatoes, wild rice and sausage. Butter a 2 quart casserole. Place ½ of the rice mixture in the pan, add ½ cup cheese. Top with remaining rice and cheese. Bake at 350° for 30 minutes.

Mrs. Gary Hanson (Jean)

Stuffed Zucchini

4 to 5 long, straight zucchini		½	cup chopped green bell pepper
Salt and to taste		Dash of Tabasco sauce	
1	pound hot bulk pork sausage, crumbled	⅔	cup Italian seasoned bread crumbs
2	tablespoons olive oil	Parmesan cheese to taste	
4	green onions, chopped		
½	cup minced celery		

Slice squash lengthwise. Scoop out pulp and chop. Lightly salt pulp. In a skillet, brown sausage, drain. Add olive oil to skillet and sauté onion, celery and bell pepper. Combine vegetables, pulp and sausage. Add Tabasco and bread crumbs. Heap mixture into shells, sprinkle with Parmesan cheese and bake at 350° for 20 minutes.

Mrs. Henry A. Pate (Patricia)

Game

Ted's Spicy Venison Chili

4 pounds venison, coarsely ground or cut into chunks
1/4 cup bacon drippings or vegetable oil
6 cloves garlic, finely minced
2 large onions, chopped
2 tablespoons vegetable oil
1 (15 ounce) can tomato sauce
1 can beef broth

About 4 cups water
6 tablespoons chili powder
2 tablespoons cumin powder
1 tablespoon paprika
2 teaspoons salt
2 teaspoons pepper
1/2 teaspoon oregano
1/2 teaspoon sugar
1/4 teaspoon cayenne pepper

Sauté venison in bacon drippings or oil in a large skillet until gray, but not brown. Place meat in a large 8 quart cooking pot. Sauté onions and garlic separately in 2 tablespoons oil and add to meat in pot. Add tomato sauce, broth, and water; bring to a boil. Turn heat down, and simmer covered for 2 hours, stirring occasionally. Add remaining ingredients; cover and cook over low heat for 1 hour, stirring occasionally. *The chili freezes well and the flavor is even better the second day.*

Mrs. LeRoy Nagel (Harriet)
Fiesta Chairman 1974-1975

Venison Stew

3 1/2 to 4 pounds venison, cut into cubes
4 ounces lean salt pork, cut into cubes
2 tablespoons butter
1/4 cup chopped onion
3 coves garlic, minced
2 tablespoons flour

Salt and pepper to taste
1 tablespoon sugar
1 1/2 bay leaves
7 peppercorns
2 1/2 cups stewed tomatoes
1 cup chopped green bell pepper
1/2 pound mushrooms, sliced

Fry salt pork in butter in a big stew pot until brown, add venison and sauté. When almost brown, add onion and garlic. Combine flour, salt, pepper, sugar, and sift into pot. Pour in stewed tomatoes, and add bay leaves and peppercorns. Cover tightly and simmer for 1 hour and 30 minutes. Add chopped green pepper and simmer another 30 minutes. Test venison for tenderness and add mushrooms about 15 minutes before serving. Remove bay leaves and peppercorns and serve hot. Serves 6 to 8.

Mrs. Larry Hall (Jane)
Fiesta Chairman 1982-1983

Bob's Venison Steak

4 to 5 small onions, chopped
3 green bell peppers, chopped
18 mushrooms, chopped
1/2 cup butter
2 bay leaves

3 to 4 pound venison steak,
   2 inches thick
Salt and pepper to taste
4 cloves garlic, mashed

In a large iron skillet, sauté the onions, green peppers and mushrooms in butter. Rub both sides of the steak with salt, pepper and mashed garlic. Fry meat with onions and peppers. Do not overcook the venison, as this will make it tough. Serves 6 to 8.

Mrs. Robert Bluntzer (Jo)

Deer Camp Venison Backstrap

1 venison back strap
Milk or buttermilk to soak
   meat
Flour

Beaten eggs
Salt and pepper to taste
Vegetable oil

Cut backstrap into serving pieces. Pound with a meat mallet or side of a saucer to tenderize. Soak in milk or buttermilk for a few hours, or overnight. Drain venison. Dip into flour, then beaten eggs, then again in flour that has been mixed with salt and pepper. Fry in hot vegetable oil until golden brown.

Mrs. LeRoy Nagel (Harriet)
Fiesta Chairman 1974-1975

Stir-Fry Venison

2 pounds venison
1/2 cup soy sauce
2 tablespoons chili powder
1/4 cup oil

2 large cloves garlic, mashed
1/2 cup picante sauce
8 flour tortillas
Guacamole to serve

Slice venison against the grain into about 2 inch wide strips. Combine soy sauce, chili powder, oil and garlic, and marinate meat for about 3 hours. Stir fry meat in 1 tablespoon oil until it is browned. Add the picante sauce. Divide meat among 8 warm flour tortillas, roll and enjoy. Serve with guacamole.

Mrs. Chris John (Anne)

Central Texas Quail

1	cup flour	1	cup dry white wine
2	teaspoons salt	1	tablespoon parsley
1/2	teaspoon garlic powder	1	tablespoon fines herbes
1	teaspoon lemon-pepper seasoning	1	teaspoon dillweed
1	teaspoon paprika	1/4	teaspoon curry powder
12 to 14 dressed quail		Salt and pepper to taste	
1/2	cup butter	2	tablespoons Cognac
		1	cup sour cream

Combine flour, salt, garlic powder, lemon-pepper and paprika; coat quail with seasoned flour. Sauté in butter in a large pot until browned. Combine white wine, parsley, fines herbes, dillweed, curry, salt and pepper, and pour over quail. Cover and simmer for 20 to 25 minutes. Baste quail occasionally with sauce. Do not overcook. Remove quail and keep warm. Stir Cognac and sour cream into pan drippings, blending well. Add more wine if the sauce cooks down too much. Pour part of the sauce over quail and serve remainder in a gravy boat.

Mrs. Larry Hall (Jane)
Fiesta Chairman 1982-1983

Quail With Vegetables And Ham

4	tablespoon vegetable oil, divided	1	carrot, scraped and cut into thin strips
1	teaspoon minced fresh ginger	4	green onion, tops and all, sliced
3	quail, split	2	broccoli stalks, peeled and cut into thin strips
Salt and pepper to taste			
3 to 4 tablespoons chicken broth		2	ounces country ham or prosciutto, cut into thin strips
1	medium zucchini, cut into thin strips		

In a large skillet, heat 2 tablespoons oil with ginger. Brown quail on all sides and season with salt and pepper. Add a little broth, cover and steam slowly for 15 minutes. Remove quail with juices and keep warm. Add 2 tablespoons oil to pot in pan and add the vegetables, sautéing for 2 to 3 minutes over medium-high heat, stirring constantly. Stir ham into vegetables, then place quail on top. Cover and steam for 4 to 5 minutes. Serves 2 to 3.

Mrs. Jack Leo (Cindy Sherrell)
Guild President 1979-1980

Sautéed Doves

12	dove	Black pepper to taste	
1	cup flour	MSG to taste	
1	cup butter	Garlic salt to taste	
1	medium onion, chopped	Onion Powder to taste	
1/2	pound mushrooms, sliced	1 1/3 cups dry sherry	

Dredge dove in flour. Sauté birds in butter until brown, about 10 minutes. Stir in onion and mushrooms, sautéing until tender. Add seasonings and sherry, mixing well. Bring to a boil, reduce heat and simmer, covered for 20 minutes or until tender.

Mrs. Charlie Cantwell (Winn)

Grilled Doves

3 to 4 doves per person to serve
Italian dressing or your favorite
  marinade
Jalapeños, quartered

Coarsely chopped onions
Bacon sices, cut into halves
Wild rice to serve

Marinate dove breasts in Italian dressing for 3 to 4 hours or overnight. Place quartered jalapeños and chopped onion in the cavity of each dove. Wrap bacon slices around dove to hold in vegetables and secure with a toothpick. Grill over coals until bacon is crisp. Drizzle marinade over doves while grilling. Check often to prevent scorching or burning. Serve with wild rice.

Mrs. William Wilson (Cora Lynn)

Stuffed Grilled Doves

12 whole doves, prepared for
  cooking
4 tablespoons butter
Juice of 1 lemon
1 to 2 tart apples, peeled and
  cut into thick slices

1 medium onion, chopped
12 slices bacon
Salt and pepper to taste
Italian dressing, optional

Combine lemon juice and butter. Coat doves, inside and out, with lemon-butter mixture. Stuff body cavity of birds with apple and onion. Close opening with a toothpick or string. Sprinkle with salt and pepper. Wrap each bird with bacon, and secure with a toothpick. Cook over low to medum charcoal fire, turning frequently. If dove seem too dry, baste occasionally with Italian dressing. Serves 4.

Mrs. LeRoy Nagel (Harriet)
Fiesta Chairman 1974-1975

"H.E.B. Lunch"

Flatonia (a Fayette county community of 1,020, some two hours drive east of San Antonio) was named after pioneer merchant F. W. Flato, ancestor of a fifth generation Texan, Malou Flato. Malou is the artist of the richly colored watercolor: "H.E.B. Lunch".

Malou was awarded a B.A. in Theatre Arts ('75), Middlebury College, Middlebury, Vermont. At Middlebury she studied design and the use of colors for theatrical productions. It was not until 1981 that Malou devoted full time to her watercolor talent. For several years she had been working in etchings on zinc. She has exhibited in shows in Texas Gallery, Houston; "New Works", Laguna Gloria Art Museum; Texas Fine Arts Association National Exhibition, Austin; Charlton Gallery, San Antonio; Arizona State University, Tempe; Amarillo Art Center, Amarillo; and Art Museum of South Texas, Corpus Christi.

Malou was the artist for the Laguna Gloria Art Museum Fiesta poster for 1982. Today she has added painting and firing wall-size ceramic tile murals to her watercolor talents.

Her watercolors are included in collections of: Harte-Hanks, San Antonio; Charles Schreiner Bank, Kerrville; City of Davis, California; Washington State Arts Commission, Arlington, Washington; Ford-Powell-Carson, San Antonio; Southwestern Bell, Dallas; 3-M Corporation, Austin; American Bank, Austin; Imperial Sugar, Sugarland; Allied Bank, Port Arthur; Texas Commerce Bank, Houston; University of Houston; Massachusetts Transit Authority, Boston; Atlantic Richfield Corporation and H.E.B. Corporation, San Antonio.

Texas Gallery, Houston is Malou's representative; in Austin her work may be viewed at Willingheart Gallery.

Breads
Cracked Wheat Bread

1½ cups boiling water
¾ cup cracked wheat
1 cup buttermilk
¼ cup molasses
2 tablespoons honey
¼ cup unsalted butter
2 teaspoons salt

2 packages dry yeast
¼ cup very warm water
½ teaspoon sugar or honey
2 to 3 cups white flour
2 cups whole wheat flour
2 tablespoons butter, melted

In a large bowl pour boiling water over wheat and let stand 1 hour. In a saucepan heat buttermilk, molasses, honey, butter and salt, just until melted. Stir to mix. Sprinkle yeast over very warm water in a large bowl. Stir in sugar and let stand 10 minutes. Add buttermilk mixture and 2 cups white flour to yeast. Beat with electric mixer for 2 minutes. Gradually add whole wheat flour and enough of remaining white flour to make a dough that holds together and pulls away from bowl. Turn dough out onto floured surface and knead 10 minutes. Place in a large greased bowl, turning to bring greased side up. Cover and let rise in a warm place until double in volume. Punch dough down, and return to lightly floured surface. Knead, then let rest 10 minutes. Divide dough in half and shape each half into a loaf and place in 2 greased loaf pans. Brush with melted butter. Cover and let rise until almost doubled. Bake at 350° for 45 minutes. Yields 2 loaves.

Mrs. Mike Metschan (Sally)
Guild President 1982-1983

Braided Bread Loaf

1 package dry yeast
1 cup warm water
3 tablespoons sugar
2 tablespoons shortening
1 egg, beaten

¾ teaspoon salt
3 to 3½ cups flour, divided
1 egg white
1 tablespoon water

In a large bowl dissolve yeast in warm water. Add sugar, shortening, egg, salt, and half the flour; beat at low speed of electric mixer until smooth. Stir in enough remaining flour to make a soft dough. Place dough in a greased bowl turning to grease top. Cover and let rise, or cover and refrigerate up to 5 days. Punch dough down; turn out onto a lightly floured board and knead 4 to 5 times. Divided dough into thirds. Shape each third into a 12 inch rope. Place ropes on a greased baking sheet; pinch ends together at one end to seal. Braid ropes and pinch other end. Cover and let rise until doubled in bulk. Combine egg white and 1 tablespoon water and beat until frothy. Gently brush over loaf. Bake at 350° for 25 to 30 minutes. Yields 1 loaf.

Mrs. Jerry Hering (Carol)
Fiesta Chairman 1979-1980

Polygrain Bread

1	cup rolled oats	1	cup plain yogurt
1	cup cracked wheat	2	tablespoons vegetable oil
1	cup boiling water	2	teaspoons salt
2	packages dry yeast	5	cups flour
1/2	cup very warm water	1	egg, slightly beaten
1	tablespoon light brown sugar		

Combine oats and wheat flour in a large mixing bowl; stir in boiling water, cool to lukewarm. Sprinkle yeast into very warm water. Stir until yeast dissolves, then stir in sugar. Let stand until bubbly and double in volume, about 5 minutes. Add yeast mixture, yogurt, oil and salt to oats and mix thoroughly. Beat in 3 cups flour until completely blended. Gradually beat in remaining flour to make a soft dough. Turn out onto lightly floured surface; knead until smooth and elastic, adding only enough additional flour to keep dough from sticking. Place in a lightly oiled bowl; turn to coat, cover and let rise until double in size. Punch down, turn out onto a lightly floured surface; invert bowl over dough; allow to rest 10 minutes. Divide in half and knead each half. Roll each half into a 15x10 inch rectangle, then roll up from long side jelly roll style. Place into 2 oiled loaf pans and let rise 30 to 45 minutes. Brush tops with slightly beaten egg. Bake at 375° for 50 minutes. Yields 2 loaves.

Mrs. Ron Mullen (Carole)
Guild President 1981-1982

Light Yeast Bread

2	packages dry yeast	1	teaspoon salt
1/2	cup warm water	1/3	cup vegetable oil
3/4	cup milk, scalded	2	eggs, beaten
1/4	cup sugar		4 to 4 1/2 cups flour

Dissolve yeast in warm water; let stand 5 minutes. Combine milk, sugar and salt in a large bowl; mix well. Cool. Add oil, eggs and 1 cup flour to yeast mixture and mix well. Gradually stir in enough of the remaining flour to make a soft dough. Turn dough out on a floured surface and knead until smooth and elastic. Place in a well greased bowl, turning to grease top. Cover and let rise in a warm place for 50 to 60 minutes. Punch down and place into 2 greased loaf pans and let rise until doubled in size. Bake at 400° for 30 minutes. Yields 2 loaves.

Mrs. Larry Hall (Jane)
Fiesta Chairman 1982-1983

Rosie's Italian Bread

2	packages dry yeast	6	cups luke warm water
3	tablespoons salt	20	cups flour

Place all ingredients in a large bowl and stir with your hands, dip hand in a pan of water when you need more moisture. After dough is thoroughly mixed take out of pan, rinse and dry pan. Place the dough back in pan and knead or punch for 30 minutes, until bubbles appear when dough is cut. Cover and let rise in a warm place for 4 hours. Flour cookie sheets. Form large 6 to 8 inch loaves and place on sheets and let rise 45 minutes to 1 hour, covered. Preheat oven to 550°. Place loaves in oven; after 10 minutes lower to 450°; after 5 minutes lower to 400°; after 15 minutes lower to 300°, bake for 30 minutes. Cool loaves on a rack. Yields 4 loaves. *Rosie is a delightful Italian woman who makes this bread by "feel" every week. She taught me how to make it one day, so I had to measure everything she did. This is a hard crusted Italian style Peasant bread. If you prefer whole wheat bread, use 7½ cups whole wheat flour and 9 cups flour.*

Mrs. Richard Musci (Linda)

French Bread

1½ cups warm water, divided	1½ cups flour
1½ packages dry yeast	2 teaspoons salt
2 teaspoons sugar, divided	

In a small bowl, mix ½ cup water, yeast and 1 teaspoon sugar; let soften 5 minutes. In a food processor blend flour, salt and 1 teaspoon sugar. Add yeast mixture to food processor and mix until well blended. Then slowly add 1 cup warm water. Blend until dough climbs up sides of work bowl. Remove dough and put on floured board. Knead dough just long enough to incorporate small amount of flour and form into a ball. Place dough in a 21 inch bagette pan that has been lightly oiled. Make ¼ inch deep slashes 2 inches apart along top of dough. Cover and let rise in warm place for 45 minutes to 1 hour. Preheat oven to 450°. Place shallow pan of water on bottom rack. Place bread on rack directly above water. Bake at 450° for 10 to 15 minutes. Lower oven temperature to 400° and bake for another 10 to 15 minutes. Let cool before slicing. Yields 1 loaf. *If the bread seems to be browning too quickly, I make a tent of foil and lay over the bread. Do not omit the shallow pan of water. This is what makes the wonderful crust on the bread. Freezes beautifully.*

Mrs. William A. Bradley (Alicia)

Russian Bread

2	packages dry yeast	4	cups rye flour, divided
2	teaspoons salt	3	cups flour, divided
1	teaspoon sugar	1/4	cup white vinegar
2	teaspoons instant coffee powder	1/4	cup dark molasses
2	teaspoons onion powder	1	square unsweetened chocolate, cut in small pieces
2	tablespoons caraway seeds, crushed	4	tablespoons margarine
1	teaspoon fennel seeds, crushed	21/2	cups boiling water
		1/4	cup cold water
2	cups 100% Bran Buds	1/2	teaspoon cornstarch

Thoroughly mix yeast, salt, sugar, coffee powder, onion powder, caraway seeds, fennel seeds, bran buds, 1 1/3 cups rye flour and 1 cup flour; set aisde. Combine vinegar, molasses, chocolate, margarine and boiling water, then add to the dry ingredients and beat with a whisk for 3 minutes. Add 1/2 cup flour and beat for another 3 minutes using either whisk or wooden spoon. Stir in enough flour, alternating between the rye and all purpose flour, to make soft dough. Turn out onto lightly floured board. Cover with bowl and let rest 15 minutes. Knead for about 15 minutes until smooth and elastic. Place in a greased bowl, turning once to grease top. Cover bowl with tea towel and set in a warm place until double in bulk. Punch dough down, turn out onto lightly floured board and knead for a couple of minutes. Divide dough in half. Shape each half into a ball about 5 inches in diameter. Place each ball in the center of greased 8 inch round cake pan. Cover and let rise in a warm place until doubled in volume. Bake in a preheated 350° oven for 50 minutes. To make the glaze combine cornstarch and cold water. Cook over medium heat, stirring constantly, until mixture boils. Cook 1 more minute, stirring constantly. As soon as the bread is out of the oven, brush glaze over top. Return to oven for an extra 3 minutes or until glaze is set. Remove from pan and cool on wire racks. Yields 2 loaves.

Mrs. Gene Reinhart (Pamela)

Alabama Biscuits

1	package dry yeast	1 1/4	teaspoons salt
1/3	cup warm water	2 1/2	heaping tablespoons sugar
1	cup lukewarm milk	3	cups flour
4	tablespoons vegetable oil	2	teaspoons baking powder

Mix yeast and warm water. Let stand 5 minutes. Add remaining ingredients and knead 5 minutes. Roll out on waxed paper and cut with biscuit cutter. Let rise 1 hour and 15 minutes. Bake in a preheated 400° oven for 15 minutes. Yields 2 dozen biscuits. *These biscuits can be frozen after baking and reheated.*

Mrs. Pat Rick (Marlene)

Rich Dinner Rolls

1 cup milk, scalded	1/2 cup very warm water
1/4 cup sugar	2 eggs, beaten
1 teaspoon salt	5 to 51/4 cups flour
1/4 cup butter or margarine	Melted butter
2 packages dry yeast	

Scald milk; stir in sugar, salt and butter. Cool to lukewarm. Soften yeast in very warm water. Add milk mixture, eggs and 2 cups flour; beat until smooth. Add enough remaining flour to make a soft dough. Turn out on a lightly floured board; knead about 8 to 10 minutes. Place in a greased bowl, turning to grease top. Cover and let rise in a warm place until doubled in bulk. Punch down. Return to floured board and shape into cloverleaf, crescent or pan rolls. Cover and let rise until doubled. Brush with melted butter. Bake at 400° for 10 to 15 minutes. Yields 3 dozen rolls.

Mrs. Scott Chapman (Vicki)
Fiesta Chairman 1980-1981

Refrigerator Rolls

3/4 cup hot water	2 packages dry yeast
1/2 cup sugar	1 cup very warm water
1 tablespoon salt	1 egg, beaten
3 tablespoons butter or margarine	5 to 51/4 cups flour
	Melted butter

Combine hot water, sugar, salt and butter; cool to lukewarm. Soften yeast in very warm water. Add sugar mixture, eggs and half of the flour; beat until smooth. Add enough remaining flour to make a soft dough. Turn dough out on a lightly floured board; knead about 10 minutes. Place in a greased bowl, turning to grease top. Cover tightly with waxed paper. Store in refrigerator until doubled in bulk. To use, punch dough down, and turn out on a lightly floured board. Shape into crescent, cloverleaf or pan rolls. Cover and let rise until doubled in bulk. Brush with melted butter. Bake at 400° for 10 to 15 minutes. Yields 3 dozen rolls. *The dough may be kept in the refrigerator for 4 to 5 days.*

Mrs. Kyle Baker (Linda)

• *For perfect bread, it is important to let the dough rise exactly the right amount. To test, press your finger into the dough. If the imprint remains, the dough is ready.*

Danish Pastry

1½ cups butter, softened	1 egg, beaten
3¾ cups flour, divided	¾ cup cold milk
½ cup warm water	⅓ cup sugar
2 packages dry yeast	½ teaspoon salt

In a medium bowl cream butter with a wooden spoon until smooth. Add ¼ cup flour, stirring until blended. Place butter mixture on waxed paper and cover with second sheet of waxed paper. Roll out to an 11x9 inch rectangle and refrigerate for 20 to 30 minutes. Meanwhile sprinkle yeast over water, stirring until dissolved. Add egg, milk, sugar and salt, mix well. Beat in 3 cups flour until smooth and elastic, about 5 minutes. Stir in remaining ½ cup flour and beat 2 minutes. Dough will be soft. Refrigerate dough, covered 10 minutes. Sprinkle pastry cloth generously with flour. Turn dough onto cloth and sprinkle with more flour. Use no more than ¼ cup flour for the sprinklings. Roll to a 14x12 inch rectangle. Brush off excess flour with a pastry brush. Remove waxed paper from butter rectangle, invert over dough leaving ½ inch margin on sides. Starting with unbuttered third, fold dough into thirds, making 3 layers. As you fold brush off excess flour. Turn dough a quarter turn to right, folded side will be at right; then starting from center roll out into a 14x12 inch rectangle. If butter breaks through, brush spot very lightly with flour. From short side fold dough into thirds. Carefully lift onto a cookie sheet, cover with foil and chill for 15 minutes. Repeat rolling and chilling the dough 3 more times. On a floured surface, roll pastry into a 18x16 inch rectangle and cut into shape desired. Fill with thick jelly or almond paste and place on greased cookie sheets, cover and refrigerate overnight. Preheat oven to 400°. Brush rolls with a beaten egg. Bake 5 minutes at 400°, then reduce heat to 350° and bake 15 minutes more until puffed and golden brown. Frost with a powdered sugar glaze. Serve warm.

Mrs. Brad Pfluger (Deborah Kaster)

Yeast Waffles

2 cups milk	1 teaspoon sugar
1 package dry yeast	3 cups flour
½ cup warm water	2 eggs, slightly beaten
⅓ cup melted butter	½ teaspoon baking soda
1 teaspoon salt	

Scald milk and cool to lukewarm. Sprinkle yeast on warm water and stir to dissolve. Add milk, melted butter, salt, sugar and flour. Mix thoroughly with electric mixer. Cover and let stand at room temperature overnight. When ready to bake in waffle iron, add eggs and baking soda and beat well. Serves 6 to 8.

Mrs. Brian Sullivan (Cynthia)

Glazed Orange Rolls

1	cup milk, scalded	3	eggs, beaten
9	tablespoons butter, divided	4½	cup flour
1	cup sugar, divided	2 to 3	teaspoons grated orange
½	teaspoon salt		peel
1	package dry yeast	2	cups powdered sugar
		3 to 4	tablespoons orange juice

Scald milk and cool to lukewarm. Add 3 tablespoons butter, ½ cup sugar, salt and yeast. Let stand 3 minutes. Add eggs and 1 cup flour. Beat well. Add remaining flour and mix to make stiff dough. Turn out on lightly floured surface and knead about 10 minutes. Place in a greased bowl turning to coat surface, cover and let rise until double in size. Punch down and return to floured surface, half dough and roll each to a 12x8 inch rectangle. Stir together 6 tablespoon butter, ½ cup sugar and orange peel. Spread over dough and roll up starting with long end. Seal seams. Slice each into 18 rolls. Place cut side down in greased 2½ inch muffin pans. Let rise until double. Bake at 375° for 15 minutes. Combine powdered sugar and orange juice to make glaze and drizzle over warm rolls. Yields 36 rolls.

Mrs. Marcus Bone (Beverly)
Fiesta Chairman 1983-1984

Thursday Therapy Cinnamon Bread

1	cup lukewarm milk	2	eggs
1	package dry yeast	4	cups flour
½	cup sugar, divided		Melted butter
1	teaspoon salt	2	teaspoons cinnamon
¼	cup butter, softened		

In a bowl put lukewarm milk and yeast, let stand for 5 minutes. Add ¼ cup sugar, salt, soft butter and eggs. Beat thoroughly with a beater. Gradually add flour. Knead on a floured board until smooth, like velvet to the touch. Place in a lightly greased bowl. Turn bread dough over in bowl so top surface is lightly greased. Cover with a damp cloth and let rise 1 hour or so until double in size. Punch down and divide into 2 to 3 small pieces. Shape into rectangles slightly more narrow than the length of bread pans and ¼ inch thick. Brush each with melted butter and sprinkle with a mixture of ¼ cup sugar and cinnamon. Roll up like a jelly roll and place in buttered 9x5 inch bread pans. Cover with a damp cloth and let rise until double in size. Brush with melted butter and bake at 400° for 30 minutes. Yields 2 standard loaves or 3 small loaves.

Sylvia Stevens

• *Always knead pastry with the heel of the hand. It's the coolest part of the hand.*

My Favorite Cinnamon Rolls

2 cups butter or margarine, divided	3 tablespoons dry yeast
1 cup sugar	½ cup warm water
¼ cup dry milk	Cinnamon
1½ cups hot water	Sugar
4 eggs	3 cups powdered sugar
8 to 10 cups flour	1 teaspoon butter flavoring
	1 teaspoon vanilla extract

Combine 1 cup butter with sugar and dry milk in mixer. Add 1½ cups hot water and mix well. Add eggs, one at a time, beating several minutes after each addition. Dissolve yeast in ½ cup warm water and set aside. Add half the flour and mix well. Add yeast and remaining flour. The batter will almost pull away from sides of bowl. Let the dough rise in the bowl until double in bulk. Punch down and divide the dough in half. Roll each half into an oblong 12x14 inch shape. Generously cover each with ½ cup of melted butter. Sprinkle dough with a mixture of cinnamon and sugar. Roll up jellyroll fashion and cut into 1 inch slices. Place slices in a 9x13 inch glass dish, and let double in size. Bake at 325° for 20 to 30 minutes. Combine together ½ cup butter, powdered sugar, butter flavoring and vanilla. Pour over rolls as soon as they come out of the oven.

Mrs. Paul Loftin (Liz)

Whole Wheat Rolls

1 package dry yeast	¾ teaspoon salt
2 cups whole wheat flour	¼ cup butter or margarine
¾ cup flour, divided	1¼ cups very warm milk
2 tablespoons packed brown sugar	

In a medium bowl mix yeast, whole wheat flour, ½ cup flour, sugar and salt; set aside. Add butter to milk, stirring until melted. Pour over flour mixture; beat with spoon until well blended. Turn out on lightly floured surface; knead until smooth and elastic, about 5 minutes. Place in a greased bowl; turn to grease top. Cover and let rise until doubled. Punch down; knead on lightly floured board until smooth and elastic. Add remaining flour if necessary to prevent sticking. Divide dough in half and shape each into a roll; then cut into 10 equal pieces. Shape in 3 inch oval roll. Place 1 inch apart on a greased cookie sheet. Let rise until doubled in size. Bake at 400° for 10 to 12 minutes. Yields 20 rolls.

Mrs. Robert Bluntzer (Jo)

Irish Soda Bread

2 cups flour	3 tablespoons shortening
1/2 teaspoon baking soda	1 tablespoon caraway seeds
1/4 teaspoon baking powder	1/2 cup raisins
1 tablespoon sugar	1 cup buttermilk or sour
1/2 teaspoon salt	milk

Sift together flour, soda, baking powder, sugar and salt. Cut in shortening; add caraway seeds, raisins, and milk. Turn onto floured board and knead 15 times. Place into greased 8 inch cake pan. Bake at 350° for 35 minutes.

Mrs. Bill Balcezak (Sharon)

Family Waffles

3 eggs, separated	4 1/2 tablespoons baking powder
2 1/4 cups flour	2 cups milk
3/4 teaspoon salt	3/4 cup butter or margarine,
1 1/2 tablespoons sugar	melted

Beat egg whites until stiff. Mix together egg yolks, flour, salt, sugar, baking powder and milk. While beating, slowly add butter or margarine. Fold in beaten egg whites. Cook in a hot waffle iron. Serves 4.

Mrs. Tim Cahalane (Kathy)

Sour Cream Pancakes

1 cup sour cream	1 teaspoon salt
1 cup flour	1 egg, slightly beaten
1 tablespoon sugar	1/2 cup milk
1 teaspoon baking soda	1/4 cup wheat germ, or more
1 tablespoon vegetable oil	to taste

Preheat an electric griddle to 375°. Place all ingredients except wheat germ in a blender and blend. Stir in wheat germ. Cook on griddle. Yields about 12 (4 inch) pancakes.

Nancy Scanlan

• *A crack down the center of a nut loaf is no mistake. It's typical.*

French Breakfast Puffs

½ cup sugar
⅓ cup butter
1 egg, slightly beaten
1½ cups flour
1½ teaspoons baking powder

½ teaspoon salt
¼ teaspoon nutmeg
¾ cup milk
½ cup sugar
1 teaspoon cinnamon

Preheat oven to 350°. Cream togehter sugar, butter and egg. Sift together flour, baking powder, salt and nutmeg. Add to creamed mixture alternating with milk. Beat well and spoon into muffin pans lined with cupcake papers. Combine sugar and cinnamon and sprinkle on top. Bake at 350° for 20 to 25 minutes. Yields 12 muffins.

Mrs. J. Douglas Hirsh (Patti)

Mile High Biscuits

2 cups flour
1 cup whole wheat flour
4½ teaspoons baking powder
2 tablepoons sugar
½ teaspoon salt

¾ teaspoon cream of tartar
¾ cup butter
1 egg, beaten
1 cup milk

Preheat oven to 450°. In a bowl combine the flours, baking powder, sugar, salt and cream of tartar. Cut in butter until mixture resembles coarse cornmeal. Add one egg and milk, stirring quickly and briefly. Knead lightly on a floured board, then roll or pat gently to 1 inch thickness. Cut into 1 to 2 inch biscuit rounds. Place in a greased 9 inch square pan. For crusty biscuits, separate on a cookie sheet. Bake at 450° for 12 to 15 minutes. Yields 2 dozen biscuits.

Mrs. Steve Bradley (Pam)

Buttermilk Biscuits

1½ cups flour
½ teaspoon salt
¼ teaspoon baking soda

2 teaspoons baking powder
⅓ cup shortening
½ cup buttermilk

Preheat oven to 450°. Sift together flour, salt, baking soda and baking powder. Cut in shortening until mixture resembles coarse crumbs. Add buttermilk and stir with fork just until dough holds together. On a floured surface, pat or gently roll dough out to ½ inch thickness. Cut with 1½ inch cutter. Place biscuits on heavy baking sheet and bake at 450° for 10 minutes. Yields 12 biscuits.

Mrs. Dan Jardine (Lisa)

Yummy Bran Muffins

1½ cups bran cereal
1   cup milk
1   egg, beaten
2   cups flour
3   teaspoons baking powder
¼   teaspoon baking soda

¼   cup sugar
1   cup raisins
½   cup blueberries, optional
¼   cup chopped pecans
¼   cup vegetable oil

Preheat oven to 350°. Soak bran cereal in milk. In a separate bowl combine egg, dry ingredients, raisins, blueberries, pecans and oil. Add cereal and milk; mix together, do not over beat. Pour into greased muffin pans and bake at 350° for 20 minutes. Yields 24 muffins.

Mrs. M. K. Hage (Nettie)

Oatmeal Muffins

1   cup quick cooking oats
1   cup buttermilk
1   egg, beaten
½   cup packed brown sugar
½   cup vegetable oil
1   cup flour

1   teaspoon baking powder
½   teaspoon salt
½   teaspoon baking soda
½   cup chopped walnuts or
     pecans, optional
½   cup chopped dates, optional

Preheat oven to 400°. Mix all ingredients together. Bake in greased and floured muffin pans at 400° for 15 to 20 minutes. Yields 12 to 15 muffins.

Mrs. William A. Bradley (Alicia)

Buttermilk Cornbread

1   cup corn meal
½   cup flour
1   teaspoon baking powder
1   teaspoon salt

½   teaspoon baking soda
1   cup buttermilk
1   egg, slightly beaten
¼   cup melted shortening

Preheat oven to 450°. Combine dry ingredients and mix well. Combine buttermilk, egg and melted shortening and add to dry mixture. Stir well and spoon into hot greased 10 inch baking pan or corn stick pan. Bake at 450° for 15 to 20 minutes or until bread is brown. Yields 6 to 8 servings.

Mrs. David Hart (Sue)
Fiesta Chairman 1985-1986

Mexican Cornbread

1/3	cup bacon drippings	1	(16 ounce) can cream corn
1	cup yellow corn meal	1	cup grated American cheese
1/2	teaspoon baking soda	1	(4 ounce) can whole green
1/2	teaspoon salt		chilies, seeds removed
3/4	cup buttermilk	1	cup grated Monterey Jack
2	eggs, beaten		cheese

Preheat oven to 400°. Melt bacon drippings in an 8x11 inch pan and roll around to coat on all sides. Remove and reserve drippings after coating sides. In a medium bowl mix corn meal, soda, salt, buttermilk, eggs, cream corn and extra drippings. Spread 1/2 mixture in pan. Spread with American cheese, layer with green chilies then Monterey Jack cheese. Top with remaining corn meal mixture. Bake at 400° for 35 minutes. Serves 8.

Becky Allen

Prize Popovers

1	cup flour	1	tablespoon unsalted butter,
1/4	teaspoon salt		melted
3	large eggs	2	tablespoons unsalted butter,
1	cup milk		cut into 6 even pieces

Preheat oven to 425°. Oil or spray popover pans and heat in oven for about 2 minutes. Blend with an electric mixer flour, salt, eggs, milk and melted butter until mixture is the consistency of heavy cream, about 1 to 2 minutes. Place 1 small piece of butter in each cup and place pans back in oven until butter is bubbly, about 1 minute. Fill each cup half full with batter and bake for 20 minutes. Reduce heat to 325° and continue baking 15 to 20 minutes. Yields 6.

Mrs. Mark Veltri (Pam)

Hush Puppies

2	cups corn meal	1/2	teaspoon baking powder
	Hot water	2	tablespoons water
	Salt to taste		Oil for frying
2	tablespoons bacon		
	drippings		

Mix enough water to corn meal to make a very dry mixture. Add salt and bacon drippings; let stand 20 minutes. Mix the baking powder with the 2 tablespoons water and combine with corn meal mixture. Pat into circles, about half dollar size. Fry in deep oil until brown.

Mrs. Paul Loftin (Liz)

Applesauce Bread

1/2 cup shortening	1/2 teaspoon baking soda
1 cup sugar	1/2 teaspoon cinnamon
2 eggs, beaten	1/2 teaspoon nutmeg
1 3/4 cups flour	1 cup sweetened applesauce
1 teaspoon salt	1/2 cup chopped walnuts,
1 teaspoon baking powder	optional

Preheat oven to 350°. Stir shortening to soften, gradually add sugar, creaming until light. Add eggs, beat until light and fluffy. Sift together dry ingredients, add creamed mixture alternately with applesauce, beating after each addition. Stir in walnuts. Pour into a 9x5x3 loaf pan sprayed with non stick spray or lined with waxed paper. Bake at 350° for 1 hour. Cool in pan 10 minutes and remove. Yields 1 loaf. *This bread is a great treat for breakfast when toasted and spread with butter.*

Mrs. Rowland V. Firth (Susan)

Spiced Applesauce Bread

1 1/4 cups applesauce	3/4 cup chopped pecans,
1 cup sugar	divided
1/2 cup vegetable oil	1 teaspoon cinnamon,
2 eggs, beaten	divided
3 tablespoons milk	1/4 teaspoon salt
2 cups flour	1/4 teaspoon nutmeg
1 teaspoon baking soda	1/4 teaspoon allspice
1/2 teaspoon baking powder	1/4 cup brown sugar

Preheat oven to 350°. Combine applesauce, sugar, oil, eggs and milk. Sift flour, soda, baking powder, 1/2 teaspoon cinnamon, salt, nutmeg and allspice. Stir into applesauce mixture and beat well. Fold in 1/2 cup pecans. Pour into well greased 9x5x3 inch loaf pan. Combine 1/4 cup pecans, brown sugar and 1/2 teaspoon cinnamon. Sprinkle over batter in pan. Bake at 350° for 1 hour. Remove from pan and cool on a rack. Yields 1 loaf.

Mrs. Chris John (Anne)

• *Breads become stale more quickly in the refrigerator than they do at room temp. Freeze extra loaves rather than storing them in the refrig.*

Apricot Nut Bread

1   cup dried chopped apricots
1¼ cups sugar, divided
2   tablespoons shortening
1   egg, beaten
½ cup orange juice

2   cups flour
2   teaspoons baking powder
1   teaspoon baking soda
1   teaspoon salt
1   cup chopped pecans

Soak apricots for 20 minutes in water. Preheat oven to 300°. Cream together 1 cup sugar, shortening and egg. Stir in ¼ cup sugar and orange juice. Sift together flour, baking powder, baking soda and salt. Add to sugar mixture and blend well. Drain apricots and stir into batter with pecans. Bake in a greased and floured loaf pan at 300° for about 65 minutes or until toothpick comes out clean. Yields 1 loaf. *Slice thickly and serve with whipped cream.*

Mrs. Henry A. Pate (Patricia)

Spicy Banana Bread

½ cup butter, softened
1   cup sugar
2   eggs, beaten
1   teaspoon baking soda
2   cups flour
Pinch of salt
1   teaspoon cinnamon

1   teaspoon cloves
½ teapoon ginger
½ teaspoon allspice
2   tablespoons plain yogurt
3 to 4 bananas, mashed
1   cup whole pecan halves

Preheat oven to 350°. Cream together butter and sugar; add beaten eggs. Add flour, salt, soda and spices. Add yogurt and beat well. Blend in mashed bananas and pecans. Bake at 350° in a greased 9x5 loaf pan for 1 hour and 30 minutes. Yields 1 loaf.

Mrs. Charles Herring Jr. (Anna)

Banana Nut Bread

1½ cups sugar
½ cup butter, softened
2   eggs, separated
2   cups flour
1½ teaspoons baking soda
1   teaspoon vanilla extract

¼ cup milk
3   medium ripe bananas, mashed
1   cup chopped pecans or walnuts

Cream butter and sugar; add egg yolks, soda, vanilla, milk, bananas and flour mixing well. Add pecans and fold in whipped egg whites. Pour into 2 small oiled loaf pans or 1 oiled bundt pan. Bake at 300° for 1 hour. Refrigerate after cooled. Yields 2 small loaves.

Becky Allen

Blueberry Quick Bread

2½ cups flour
¾ cup sugar
1 tablespoon baking powder
½ teaspoon salt
6 tablespoons butter or margarine

¾ cup chopped walnuts, optional
2 eggs, beaten
1 cup milk
1 teaspoon vanilla extract
1½ cups blueberries

Preheat oven to 350°. Grease and flour a 9x5 inch loaf pan. In a large bowl, with fork, mix flour, sugar, baking powder and salt. With pastry blender or 2 knives, cut in butter or margarine until mixture resembles fine crumbs. Stir in walnuts. In a small bowl beat eggs slightly; stir in milk and vanilla. Stir egg mixture into flour mixture until flour is just moistened. Gently stir blueberries into batter. Spoon evenly into loaf pan. Bake at 350° for 1 hour and 20 minutes. Cool bread in pan on wire rack 10 minutes. Yields 1 loaf or 24 muffins.

Mrs. Rowland V. Firth (Susan)

Cinnamon Flop

1 cup sugar
2½ cups flour
2 teaspoons baking powder
1 cup milk
1 egg, beaten

5 tablespoon melted butter, divided
1 cup brown sugar
Cinnamon

Preheat oven to 350°. Sift together sugar, flour and baking powder. Add milk, egg and 1 tablespoon melted butter. Mix well. Pour into 2 greased and floured 8 inch pans. Spread each with ½ cup brown sugar and then sprinkle generously with cinnamon. Then pour 2 tablespoons melted butter over cinnamon and sugar. Bake at 350° for 20 to 25 minutes. Yields 2 loaves.

Mrs. Don Cooper (Coleen)

Carrot Bread

1 cup sugar
⅔ cup vegetable oil
2 eggs, beaten
1½ cups flour
1 teaspoon baking soda

1 teaspoon baking powder
1 teaspoon cinnamon
¼ teaspoon salt
1 cup junior food carrots
½ cup chopped pecans

Preheat oven to 350°. Mix together all ingredients in order listed. Bake in a greased loaf pan at 350° for 1 hour. Yields 1 loaf. *My family loves to spread cream cheese on this bread when eating.*

Mrs. Ross Burgh (JoLynne)
Guild President 1980-1981

Cranberry Bread

2 cups flour	1 tablespoon freshly grated
1 cup sugar	orange rind
1½ teaspoons baking powder	2 tablespoons corn oil
½ teaspoon baking soda	1 egg, well beaten
1 teaspoon salt	½ cup chopped pecans
¾ cup orange juice	1½ cups fresh or frozen
	cranberries, halved

Preheat oven to 350°. Sift together flour, sugar, baking powder, soda and salt. Combine orange juice, grated rind and oil; then stir in beaten egg. Pour this mixture into dry ingredients, mixing just enough to dampen. Fold in halved cranberries and pecans. Spoon into well greased loaf pan, spreading evenly, making corners slightly higher than center. Bake at 350° for 50 to 60 minutes. Cool; remove from pan and store overnight for easier slicing. Yields 1 loaf.

Mrs. Dan Bullock (Gayle)

Lemon Bread

⅓ cup shortening	¼ teaspoon salt
1⅔ cups sugar, divided	½ cup milk
2 eggs, beaten	Grated rind of 1 lemon
1½ cups flour	½ cup chopped pecans
1½ teaspoons baking powder	Juice of 2 lemons

Preheat oven to 350°. Beat together shortening and 1 cup sugar until light and fluffy. Add eggs, one at a time, beating well after each. Sift the dry ingredients and add alternately with the milk to the sugar mixture, beating well after each addition. Add the lemon rind and pecans. Turn into a greased large loaf pan or 2 small ones. Bake at 350° for 45 to 60 minutes. Transfer immediately to a serving plate. Mix the juice of 2 lemons and ⅔ cup of sugar and spread over top and sides. Yields 1 large loaf or 2 small loaves.

Mrs. Roger W. Marcum (Debbie)

• *To substitute plain gelatin for a 3 ounce package of flavored gelatin, add about ¼ cup sugar to one envelope unflavored gelatin.*

Fresh Peach Muffins

1 egg, beaten	2 cups flour
1 cup milk	3 teaspoons baking powder
1/4 cup vegetable oil	1/2 teaspoon salt
1 teaspoon lemon juice	1/4 teaspoon cinnamon
1/4 teaspoon vanilla extract	1 cup unpeeled, chopped
2/3 cup sugar	fresh peaches

Preheat oven to 450°. Beat egg, stir in milk, oil, lemon juice and vanilla. Add sugar; mix well. Sift dry ingredients together; stir in milk mixture just until blended. Do not over mix. Fold in peaches. Fill greased muffin cups 2/3 full and bake at 450° for 20 minutes. Yields 12 muffins.

Mrs. Boyd Morgan (Sherry)

Chopped Pear Bread

3 eggs, beaten	2 teaspoons cinnamon
2 cups sugar	1/4 teaspoon nutmeg, optional
2 teaspoons vanilla extract	1/4 teaspoon cloves, optional
1 cup vegetable oil	1/4 teaspoon allspice, optional
3 cups flour	1 cup chopped pecans
1 teaspoon baking soda	3 cups pared, cored and
1/2 teaspoon salt	chopped pears

Preheat oven to 350°. Beat eggs; then add sugar, vanilla and oil. Beat well. Add flour, soda, salt, cinnamon and other optional spices. Batter may be very thick. Add pecans and pears, mixing well. Pour into 2 well greased and floured loaf pans and bake approximately 1 hour. Yields 2 loaves. *For Pear Apple bread, use 2 cups pears and 1 cup pared, cored and chopped apple.*

Mrs. Kent Conlan (Sandra)

Nan's Pumpkin Bread

4 eggs, beaten	1 teaspoon nutmeg
3 cups sugar	1 cup canned pumpkin
1 1/2 teaspoons salt	2/3 cup water
1 cup vegetable oil	2 teaspoons baking soda
1 teaspoon cinnamon	3 cups flour

Preheat oven to 350°. Mix together eggs, sugar, salt, oil, cinnamon and nutmeg. Stir in remaining ingredients and mix well. Pour into two greased and floured loaf pans and bake at 350° for one hour. Yields 2 loaves.

Mrs. Danny Pounds (Charlotte)

Raspberry Streusel Muffins

1¾ cups flour, divided
¼ cup sugar
¾ cup firmly packed dark brown sugar, divided
2 teaspoons baking powder
¼ teaspoon salt
2 teaspoons cinnamon, divided
1 egg, slightly beaten
10 tablespoons unsalted melted butter, divided
½ cup milk
1¼ cups fresh or frozen raspberries
2 teaspoons grated lemon zest, divided
½ cup toasted chopped pecans
½ cup powdered sugar
1 tablespoon lemon juice

Preheat oven to 350°. Line 12 muffin cups with paper liners. Sift together 1½ cups flour, sugar, ¼ cup brown sugar, baking powder, salt and cinnamon into a medium sized mixing bowl. Make a well in the center. Put the egg, 8 tablespoons melted butter and milk in the well. Stir with a wooden spoon just until ingredients are combined. Quickly stir in the raspberries and 1 teaspoon lemon zest. Fill each muffin cup ¾ full with batter. Combine pecans ½ cup brown sugar, ¼ cup flour, 1 teaspoon cinnamon and 1 teaspoon lemon zest in a small bowl. Pour in 2 tablespoons melted butter and stir to combine. Sprinkle mixture evenly over the top of each muffin. Bake at 350° for 20 to 25 minutes. Mix lemon juice with powdered sugar and drizzle over muffins while warm. Yields 12 muffins.

Mrs. Garrel Fleming (Ginny Puryear)

Pecan Sour Cream Coffee Cake

1 cup butter
1¼ cups sugar
2 eggs, beaten
1 cup sour cream
2 teaspoons vanilla extract, divided
½ teaspoon salt
1½ teaspoons baking powder
2 cups flour
1 cup chopped pecans
2 tablespoons brown sugar
2 tablespoons softened butter

Preheat oven to 350°. Cream butter and sugar; add eggs, sour cream and 1 teaspoon vanilla. Mix together salt, baking powder and flour. Combine flour mixture with butter mixture and stir well, set aside. Mix together pecans, brown sugar, 1 teaspoon vanilla and 2 tablespoons softened butter. Pour half of the batter into a well greased and floured bundt pan, then top with pecan filling, then the other half of batter. Bake at 350° for 50 minutes. Serves 12 to 14.

Laura Juvé

• *Pecans contain protein, carbohydrates, calcium, iron, Vitamin A, ascorbic acid and small quantities of thiamine, riboflavin and niacin.*

Fresh Strawberry Bread

2 cups flour	1 cup chopped pecans
1/2 cup brown sugar	2 cups fresh mashed
1/2 cup sugar	strawberries, with juice
1/3 teaspoon baking powder	2 tablespoons melted butter
1/2 teaspoon salt	2 eggs, beaten
1/2 teaspoon baking soda	

Preheat oven to 300°. In a large bowl, mix dry ingredients. Combine strawberries, butter and eggs. Mix slowly by hand, then add pecans. Pour into 2 well greased loaf pans. Bake at 300° for about 40 minutes or until toothpick comes out clean. Yields 1 loaf.

Mrs. Henry A. Pate (Patricia)

Strawberry Bread

1 (20 ounce) package frozen	1 teaspoon baking soda
strawberries, thawed	1 teaspoon salt
4 eggs, beaten	3 teaspoons cinnamon
1 1/4 cups vegetable oil	2 cups sugar
3 cups flour	1 cup chopped pecans

Mix together undrained strawberries, eggs and oil. Sift dry ingredients into strawberry mixture, reserving about 1/2 cup flour. Stir to blend thoroughly. Stir pecans into reserved flour to keep them from sinking to bottom of loaf and add to bread batter. Stir well. Pour into 2 well greased and lightly floured loaf pans. Bake at 350° for 1 hour. Yields 2 loaves.

Mrs. Maitland Huffman (Pepper)
Guild President 1971-1972

Linda's Zucchini Bread

3 eggs, beaten	2 cups flour
1 1/2 cups sugar	1 cup whole wheat flour
1 cup vegetable oil	1 teaspoon salt
2 cups peeled and grated	1 teaspoon baking soda
zucchini	1/4 teaspoon baking powder
3 teaspoons vanilla extract	3 teaspoons cinnamon
	1 cup chopped pecans

Preheat oven to 350°. Beat eggs until light and foamy. Add the sugar, oil, zucchini and vanilla mixing lightly but well. Combine flour, salt, soda, baking powder and cinnamon and add to the egg mixture. Stir until well blended then add pecans and pour into two greased 9x5 inch loaf pans. Bake at 350° for 1 hour. Cool on rack. Yields 2 loaves.

Mrs. Richard Musci (Linda)

Poppy Seed Bread

2 eggs
1½ cups sugar
1 teaspoon baking powder
2 cups flour
1 cup evaporated milk

¼ cup poppy seeds
1 teaspoon salt
1 teaspoon vanilla extract
¾ cup vegetable oil

Preheat oven to 350°. Sift together flour, baking powder and salt. Beat eggs and add sugar and oil; mix well. Add vanilla and seeds. Alternately, add flour and milk. Bake in a greased and floured loaf pan at 350° for one hour. Yields 1 loaf. *This will melt in your mouth. You can also double this recipe and bake in 3 smaller loaf pans.*

Mrs. Steve Robirds (Gay)

Spanish Coffee Cake

2½ cups flour
¾ cup sugar
1 cup brown sugar
1 teaspoon salt
1 teaspoon cinnamon

¾ cup vegetable oil
1 egg, beaten
1 cup buttermilk
1 teaspoon baking soda
1 teaspoon baking powder

Preheat oven to 350°. Mix together flour, sugar, brown sugar, salt, cinnamon and oil. Take out 1 cup of mixture and set aside. Beat remaining ingredients into flour mixture and beat 4 minutes or until smooth. Pour into greased and floured 9x13 inch pan. Top with 1 cup flour mixture. Bake at 350° for 35 to 45 minutes.

Mrs. B. L. (Linda)

My Grandmother's Scones

2 cups flour
4 teaspoons baking powder
2 teaspoons sugar
½ teaspoon salt
4 tablespoons butter
Raisins or currants, optional

2 eggs, reserving 1 teaspoon
   egg white
⅓ cup half and half cream
Sugar
Butter and jam to serve

Preheat oven to 375°. Sift together flour, baking powder, sugar and salt. Blend in butter. Add raisins or currants if desired. Add well beaten eggs and cream. Stir together for one minute. On a floured board, pat and roll to ¾ inch thick. Cut into squares; brush with reserved slightly beaten egg white and sprinkle top very lightly with sugar. Bake at 375° for 15 minutes or until lightly browned. Serve with butter and jam. *These scones may be kept frozen for several weeks.*

Mrs. Jay Matthews (Babs)
Guild President 1958-1959

with that from the earth, beauty i will create. with that beauty, my soul i will give...

amado maurilio peña, jr ©1980 us

"Artesanos"

(Craft Workers)

For more than a decade, viewers have been drawn to the vibrant colors and unmistakable style of Austin's Amado Maurilio Peña, Jr. His acclaimed images are about: "persons from my past and from my present; Mexicans, Indians, children, friends and the peoples of the Southwest", he said. Peña's Laguna Gloria Art Museum Fiesta posters of 1982, and 1984 sold thousands of prints and are still in demand. Peña has already agreed to paint the 1986 Fiesta Poster.

The strength of these images have found no boundaries; many contribute this remarkable reservoir of talent to his heritage from his Chicano-Yaqui lineage. The Yaquis had villages on the Yaqui River, which is in the Mexican State of Sonora. Amado is not only a master printmaker in the field of serigraphy, but he has also been able to explore and successfully expand many other media.

His learning years were founded on several earned degrees in Art and an innovative career as an educator. The force of his desire to excel in his art career has grown from the small Austin East Avenue studio to the expansion of three prominent "El Taller Galleries" in Austin, Santa Fe and Taos, New Mexico.

Peña's comment about his serigraph "Artesanos": "with that from the earth's beauty I will create, with that beauty, my soul I will give . . ." thus his vision to capture the essence of a people's culture and their relationship to the earth has been the factor in adding yet another name on the Southwest banner of success.

Cakes

Amaretto Pound Cake

Thinly sliced almonds
1/2 cup butter
1/2 cup shortening
3 cups sugar, divided
6 eggs

2 cups sifted flour
2 teaspoons Amaretto liqueur
1/4 cup water
2 tablespoons Amaretto liqueur

Preheat oven to 325°. Generously grease a 10 inch tube pan and press almond slices onto sides and bottom. Set aside. Cream together butter, shortening, 2 cups sugar, then add eggs, one at a time, continuing to beat. Gradually add flour and 2 teaspoons Amaretto. Beat at high speed until batter is fluffy. Pour into prepared pan and bake at 325° for 60 minutes or until done. Boil 1 cup sugar and water for 1 minute. Remove from heat. Add 2 tablespoons Amaretto and pour over lukewarm cake. Leave cake in pan until it has cooled completely. Serves 12 to 16.

Mrs. Glenn Johnson (Debbie)

Chocolate Chip Pound Cake

8 ounces cream cheese, softened and cut into 1-inch cubes
1 cup unsalted butter, softened and cut into 8 pieces
1 1/2 cups sugar
4 large eggs

2 tablespoons sour cream
2 tablespoons vanilla extract
2 1/4 cups cake flour
2 teaspoons baking powder
1/4 teaspoon salt
1 cup semi-sweet chocolate chips
Powdered sugar

Preheat oven to 325°. Blend cream cheese, butter and sugar until smooth. If using a food processor this will take about 30 seconds. Add eggs, blending well. With the motor running, process the eggs for about 40 seconds. Add the sour cream and vanilla, blending again or processing for 10 seconds. Combine flour, baking powder, salt and chocolate chips and add to batter, mixing just until flour is incorporated. Pulse only 8 to 10 times with the processor. Spoon batter into a greased and floured 10-cup tube pan and bake at 325° for about one hour or until done. Remove cake to a wire rack to cool and dust with powdered sugar if desired. Serves 12 to 16.

Ada Smyth

Buttermilk Walnut Cake

1 cup butter	3 tablespoons vanilla extract
2 cups sugar	3 cups flour
3 eggs	1/2 teaspoon salt
1 cup buttermilk	1 cup chopped walnuts
1/2 tablespoon baking soda	

Preheat oven to 350°. Cream together butter and sugar, then add eggs and mix until light. Combine buttermilk, baking soda and vanilla together and let stand. Mix flour, salt and walnuts and add to the creamed mixture alternating with the buttermilk solution. Mix well. Bake at 350° in a greased and floured bundt pan for about 50 to 60 minutes or until done. Glaze with a frosting of powdered sugar, milk and a little vanilla extract or orange extract mixed together. Serves 12 to 16.

Mrs. Charles Boner (Grace)

Gram's Pound Cake

1 1/2 cups egg, beaten (about 6 large eggs)	1 1/2 cups butter
2 teaspoons baking powder	3 cups flour
2 1/2 cups sugar	1 teaspoon vanilla extract
	1 teaspoon lemon extract

Preheat oven to 300°. Combine eggs and baking powder. Gradually add sugar. In another bowl cream butter, add flour. Blend in egg-sugar mixture and flavorings. Pour batter into a greased and floured bundt pan and bake at 300° for 1 hour and 30 minutes. Serves 12 to 16.

Mrs. Dan Jardine (Lisa)

Swedish Pound Cake

1 cup butter, softened	2 cups sifted flour
2 cups sugar	1 teaspoon vanilla extract
5 eggs	

Preheat oven to 325°. Cream butter and sugar. Add eggs, beating well for 2 to 3 minutes. Stir in flour and vanilla. Bake at 325° in a greased and floured bundt pan for 50 to 60 minutes or until done. Serves 12. *This is a very moist cake. The taste is similar to the commercial frozen cake only better!*

Mrs. Paul Loftin (Liz)

Easy Chocolate Cake

1½	cups flour	1	teaspoon white vinegar
3	tablespoons cocoa	1	teaspoon vanilla extract
1	cup sugar	5	tablespoons corn oil
½	teaspoon salt	1	cup water (or juice for
1	teaspoon baking soda		variety)

Preheat oven to 350°. Sift flour, cocoa, sugar, baking soda and salt into a 8" square cake pan. Make three holes in dry ingredients; pour vinegar into one, vanilla into second and oil into third. Pour water (or juice) over all and mix well until smooth. Bake at 350° for 25 to 35 minutes or until done. Frost when cool.

Frosting:

½	cup butter or margarine, softened	½	cup unsweetened cocoa
1	(16 ounce) box powdered sugar, sifted	1½	teaspoons vanilla extract
		2	egg yolks
Dash of salt		Small amount of milk	

Combine butter, powdered sugar, salt, cocoa, vanilla and egg yolks. Beat until well mixed and fluffy, adding only enough milk until it is easy to spread. Serves 12.

Mrs. Edward Konop (Rita)

Inside Out Chocolate Bundt Cake

1	(4½ ounce) box chocolate instant pudding and pie filling	1	(12 ounce) package chocolate baking chips
1	package chocolate cake mix	2	eggs
1¾	cups milk	Powdered sugar	

Preheat oven to 350°. Combine pudding mix, cake mix, chips, milk and eggs in a bowl. Mix by hand until well blended (about 2 minutes). Pour into greased and floured 12 cup bundt pan. Bake at 350° for 50 to 55 minutes or until cake springs back when lightly pressed with a finger. Do not overbake. Cool 15 minutes in pan; remove and cool on rack. Ice or sprinkle with powdered sugar.

Susan Hasslocher
Guild President 1984-1985

Chocolate Rum Cake

1 box chocolate cake mix with pudding	2 cups whipping cream
3 eggs	1/3 cup unsweetened cocoa
1 cup dark rum, divided	1/2 cup powdered sugar
1/2 cup water	1 teaspoon vanilla extract
1/3 cup vegetable oil	Chocolate curls to garnish
1/2 cup slivered almonds, optional	

Combine cake mix, eggs, 1/2 cup rum, water, oil and almonds, blending well. Beat at medium speed 2 minutes. Pour into two 9 inch greased and floured cake pans and bake at 350° for 30 minutes. Cool in pans for 10 minutes. Remove cake from pans and split horizontally in half. Combine cream, cocoa, powdered sugar and vanilla in a mixing bowl. Beat until stiff. Fold in rum. Spread 1 cup filling between each cake layer and over the top. Keep cake chilled and serve cold. Serves 12.

The almonds may also be slightly toasted and placed between the cake layers and on top to garnish.

Mrs. Ron Tobin (Bonnie)

Chocolate Pistachio Cake

1 box white cake mix	4 eggs
1 small package pistachio pudding	1/2 cup vegetable oil, not corn oil
1/2 cup orange juice	1 (5 1/2 ounce) can chocolate syrup
1/2 cup water	

Preheat oven to 350°. Mix cake mix, pudding, orange juice, water, eggs and oil, beat for 2 minutes. Divide batter in half. To one half add the chocolate syrup. Layer batter in a greased and floured bundt pan using half of the chocolate batter first, all of the pistachio batter next, and remaining chocolate batter on top. Bake at 350° for 1 hour. Remove cake from pan when cool and top with chocolate glaze. Serves 12.

Glaze:

2 tablespoons unsweetened cocoa	1/2 teaspoon vanilla extract
2 tablespoons water	1 cup sifted powdered sugar
1 tablespoon white corn syrup	1 tablespoon shortening

Combine all ingredients except sugar in saucepan. Stir over low heat until mixture is smooth. Beat in powdered sugar.

Mrs. Jeff Stewart (Anna)

German Chocolate Cake

2 cups sugar
1 cup butter or margarine
5 eggs, separated
1 cup buttermilk
1 teaspoon baking soda
2½ cups cake flour

Pinch of salt
1 (4 ounce) bar German sweet chocolate
½ cup water
1 teaspoon vanilla extract

Preheat oven to 325°. Cream sugar and butter, add egg yolks and blend well. Stir baking soda into buttermilk, and add salt to flour. Add flour and buttermilk alternately to the creamed batter. Melt chocolate in water and vanilla and add to the mixture. Fold in beaten egg whites. Bake in two 9 inch layer pans at 325° for 30 to 35 minutes. Cool and frost with the coconut/pecan icing.

Coconut-Pecan Icing:

1 cup sugar
1 (12 ounce) can evaporated milk
3 egg yolks

1 tablespoon butter, softened
1 cup coconut
1 cup chopped pecans

Cream together sugar, milk, egg yolks, and butter and boil until thick. Stir while cooking. Add coconut and pecans. Serves 12 to 16.

Susan Hasslocher
Guild President 1984-1985

French Chocolate Cake

½ cup butter, softened
⅔ cup sugar
½ teaspoon almond extract
4 eggs, separated

5 (1 ounce) squares semisweet chocolate
2 tablespoons Kahlua
1 cup sifted cake flour
Powdered sugar to serve

Preheat oven to 350°. Beat butter until creamy. Slowly add sugar, almond extract and egg yolks. Beat until fluffy. Melt chocolate in Kahlua and add to batter, blending well. Beat egg whites until stiff and add one fourth of the whites to lighten the batter. Carefully fold in the remaining egg whites. When partly blended, add the flour and carefully mix under. This is a delicate batter. Do not beat. Pour into an 8 inch greased and floured layer pan. Bake at 350° for 30 minutes. Let cool on a rack for one hour. Sprinkle with powdered sugar. Serves 8 to 10.

Mrs. Loy G. White (Marsha)

Chocolate Mousse Cake

7   large eggs, separated, at
    room temperature
1/2 cup unsweetened cocoa
3/4 cup boiling water
1 3/4 cups sifted cake flour
1 3/4 cups sugar

1 1/2 teaspoons baking soda
1   teaspoon salt
1/2 cup vegetable oil
2   teaspoons vanilla extract
1/2 teaspoon cream of tartar

Preheat oven to 325°. Stir water into cocoa and blend until smooth. Cool for 30 minutes. Sift flour with sugar, soda and salt. Make a well in the center and pour in oil, egg yolks, vanilla and cocoa mixture. Beat just until smooth. Sprinkle cream of tartar over egg whites, beat until very stiff peaks form. Do not underbeat. Pour batter over egg whites and fold together with an over and under motion. Pour into an ungreased tube pan and bake at 325° for 60 to 65 minutes or until top springs back when pressed. Invert pan over the neck of a bottle and cool 1 hour and 30 minutes. Remove cake from pan and cool on a rack.

Cut a 1 inch slice from top of cake and set aside. Carefully remove the inside of the cake, leaving 1 inch thick walls on the outside, bottom and sides. Reserve 1 1/2 cups crumbled cake. Fill this cavity with the chocolate gelatin filling mixture and replace top. Fill center hole with a mixture of 1/2 cup filling and reserved crumbled cake. Frost sides and top of cake with remaining chocolate filling. Serves 12.

Chocolate Filling:

3   cups whipping cream
1 1/2 cups sifted powdered sugar
3/4 cup unsweetened cocoa

2   teaspoons vanilla extract
1/4 teaspoon salt
1   teaspoon unflavored gelatin

Combine and let stand in the refrigerator for one hour the cream, sugar, cocoa, vanilla and salt. Beat until stiff. Soften gelatin in 2 tablespoons water and then heat stirring often to dissolve. Combine 2 1/2 cups chocolate filling and gelatin, and use to fill the cavity.

Mrs. Bill von Rosenberg (Susan)

- *Lightly dust cake pans with cocoa instead of flour when making chocolate cake.*

- *Recipes using plenty of eggs are always popular with Art Guild members. Cascarones, confetti stuffed and tissue capped egg shells are always popular and a tradition at fiesta.*

Apple Cake

2	cups flour	1	teaspoon vanilla extract
1	teaspoon baking soda	4	cups chopped apples
1/2	teaspoon salt	1/2	cup chopped pecans
2	cups sugar	1 1/2	cups powdered sugar
2	teaspoons cinnamon	1	(8 ounce) carton whipped
3	eggs		topping
1	cup vegetable oil		

Preheat oven to 350°. Combine flour, baking soda, salt and sugar. Mix eggs, oil, vanilla in another bowl. Add apples and pecans. Add dry ingredients and blend only enough to moisten all of the ingredients. Spread in a 9x13 inch pan or a bundt pan and bake at 350° for 45 to 60 minutes or until an inserted toothpick comes out clean. Blend 1 1/2 cups powdered sugar and whipped topping together and spread over cooled cake. Store in refrigerator. This cake freezes beautifully.

Optional Glaze:

1/2	cup apple cider	2	cups powdered sugar

Combine ingredients and bring to a boil. Pour immediately over hot cake while still in the pan. Serves 12 to 16.

Mrs. Paul Loftin (Liz)

Apple Pie Cake

1/4	cup butter	3	tablespoons orange juice
1	cup sugar	1	teaspoon vanilla extract
2	eggs	2 1/2	cups peeled and finely
1	cup flour		chopped apples
1	teaspoon baking soda	1/2	cup raisins
1/4	teaspoon salt		Sweetened whipped cream to
1	teaspoon ground cinnamon		serve
1/2	teaspoon ground nutmeg		

Preheat oven to 350°. Cream butter, gradually add sugar, then add eggs mixing well. Combine flour, baking soda, salt, cinnamon and nutmeg. Add to creamed mixture alternately with the orange juice, beginning and ending with the dry ingredients. Fold in vanilla, apples and raisins. Spread in a greased and floured 9 inch pie pan and bake at 350° for 45 minutes. Top with sweetened whipped cream. Serves 12.

Mrs. Ron Tobin (Bonnie)

Banana Nut Cake

1½ cups sugar
½ cup shortening
1½ cups flour
½ cup buttermilk
1 teaspoon baking soda

2 eggs, slightly beaten
1 cup mashed banana
1 cup chopped pecans
1 teaspoon vanilla extract

Preheat oven to 350°. Cream together sugar and shortening. Gradually add the flour and blend well. Mix buttermilk and baking soda together, then add to batter. Add eggs, mashed banana, pecans, and vanilla. Pour into greased and floured bundt pan and bake at 350° for 45 minutes or until done.

Carmel Icing:

½ cup butter or margarine
1 cup packed brown sugar
¼ cup milk

2 cups sifted powdered sugar
1 teaspoon vanilla extract
1 cup chopped pecans

Melt butter, stir in brown sugar. Cook and stir over low heat for 2 minutes. Add milk and continue stirring until boiling. Remove from heat. Let cool until lukewarm, then pour into mixing bowl. Add powdered sugar and vanilla and beat at medium speed. Then beat on high speed about 2 minutes. Add pecans. Pour over cooled cake. Serves 12 to 16.

Mrs. Leroy Wilkins (Linda)

Piña Colada Cake

1 box yellow cake mix
1 can cream of coconut
1 can sweetened condensed milk

1 (8 ounce) container whipped topping
1 (3½ ounce) can coconut

Preheat oven to 350°. Bake yellow cake mix according to package directions in a 9x13 inch pan until done. While still hot, make holes in cake with a fork. Combine cream of coconut and condensed milk and pour evenly over the cake. Let stand for several hours. Combine whipped topping and coconut and spread over cake. Keep cake refrigerated, but set out about 30 minutes before serving. Serves 12.

Mrs. Clark Covert (Melinda)

Deluxe Carrot Cake

3 cups flour	1/2 cup chopped pecans
2 cups sugar	1/2 cup raisins
2 teaspoons baking powder	1/2 cup coconut
2 teaspoons baking soda	2 cups grated carrots
2 teaspoons cinnamon	1 (8 ounce) can crushed
1/2 teaspoon salt	pineapple, with juice
11/4 cups vegetable oil	3 eggs
2 teaspoons vanilla extract	

Preheat oven to 350°. Sift together flour, sugar, baking powder, baking soda, cinnamon, and salt. Add oil and vanilla, then pecans, raisins, coconut and crushed pineapple, juice and all. Beat in eggs, one at a time. Pour in a greased and floured bundt or tube pan and bake at 350° for 50 to 60 minutes or until done. After cooling, turn cake out of pan and frost.

Moravian Cream Nut Icing:

1 egg, separated	2/3 cup sifted powdered sugar
2/3 cup sour cream	1 cup finely chopped pecans
1 teaspoon vanilla extract	

Add beaten egg yolk to sour cream and beat. Add vanilla and sugar and beat again until thick. Fold in pecans and stiffly beaten egg white. Chill.

Mrs. Charles Boner (Grace)

Jamaica Cake

3 cups flour	11/2 cups vegetable oil
1 teaspoon baking soda	11/2 teaspoons vanilla
2 cups sugar	3 beaten eggs
1 teaspoon salt	2 cups mashed bananas,
1 teaspoon cinnamon	approximately 3 bananas
1 (8 ounce) can crushed pineapple	

Preheat oven to 325°. Sift flour, baking soda, sugar, salt and cinnamon in a large bowl. Add undrained pineapple, oil, vanilla, eggs and banana pulp. Stir well but do not beat. Pour into a greased 10 inch tube pan and bake at 325° for about one hour or until done. Serves 12.

Mrs. Dan Green (Susan)

Christmas Date Cake

1 cup hot water	1 teaspoon unsweetened
1 cup chopped dates	cocoa
1 egg, lightly beaten	1/2 teaspoon ground cinnamon
1 1/4 cups flour, sifted	1/4 teaspoon ground cloves
1 cup sugar	Dash of salt
1 teaspoon baking soda	1 cup chopped walnuts

Before beginning, pour hot water over chopped dates. Put egg in bowl and beat for 2 minutes. Sift in all dry ingredients and beat another 2 minutes. Add nuts and dates and mix for 1 minute. Place batter into greased and floured small loaf pans. Bake at 350° for 45 minutes. Watch carefully as these will burn easily. Cool and wrap air tight in foil if not serving right away. Serves 12. *These freeze very well and are great served with ice cream or thick egg nog as a topping.*

Mrs. Owen Messenger (Nancy)

Cranberry Orange Date Cake

2 1/2 cups flour	2 tablespoons grated orange
1 cup sugar	peel
1/2 teaspoon baking soda	2 eggs, beaten
1 teaspoon baking powder	3/4 cup corn oil
1 (8 ounce) package chopped	1 cup buttermilk
dates	1/3 cup orange juice
1 (12 ounce) package fresh	concentrate, thawed
whole cranberries	1/3 cup sugar
1 cup chopped walnuts	

Preheat oven to 350°. In a large bowl, mix together flour, 1 cup sugar, soda, and baking powder. Stir in dates, cranberries, orange peel and walnuts. Combine the eggs, oil and buttermilk and stir this into batter. Pour into well greased bundt pan and bake 1 hour. Cool 10 minutes in pan and then invert onto a serving plate. While cake is cooling, combine orange juice concentrate and 1/3 cup sugar in a small saucepan and boil very gently for 4 minutes. Immediately brush glaze over top and sides of warm cake. Serves 12 to 16. *This cake is so pretty for holiday entertaining or gifts!*

Mrs. Edward Konop (Rita)

Date Cake

¾ cup butter	½ teaspoon salt
1½ cups dark brown sugar	1 cup boiling water
1 (8 ounce) package chopped dates	1 teaspoon baking soda
	2 tablespoons rum
1 cup flour	Whipped cream to serve
1 cup chopped pecans	Toasted pecans to serve
2 eggs, beaten	

Preheat oven to 350°. Line bottom of 10 cup tube pan with paper. Cream butter with brown sugar until light and fluffy. Blend in dates, flour, pecans, eggs and salt. Combine water with baking soda. Pour into batter. Blend well. Transfer to prepared pan and bake at 350° for 60 minutes. Pour rum over top. Cool until warm. Invert to platter. Serve with whipped cream and toasted pecans. Freezes well. Serves 16.

Mrs. Henry Mayes (Kathy)

Gingerbread With Lemon Sauce

½ cup butter	½ teaspoon baking soda
½ cup brown sugar	½ teaspoon salt
1 cup dark molasses	1 teaspoon ground ginger
2 eggs	1 teaspoon ground cinnamon
2½ cups flour	½ teaspoon ground nutmeg
2 teaspoons baking powder	½ teaspoon ground cloves
¼ cup unsweetened cocoa	¾ cup strong hot coffee

Preheat oven to 350°. Cream together the butter and sugar; add molasses, blending well. Add eggs, one at a time, beating well. Sift together the flour, baking powder, cocoa, baking soda, salt and spices. Add to creamed mixture alternating with the hot coffee. Beat until smooth. The batter will be thin. Pour into a 9 inch square dish and bake at 350° for 30 minutes. Serve with lemon sauce. Serves 8 to 10.

Lemon Sauce:

½ cup sugar	1 teaspoon lemon rind
¼ teaspoon salt	2 tablespoons butter
1 tablespoon cornstarch	3 tablespoons lemon juice
1 cup boiling water	

Mix sugar, salt and cornstarch. Add boiling water and cook until clear. Add rind and cook 1 minute more. Remove from heat, stir in butter and lemon juice. Serve hot.

Mrs. Larry Hall (Jane)
Fiesta Chairman 1982-1983

Prune Cake

2 cups sugar	1 teaspoon nutmeg
3 eggs, beaten	1 teaspoon cinnamon
1 cup vegetable oil	1 teaspoon allspice
2 cups flour, sifted at least three times	1 junior size jar baby food prunes
2½ teaspoons baking powder	½ cup chopped pecans
¼ teaspoon salt	

Preheat oven to 325°. Cream sugar, eggs, and oil. Sift flour with baking powder, salt, nutmeg, cinnamon and allspice. Add flour mixture to creamed mixture along with the prunes and pecans. Blend well. Pour into a greased and floured bundt pan and bake at 325° for 1 hour and 15 minutes. This cake freezes well. Serves 12 to 16.

Mrs. Bill Rhoades (Dixie)

Mrs. Ferguson's Prune Cake

1 cup corn oil	1 teaspoon ground cloves
2 cups sugar	1 teaspoon ground nutmeg
3 eggs, beaten	1 teaspoon ground cinnamon
1 cup buttermilk	1 package pitted prunes, cut up
1 teaspoon baking soda	1 cup coarsely chopped pecans
2 cups flour	
1 teaspoon salt	
1 teaspoon ground allspice	

Mix together the oil and sugar, then add the eggs, blending well. Add baking soda to buttermilk. Sift together the flour and spices and add to oil mixture alternating with the buttermilk. Fold in pecans and prunes. Pour into a greased and floured tube pan and bake at 350° for 1 hour and 15 minutes, or until a tester inserted in center comes out clean. Cool thoroughly before removing from pan. *This is a 22 year family favorite. I bake about 10 to 15 of these cakes each year as gifts for the Christmas season.*

Mrs. Edward Konop (Rita)

Dump Cake

1 (22 ounce) can cherry pie filling	1 cup chopped pecans
1 (20 ounce) can crushed pineapple	1 package white or yellow cake mix
	1 cup margarine, melted

Preheat oven to 450°. Pour the following ingredients into an ungreased 9x13 inch pan as follows: cherry pie filling, crushed pineapple, half of the cake mix, chopped pecans, remaining half of cake mix, and melted margarine on top. Bake at 450° for 10 minutes, then decrease the heat to 350° and bake for 30 to 35 minutes. Serve cool. Serves 12.

Mrs. Robert Storey (Carolyn)

Poppy Seed Cake

1 package yellow cake mix	3/4 cup vegetable oil
1 small package instant butterscotch pudding	1/4 cup poppy seeds
4 eggs	3/4 cup sherry

Combine all ingredients and mix well. Pour into a well greased bundt or tube pan and bake at 350° for 50 to 60 minutes. After removing cake from the oven, punch holes in cake using a fork. Pour glaze over top. Serves 12 to 16.

Glaze:

1/4 cup sherry	1 cup powdered sugar

Combine ingredients and pour over hot cake.

Mrs. D. Maitland Huffman (Pepper)
Guild President 1971-1972

• *Sunday morning breakfasts have always been a popular time for the "die-hard" Fiesta volunteer. They usually begin around 6:30 and include a hearty meal to help start the long day.*

Tia Maria Cream Torte

1 baked angel cake	Sliced toasted almonds to
3 cups whipping cream	garnish
2 teaspoons vanilla extract	Grated chocolate or chocolate
1/2 cup powdered sugar	curls to garnish
1/2 cup Tia Maria coffee	
liqueur	

Slice off top of cake about 1 1/4 inches down. Scoop out the inside of the cake leaving a 1 inch thick wall all around. Whip the cream until stiff. Blend in vanilla, sugar, then slowly mix in Tia Maria. Fill the cake with 2/3 of the cream mixture. Replace top on cake and frost with remaining cream mixture. Sprinkle with almonds, grated chocolate or chocolate curls. Freeze until firm, then serve. Serves 12. *If storing in freezer, freeze first, then wrap tightly in moisture proof wrapping.*

Mrs. Allen L. Williams (Rose Betty)

Peanut Butter Cups

1 3/4 cups flour	1/3 cup shortening
1/4 cup firmly packed brown	1/3 cup peanut butter
sugar	1 teaspoon vanilla extract
3 teaspoons baking powder	2 eggs
1 teaspoon salt	24 miniature chocolate
1 cup milk	covered peanut butter cups

Preheat oven to 350°. Line 24 muffin cups with paper baking cups. Mix all ingredients except peanut butter cups at low speed until moist. Beat 2 minutes at medium speed. Fill muffin cups two thirds full. Press peanut butter cups into batter until top edges are even with batter. Bake at 350° for 16 to 18 minutes or until cupcake springs back when touched. Yields 24 cupcakes.

Mrs. Paul Loftin (Liz)

• *An angel food cake will slice neatly without crumbling if you freeze it first, then thaw it.*

Cookies

World's Best Brownies

1 cup butter or margarine	1½ cups flour
3 squares unsweetened chocolate	1 teaspoon baking powder
	2 teaspoons vanilla extract
2¼ cups sugar	1 cup chopped pecans,
4 eggs, slightly beaten	optional

Preheat oven to 350°. Melt butter and chocolate over hot water or low heat. A microwave is great for this. Add sugar and eggs; mix thoroughly. Mix flour and baking powder, stir into creamed mixture. Add vanilla and optional pecans. Bake in a greased 9x13 inch pan at 350° for 35 to 40 minutes. Cool slightly and frost. When frosting has set and brownies are cool, cut into squares. Yields 24 average-sized brownies. *I have frozen these and they seem to be fine if frozen in the pan before they are cut.*

Frosting:

4 tablespoons butter or margarine	2 cups powdered sugar
	3 tablespoons hot milk
2 squares unsweetened chocolate	1 teaspoon vanilla extract

Melt butter and chocolate over hot water or low heat (or microwave). Stir in powdered sugar. Add hot milk and vanilla. Beat well. If mixture seems too dry, add another tablespoon of hot milk. Spread over warm brownies.

Mrs. Ben Morgan (LaRee)

• *Store soft cookies in a tightly covered container. An apple slice will mellow cookies and keep them moist.*

Cream Cheese Brownies

1/2 cup butter	1 cup chopped pecans, optional
2 squares unsweetened chocolate	1 1/2 teaspoons vanilla extract, divided
3 eggs, divided	8 ounces cream cheese, softened
1/2 cup flour	
1 1/3 cups sugar, divided	

Preheat oven to 350°. Melt butter and chocolate in saucepan over low heat. Beat 2 eggs and stir into chocolate. Stir in flour and 1 cup sugar. Add pecans and 1 teaspoon vanilla, stirring well. Pour all but one half cup into a greased 9x13 inch pan. Mix together cream cheese, 1/3 cup sugar, 1 egg, and 1/2 teaspoon vanilla. Cover brownie mixture in pan with this cream cheese mixture. Spoon reserved one half cup brownie mixture over cream cheese. Cut through batter with a knife for a marbled effect. Bake at 350° for 35 minutes or until done. Cool and cut into squares. Yields 24 average brownies.

Mrs. Doug Beaty (Joan)

Peppermint Chocolate Chip Squares

1 cup butter	1 teaspoon baking soda
3/4 cup sugar	1/2 teaspoon salt
3/4 cup firmly packed brown sugar	12 ounces semisweet chocolate chips
2 eggs	1 cup chopped pecans
1 teaspoon vanilla extract	3/4 cup crushed peppermint candy
2 1/4 cups flour	

Preheat oven to 350°. Cream butter and sugar until light. Beat in eggs and vanilla. Combine flour, soda and salt; gradually blend into creamed mixture. Stir in chocolate chips and pecans. Spread dough evenly in a well buttered 15x10 inch jelly roll pan and bake at 350° for 20 to 25 minutes or until inserted toothpick comes out clean. Remove from oven and sprinkle at once with crushed candy. Press into top. Cool completely. Cut into squares. Yields 4 dozen squares.

Mrs. Henry A. Pate (Patricia)

Texas Chewy Pecan Squares

2	tablespoons butter	2	eggs
1	cup brown sugar	1	teaspoon vanilla extract
5	tablespoons flour		Powdered sugar to garnish
1/8	teaspoon baking soda		Pecan halves to garnish
1	cup chopped pecans		

Preheat oven to 350°. Melt butter in an 8 inch square pan. In a small bowl, mix brown sugar, flour, soda and pecans. Beat eggs in a large bowl and stir in brown sugar mixture and vanilla. Pout this over melted butter in pan. Do Not Stir. Bake at 350° for 20 minutes. Remove from oven, let cool. Cut into squares and sprinkle if desired with powdered sugar and pecan halves. Yields 16. *Sometimes the squares are difficult to remove from the pan. Use a fork and take your time. These are well worth the trouble!*

Mrs. Edward Konop (Rita)

Pecan Turtle Cookies

2	cups flour	1	cup pecan halves
1½	cups firmly packed brown sugar, divided	2/3	cup butter
½	cup butter, softened	12	ounces semisweet chocolate chips

Preheat oven to 350°. Combine flour, 1 cup brown sugar, and ½ cup softened butter. Beat until well mixed, then pat firmly into an ungreased 9x13 inch pan. Sprinkle pecan halves evenly over top. In a heavy pan combine ½ cup brown sugar and 2/3 cup butter. Cook over medium heat, stirring constantly until mixture boils. Boil 30 to 60 seconds, stirring all the time. Pour this caramel mixture over the pecans and unbaked crust. Bake at 350° for 18 to 22 minutes or until caramel layer is bubbly and crust is a light golden brown. Remove from oven and immdiately sprinkle with chocolate chips. Lightly spread chips as they melt. Cool completely. Cut into bars. Yields 24 bars.

Mrs. Felix Wolff Jr. (Rosann)

Butter Pecan Cream Cheese Bars

2 cups plus 2 tablespoons flour, divided	8 ounces cream cheese, softened
1 cup firmly packed brown sugar, divided	2 eggs
¾ cup butter, softened	6 ounces butterscotch chips
1 cup chopped pecans	1 square unsweetened chocolate, melted
½ teaspoon vanilla extract	

Preheat oven to 350°. Combine 2 cups flour, ⅔ cup brown sugar and butter until crumbly. Stir in pecans. Press mixture into an ungreased 9x13 inch pan and bake at 350° for 15 to 20 minutes or until light golden brown. Meanwhile, beat together cream cheese, ⅓ cup brown sugar and vanilla. Add 2 tablespoons flour and eggs, blending well. Pour over baked crust, sprinkle with butterscotch chips and bake for 15 to 20 minutes or until firm. Top with chocolate. Yields 32 bars.

Mrs. Paul Loftin (Liz)

Graham Cracker Praline Cookies

24 graham crackers	1 cup butter or margarine
1 cup brown sugar	1 cup chopped pecans

Preheat oven to 350°. Place graham crackers in a 11x15 inch jelly roll pan to cover bottom of pan. In a saucepan melt brown sugar and butter, bring to a boil and cook for 2 minutes. Add pecans. Pour mixture over graham crackers and bake at 350° for 10 minutes. Cool and break apart.

Mrs. Robert Storey (Carolyn)

Lemon Bars

2 cups plus 1 tablespoon flour, divided	4 eggs, beaten
½ cup powdered sugar	1 teaspoon baking powder
1 cup butter or margarine	4 tablespoons lemon juice
2 cups sugar	Powdered sugar to serve

Preheat oven to 350°. Mix together 2 cups flour, powdered sugar and butter. Pat into an ungreased 9x13 inch pan and bake at 350° for about 20 minutes. Mix together sugar, 1 tablespoon flour, eggs, baking powder and lemon juice and pour over baked crust. Bake 25 minutes longer. Cut into squares and dust with powdered sugar.

Mrs. Fred J. Markham (Marilyn)

Blarney Stones

4 eggs, divided	¼ teaspoon salt
1 cup sugar	½ cup boiling water
1 cup flour	½ teaspoon vanilla extract
1½ teaspoons baking powder	

Preheat oven to 350°. Separate eggs, reserving 1 yolk for icing. Beat 4 egg whites until stiff. Set aside. Beat 3 egg yolks until thick and lemon colored, gradually add sugar, beating continously. Sift together flour, baking powder and salt, and add to egg mixture alternating with the boiling water. Add vanilla and beat well. Fold in beaten egg whites. Pour into a 9x13 inch pan and bake at 350° for 30 minutes or until done. Let cool.

Blarney Stone Icing:

1 cup butter	Crushed salted peanuts to
2½ cups powdered sugar	garnish
1 teaspoon vanilla extract	

Cream together butter and reserved egg yolk. Gradually add powdered sugar until soft and smooth. Add vanilla. Spread icing on cooled bars and top with crushed salted peanuts. Yields 36 bars.

Mrs. David Dacy (Nancy)

Apricot Spice Bar

⅓ cup butter, softened	1 teaspoon cinnamon
1½ cups firmly packed brown sugar	½ teaspoon ground cloves
½ cup honey	1 (6 ounce) package dried apricots, finely chopped
3 eggs	1 cup chopped walnuts
1¾ cups flour	¾ cup powdered sugar
1 teaspoon baking powder	1 tablespoon lemon juice
1 teaspoon salt	

Preheat oven to 350°. Cream together butter, brown sugar and honey. Add eggs and beat well. Combine flour, baking powder, salt, cinnamon and cloves, and add to creamed mixture. Mix well, stirring in apricots and walnuts. Spread in a greased 15x11 inch jelly roll pan and bake at 350° for 20 to 25 minutes. Cool 15 minutes. Combine powdered sugar and lemon juice, and spread over warm cookies. Cut into bars. Yields 35 bars.

Mrs. Willy Scott (Janet)

Mincemeat Squares

2 cups graham cracker crumbs	1 can sweetened condensed milk
1²/₃ cups mincemeat	1 teaspoon vanilla extract
1 teaspoon cinnamon	Candied cherries and chopped nuts, optional

Preheat oven to 350°. Mix all ingredients well and pour into a greased 11x7 inch pan. Bake at 350° for about 25 minutes or until brown on top. Cool and cut into squares. *These squares freeze well and are an easy addition to your holiday assortment of treats.*

Mrs. Fred Hansen (Gayle)
Guild President 1968-1969

Strawberry Squares

1 cup flour	2 tablespoons lemon juice
¼ cup brown sugar	1 (10 ounce) package frozen strawberries, thawed
½ cup butter or margarine	
1 cup chopped pecans	1 cup whipping cream, whipped
2 egg whites	
1 cup sugar	

Preheat oven to 350°. Mix flour, brown sugar, butter and pecans. Pat thinly onto cookie sheet with sides. Cook at 350° for 15 minutes. Cool and crumble. Place one half mixture into a 9x9 inch serving dish. Beat egg whites with sugar, then add lemon juice. Fold strawberries into egg mixture, then fold in whipped cream. Spread mixture over crumbs in pan and top with remaining crumbs. Cut into squares and freeze. Remove from freezer a short time before serving.

Mrs. Jeff Wigginton (Mandy)

Walk To School Sugar Cookies

2 cups butter, no substitute	1 teaspoon vanilla extract
1 cup sugar	Powdered sugar as a topping
4 cups flour	

Preheat oven to 325°. Mix well the butter, sugar, flour and vanilla and pat into rolls. Place rolls in refrigerator to chill. Slice and bake at 325° for 10 to 12 minutes. Sprinkle with powdered sugar while hot. Yields 4 dozen.

Mrs. Allan L. Williams (Rose Betty)

Granny's Sugar Cookies

1/2 cup butter	1/2 teaspoon salt
1 cup sugar	1 cup powdered sugar for
1 large egg	glaze
1/2 teaspoon vanilla extract	5 to 6 teaspoons water
2 to 2¼ cups flour	Food coloring for glaze,
2 teaspoons baking powder	optional

Preheat oven to 375°. Cream together butter and sugar. Add egg and vanilla. Sift together flour, baking soda and salt and add to creamed mixture. Divide dough into two parts. Chill one to two hours. Roll dough, one part at a time, to 1/8 inch thickness and cut with cookie cutters. Transfer to cookie sheets and bake at 375° for 8 to 10 minutes. Glaze cookies, if desired, with a mixture of 1 cup powdered sugar, 5 to 6 teaspoons water and food coloring. Brush glaze over cookies.

Mrs. Danny Pounds (Charlotte)

Great Grandma Howell's Tea Cookies

3¾ cups flour	1⅔ cups sugar
1/2 teaspoon salt	3 eggs
1 tablespoon baking powder	3 tablespoons milk
1 cup shortening	

Preheat oven to 375°. Sift together flour, salt and baking powder. Blend shortening, sugar, eggs and milk, and add to dry ingredients. Mix with hands. Roll out to a 1/2 inch thickness. Cut out cookies using a small round cutter and bake at 375° until sides begin to slightly brown.

Dee Vargas

Potato Chip Cookies

2 cups butter	3 ounces potato chips,
3½ cups flour	crushed
1½ cups sugar	Powdered sugar
2 teaspoons vanilla extract	

Preheat oven to 350°. Beat butter until light and fluffy. Add flour, sugar and vanilla, mix thoroughly. Blend in potato chips. Drop by teaspoon onto ungreased cookie sheets. Bake at 350° for 8 to 10 minutes or until light golden brown. Cool on baking sheet for 5 minutes. Sprinkle with powdered sugar. Move to rack and cool.

Mrs. Doug Henson (Kathy)

Gingerbread Cookie People

¾ cup butter, softened	1 teaspoon ground cloves
1½ cups brown sugar	1½ teaspoons cinnamon
1½ cups molasses	3 teaspoons ground ginger
9 cups flour	1½ teaspoons salt
3 teaspoons baking soda	1 cup brewed coffee

Cream butter and sugar, and add molasses. Combine flour, baking soda, cloves, cinnamon, ginger and salt. Mix dry ingredients into creamed mixture alternating with the coffee, beginning and ending with the coffee. Roll out dough on floured pastry cloth or between two sheets of waxed paper to ⅓ inch thickness. Cut with desired cookie cutters. Bake on lightly oiled cookie sheet at 350° for 8 minutes. Let cool a few minutes on sheets before transferring to cookie racks. Decorate.

Mary Coneway

Texas Special Cookies

1 cup shortening	1 teaspoon baking powder
2 cups brown sugar	2 cups uncooked oatmeal
2 eggs	1 cup coconut
2 cups flour	2 cups orange slice candy,
¼ teaspoon salt	chopped
1 teaspoon baking soda	1 cup chopped pecans

Preheat oven to 325°. Cream shortening with brown sugar. Beat in eggs. Sift together flour, salt, soda, baking powder, and oatmeal; add to creamed mixture. Add coconut, orange slice candy, and pecans. Drop by teaspoonful on lightly greased and floured cookie sheets. Bake at 325° for 10 minutes.

Mrs. Berry Gannaway (Jackie)
Fiesta Chairman 1984-1985

Fast Peanut Butter Cookies

1 cup sugar	1 cup peanut butter
1 egg	

Preheat oven to 350°. Mix all ingredients. Roll cookies into balls and place on ungreased cookie sheets. Press down with a fork. Bake at 350° for 10 minutes.

Mrs. Steve Chalmers (Sue)

Apple Drop Cookies

½ cup shortening	2 cups flour
1⅓ cups brown sugar	1 teaspoon baking soda
½ teaspoon salt	1 cup chopped pecans
1 teaspoon cinnamon	1 cup finely chopped apples,
1 teaspoon ground cloves	about 2 medium
½ teaspoon nutmeg	1 cup raisins
1 egg	¼ cup apple juice or milk

Preheat oven to 375°. Combine shortening, sugar, salt, cinnamon, cloves, nutmeg and egg. Beat well. Sift together flour and baking soda. Add to egg mixture. Stir in nuts, apples, raisins and apple juice or milk. Drop by teaspoonful on greased cookie sheets and bake at 375° for 11 to 14 minutes or until lightly browned. Spread with frosting while hot. Yields 48 cookies.

Frosting:

1½ cups sifted powdered sugar	⅛ teaspoon salt
1 tablespoon butter, melted	2½ tablespoons half and half
½ teaspoon vanilla extract	cream

Combine powdered sugar, butter, vanilla, salt and cream. Mix to a good spreading consistency. Spread over hot cookies. *These moist and chewy cookies are a wonderful spicy treat anytime, but they are especially nice at Christmas.*

Mrs. Sammy Kurio (Frances)

Nutty Chocolate Candy Cookies

1½ cups semisweet chocolate pieces, divided	1½ teaspoons vanilla extract
4 tablespoons butter	½ cup flour
¾ cup sugar	½ teaspoon salt
1 egg	¼ teaspoon baking powder
	½ cup chopped pecans

Melt 1 cup chocolate pieces in a small pan. Cream together the butter and sugar. Add egg and vanilla, beating well. Blend in melted chocolate. Combine flour, salt and baking powder and add to chocolate mixture. Stir in pecans and remaining ½ cup chocolate pieces. Drop dough from teaspoons 2 inches apart on lightly greased cookie sheets. Bake at 350° for 8 to 10 minutes. Yields 30 cookies.

Mrs. Larry Hall (Jane)
Fiesta Chairman 1982-1983

Gingersnaps

1½ cups shortening	1 tablespoon ground ginger
2 cups sugar	4 teaspoons baking soda
2 eggs	2 teaspoons cinnamon
½ cup molasses	1 teaspoon salt
4 cups flour	Sugar to roll

Preheat oven to 350°. Cream shortening and sugar, add egg and molasses. Sift together flour, ginger, soda, cinnamon and salt. Combine with creamed mixture, blending well. Roll dough into 1 inch balls and dip top in sugar. Bake on ungreased baking sheets at 350° for 12 minutes. Tops will crack when done. Yields 9 dozen.

Mrs. Andy Tewell (Judy)

Mint Cookies

2 egg whites	½ teaspoon mint flavoring
½ teaspoon cream of tartar	6 ounces semisweet chocolate chips
¾ cup sugar	
2 to 3 drops green food coloring	

Cover cookie sheet with waxed paper. Beat egg whites and cream of tartar until stiff, adding sugar, food coloring and mint flavoring. Fold in chocolate chips. Heat oven to 375° for 15 minutes, then turn off. Drop cookies by teaspoonful on prepared cookie sheet and leave in oven at least 2 hours or overnight without opening oven door.

Mrs. Doug Beaty (Joan)

Oatmeal Cookies

1 teaspoon salt	1½ cups flour
1 cup margarine	1 teaspoon baking soda
1 cup sugar	1½ cups uncooked oatmeal
1 cup packed brown sugar	1 cup chopped pecans
2 eggs	1 (3½ ounce) can coconut
1 teaspoon vanilla extract	

Preheat oven to 325°. Blend well the salt, margarine, and sugars. Add eggs, and vanilla. Sift together flour and soda, and add to creamed mixture. Add by hand pecans, oatmeal and coconut. Drop by teaspoonfuls on an ungreased cookie sheet and bake at 325° until done. During baking, flip or bounce the pan when they rise to achieve a thin, chewy cookie.

Susan Hasslocher
Guild President 1984-1985

Pies

Chocolate Praline Pie

1 cup sugar
1/2 teaspoon cornstarch
2 eggs, slighty beaten
1/2 cup butter, melted
1/4 cup praline liqueur
1 cup chopped pecans

6 ounces semisweet chocolate chips
1 (9 inch) unbaked pastry shell
Sweetened whipped cream to serve

Preheat oven to 350°. Combine sugar, and cornstarch, and gradually add to eggs, mixing well. Stir in melted butter. Add liqueur, pecans, and chocolate chips, and mix well. Pour into unbaked pastry shell and bake at 350° for 45 to 50 minutes. Cool. Serve warm or cold with whipped cream. Stores well covered in the refrigerator. Serves 8.

Mrs. Carey Brennan (Shari)

French Silk Pie

3/4 cup butter, softened
1 cup sugar
1 1/2 squares unsweetened chocolate, melted
1 teaspoon vanilla extract

4 eggs
1/2 cup chopped pecans
1 (9 inch) baked pastry shell
Sweetened whipped cream to serve

Cream butter, sugar and cooled melted chocolate. Add vanilla. Add two eggs and beat on high speed for 5 minutes. Add remaining two eggs and beat again for 5 minutes. Line the bottom of the pastry shell with the chopped pecans, then pour in the chocolate mixture. Pour into cooled crust and refrigerate overnight. Top with whipped cream and chill before serving. Serves 6 to 8.

Linda Cassidy

• *Pecans contain protein, carbohydrates, calcium, iron, Vitamin A, ascorbic acid and small quantities of thiamine, riboflavin and niacin.*

Fresh Blueberry Sour Cream Pie

1	cup sour cream	1	(9 inch) unbaked pastry
6	tablespoons flour, divided		shell
¾	cup sugar	3	tablespoons chilled butter
1	teaspoon vanilla extract	2	tablespoons brown sugar
¼	teaspoon salt	3	tablespoons chopped
1	egg		pecans, optional
2½	cups fresh blueberries		

Combine sour cream, 2 tablespoons flour, sugar, vanilla, salt and egg, beating well until smooth. Fold in blueberries. Pour filling into unbaked pastry shell and bake at 400° for 25 minutes. Meanwhile, combine chilled butter, 4 tablespoons flour, brown sugar and pecans, and sprinkle over pie and bake an additional 10 minutes. Chill before serving.

Mrs. Marcus Bone (Beverly)
Fiesta Chairman 1983-1984

Apple-Cranberry Pie

3	cups sliced peeled apples	1	teaspoon cinnamon
2	cups fresh cranberries,	2	teaspoons butter, melted
	halved	1	(9 inch) unbaked pastry
1½	cups sugar		shell and topping
¼	cup flour		

Preheat oven to 425°. Combine all ingredients and place in pastry shell. Top with pastry strip lattice and bake at 425° for 40 to 50 minutes. The filling can be frozen separately in a foil lined 9 inch pie plate for up to three months. When ready to bake, place in prepared pastry and cook frozen in a 425° oven for 1 hour and 10 minutes. If top browns too quickly, cover loosely with foil.

Mrs. Robert Bluntzer (Jo)

Key Lime Pie

1	(6 ounce) can frozen	1	can sweetened condensed
	limeade, undiluted		milk
1	(8 ounce) carton frozen	1	(8 inch) graham cracker
	whipped topping		crust

Beat together limeade, whipped topping and condensed milk. Pour into crust and top with additional whipped topping if desired. Chill. Serves 6.

Susan Hasslocher
Guild President 1984-1985

Sour Cream Apple Pie

½ cup chopped walnuts	1 (21 ounce) can apple pie
½ cup butter	filling
1 cup flour	½ cup sour cream
8 ounces cream cheese,	⅛ teaspoon cinnamon
softened	¼ cup raisins
1 cup powdered sugar	
1 (8 ounce) carton whipped	
topping, thawed	

Preheat oven to 350°. Combine walnuts, butter and flour until well mixed. Press into a 10 inch pie pan. Bake at 350° for 25 minutes. Cool. Blend cream cheese and powdered sugar until light and fluffy. Fold in topping. Spread over crust. Top with pie filling. Combine sour cream, cinnamon and raisins. Spread over top of pie. Chill. Serves 8 to 10.

Mrs. Paul Loftin (Liz)

Banana Cream Pie

1 cup plus 2 tablespoons	1½ tablespoons butter
sugar, divided	1 teaspoon vanilla extract
¼ cup cornstarch	2 small bananas
⅛ teaspoon salt	¼ heaping teaspoon cream of
3 cups milk	tartar
3 eggs, separated	1 (9 inch) baked pastry shell

Preheat oven to 350°. Combine ¾ cup sugar, cornstarch, and salt in double boiler. Mix milk and egg yolks, gradually stir into sugar mixture. Cook over medium heat, stirring constantly until mixture thickens and boils. Boil one minute. Remove from heat, stir in butter and vanilla. Slice bananas into baked pastry shell. Pour filling over bananas. Cover filling with waxed paper.

Beat together egg whites, at room temperature, and cream of tartar for one minute. Gradually add ¼ cup plus 2 tablespoons sugar, one tablespoon at a time, beating until stiff peaks form. Spread meringue over hot filling, sealing edge. Bake at 350° for 12 to 15 minutes. Serves 6 to 8.

Mrs. Andy Tewell (Judy)

Toasted Coconut Pie

3   eggs, beaten
1½ cups sugar
½   cup butter or margarine,
    melted
4   teaspoons lemon juice
1   teaspoon vanilla extract
1⅓ cups flaked coconut

1   (9 inch) unbaked pastry
    shell
Sweetened whipped cream to
    serve, optional
Toasted coconut to serve,
    optional

Preheat oven to 350°. Thoroughly combine eggs, sugar, butter, lemon juice and vanilla. Stir in coconut. Pour filling into pastry shell and bake at 350° for 40 to 45 minutes or until knife inserted halfway between edge and center comes out clean. Cool before serving. If desired, garnish with whipped cream or dessert topping and additional toasted coconut. Serves 6 to 8.

Mrs. Adon Sitra (Carolyn)

Whole Lemon-Lemon Pie

1   (9 inch) two crust pastry
    recipe
1½ tablespoons crystal sugar
1   teaspoon nutmeg
1½ cups sugar
3   tablespoons flour
¼   teaspoon salt
⅓   cup butter, softened

3   eggs, beaten
2   tablespoons grated lemon
    rind
3   peeled lemons, very thinly
    sliced with all white
    membrane removed
½   cup cold water

Preheat oven to 400°. Make your pastry crust for a two crust 9 inch pie. Roll out half of pastry, using it to line the pie pan. Roll out other half into a 9 inch circle. On it invert a round bowl that measures 8 inches across. With a pastry wheel, trace around bowl; remove bowl and cut pastry into 6 equal wedges. Put pastry wedges on a cookie sheet and sprinkle with crystal sugar and nutmeg. Bake at 400° for 10 minutes only. Cool.

In a bowl combine sugar, flour, salt, butter, eggs, rind, sliced lemons and water. Pour into crust and bake 25 minutes. Remove from oven and arrange wedges over pie with points touching at center. Return to oven and bake 10 additional minutes. This pie is best served at room temperature. Serves 6 to 8.

Mary Coneway

Pecan Fudge Pie

12 ounces semisweet chocolate
chips
4 eggs, beaten
1/4 teaspoon salt
2 teaspoons vanilla extract
1 cup light corn syrup

2 tablespoons butter, melted
1 1/2 cups coarsely chopped
pecans
1 (10 inch) unbaked pastry
shell

Preheat oven to 350°. Melt chocolate chips over low heat stirring constantly. Combine eggs, salt, vanilla, corn syrup and butter in a mixing bowl, mix well. Slowly add chocolate to egg mixture, stirring rapidly. Stir in pecans. Pour into pastry shell, and bake at 350° for 50 to 55 minutes or until set. Cool. Serves 8 to 10.

Mrs. Paul White (Suzanne)

Coconut Banana Cream Pie

1/2 cup butter
3 cups flaked coconut
3 cups half and half cream,
divided
3/4 cup sugar, divided
4 egg yolks
3 tablespoons cornstarch

1/4 teaspoon salt
1/4 cup flour
2 drops yellow food coloring
2 teaspoons vanilla extract
2 medium bananas, sliced
1 cup whipping cream
1 tablespoon powdered sugar

Melt butter in a large skillet and sauté coconut until golden brown. Remove and press firmly into a 9 inch lightly buttered pan. Chill before adding bananas and cream mixture.

Place 2 cups of cream and 1/2 cup of sugar in a 3 quart saucepan and bring to a boil. In a small bowl, mix together egg yolks, 1/4 cup sugar, cornstarch, salt and flour. Gradually add the remaining 1 cup cream and whisk until thoroughly mixed. As the sugar mixture nears the boiling point, slowly stir in the egg mixture. Continue to cook, stirring constantly, until the custard is slightly thickened. Remove from heat, and stir in coloring and vanilla. Cover surface with plastic wrap and cool. Line bottom of prepared pie crust with bananas and pour cooled filling on top. Whip cream with powdered sugar until stiff, and spread on top of pie. Chill at least 2 hours before serving. Serves 6 to 8.

Susan Hasslocher
Guild President 1984-1985

Lemon Blueberry Tart

2 cups flour	3 tablespoons shortening, chilled
2 tablespoons sugar	
1 teaspoon grated lemon peel	1 tablespoon Cognac
Pinch of salt	2 to 4 tablespoons ice water
1/2 cup chilled unsalted butter, cut into 1/2 inch pieces	

Combine flour, sugar, lemon peel and salt in a large bowl. Cut in butter and shortening until mixture resembles coarse meal. Add Cognac, then gradually add water until mixture can be rolled into a ball. Flatten dough into a large circle, then wrap in plastic wrap and refrigerate at least one hour or up to three days.

Preheat oven to 450°. Roll dough out onto lightly floured surface into 12 to 13 inch circle. Place in buttered 10 inch tart pan and form edges. Again chill pastry until firm. Can be frozen up to one month. Prick shell and line with buttered parchment paper, then fill with dried beans or pie weights. Bake at 450° for 5 minutes. Reduce heat to 350° and bake 10 minutes more. Remove paper and weights, then continue baking until lightly browned, about 20 more minutes.

Lemon Filling:

1 1/2 cups sugar	2 egg yolks, well beaten
1/2 cup unsalted butter, melted and cooled	1 to 2 tablespoons minced lemon peel
7 tablespoons fresh lemon juice	4 cups fresh blueberries, washed
3 extra large eggs, well beaten	

Combine all filling ingredients except blueberries in a saucepan and cook, stirring constantly over low heat until thick, about 15 to 20 minutes. Do not boil. Cool. Spoon filling into crust. Arrange blueberries decoratively over top and serve. *Fresh raspberries or blackberries may be substituted for the blueberries. The unbaked pastry can be frozen and the filling can be prepared two days ahead.*

Mrs. Garrel Fleming (Ginny Puryear)

Pumpkin Chiffon Pie

1/2 pound gingersnaps, crushed	1/4 teaspoon ginger
1/4 cup butter, melted	1 cup milk
1/2 cup brown sugar	4 eggs, separated
2 envelopes unflavored gelatin	1 1/4 cups pumpkin
1/2 teaspoon salt	1/3 cup rum
1/2 teaspoon cinnamon	1/2 cup sugar
1/4 teaspoon nutmeg	1/2 cup coconut

Mix gingersnap crumbs with butter in a 9 inch pie plate, using your hands to blend thoroughly. Pat the mixture firmly to make a smooth coating on bottom and around sides of plate.

Mix brown sugar, gelatin, salt, and spices in a saucepan. Stir in milk, egg yolks and pumpkin. Cook over medium heat, stirring frequently, until mixture begins to bubble. Cook over low heat, stirring frequently, for 10 minutes or until gelatin is completely dissolved. Cool, then stir in rum. Chill until mixture thickens enough to mound slightly when dropped from a spoon. Beat egg whites until stiff. Beat in sugar a little at a time. Fold egg whites into pumpkin mixture and pour into prepared crust. Chill until firm, at least 2 hours. Spread coconut on baking sheet and brown in a 350° oven for 5 to 10 minutes. Sprinkle toasted coconut over top of pie. Serves 6 to 8.

Mrs. Jeff Wigginton (Mandy)

Mrs. Sturm's Pumpkin Pie

1 1/2 cups fresh pumpkin	2 tablespoons butter or margarine, melted
1 cup sugar	
1 teaspoon cinnamon	1 (9 inch) unbaked pastry shell
1/2 teaspoon salt	
2 eggs, slightly beaten	Sweetened whipped cream to serve, optional
1 cup milk	

Preheat oven to 400°. Cook pumpkin until tender, then mash. Mix sugar, cinnamon and salt. Stir into pumpkin. Combine eggs, milk and butter and add to pumpkin mixture. Pour into pastry shell and bake at 400° for about 40 minutes or until filling is set. Serve with whipped cream, if desired. Serves 6 to 8.

Dee Vargas

Sour Cream Raisin Pie

1	cup sour cream	1	tablespoon butter
1	cup sugar	3	ounces cream cheese,
2	eggs		softened
1	cup raisins	1/2	cup powdered sugar
1/2	teaspoon cinnamon	1	cup whipping cream,
1/4	teaspoon ground cloves		whipped
1/4	teaspoon salt	1	(8 inch) baked pastry shell

Mix together in a saucepan the sour cream, sugar, eggs, raisins, cinnamon, cloves, salt and butter. Cook until thick, then chill thoroughly. Beat together the cream cheese and powdered sugar. Fold whipped cream into mixture. Spread half of the mixture in the bottom of the pastry shell, then pour raisin filling on top and and spread evenly. Place the remaining half of the topping over the filling and chill before serving. Serves 6.

Susan Goodsell

Red Raspberry Pie

4	cups fresh raspberries, picked over, not soaked	1	tablespoon lemon juice
			Pinch of salt
1	cup sugar	1	recipe for two crust pastry
1/3	cup creme de Cassis	2	tablespoons unsalted butter
4	tablespoons cornstarch	3	paper thin slices lemon

Preheat oven to 425°. Toss raspberries and sugar together in a mixing bowl. Whisk Cassis and cornstarch together in a small bowl until smooth. Stir Cassis mixture, lemon juice and salt gently into berries.

Roll out 2/3 of the pastry and line a 9 inch pie pan, leave edges untrimmed. Spoon in the berries, dot with butter and arrange lemon slices, overlapping slightly, in the center of the berries. Roll out remaining pastry into a 10 inch round and cut into 1/2 inch strips. Arrange over berries in a lattice pattern. Trim edges and bring lower crust over lattice and crimp. Bake in the middle of the oven at 425° for 15 minutes, then lower the temperature to 350° and continue to bake for another 30 to 40 minutes or until crust is golden brown and filling is bubbling. Serves 6 to 8.

Mrs. Garrel Fleming (Ginny Puryear)

Tollhouse Pie

2 eggs, well beaten	6 ounces semisweet chocolate
1/2 cup flour	chips
1/2 cup sugar	1 cup chopped pecans
1/2 cup brown sugar	1 teaspoon vanilla extract
1 cup butter, melted	1 (9 inch) unbaked deep dish
	pastry shell

Preheat oven to 325°. Beat together eggs, flour and sugars, until well blended. Add cooled butter. Stir in chips, pecans and vanilla. Pour into pastry shell and bake at 325° for about 50 to 60 minutes. Allow to set before slicing. This pie is best served warm. Serves 6 to 8.

Mrs. Paul Loftin (Liz)

Impossible Pie

4 eggs	1/2 cup sugar
1/2 cup margarine	1/2 cup coconut
1/2 cup flour	2 cups milk
2 teaspoons vanilla extract	Pinch of salt

Preheat oven to 350°. Put all ingredients in a blender and beat for 30 seconds. Pour into a greased 10 inch pie pan and bake at 350° for 40 minutes. Serves 8 to 10.

Mrs. David Hart (Sue)
Fiesta Chairman 1985-1986

Never Fail Pastry

1 cup shortening	1/2 cup cold water
3 cups sifted flour	1 tablespoon white vinegar
1 teaspoon salt	1 egg

Cut shortening into a mixture of flour and salt until you get a cornmeal consistency. Beat together the water, vinegar and egg. Blend with flour mixture to form a smooth dough. Divide dough into thirds and gently roll into circular pie shell. Yields three 9 inch pie shells.

Susan Hasslocher
Guild President 1984-1985

Desserts

Oreo Cheesecake

1 cup fine chocolate wafer crumbs

3 tablespoons unsalted butter, melted

1/2 teaspoon cinnamon

4 (8 ounce) packages cream cheese, softened

1 3/4 cups sugar, divided

4 tablespoons flour

4 extra large eggs

2 large egg yolks

1 1/3 cups whipping cream, divided

3 teaspoons vanilla extract, divided

1 1/2 cups coarsely chopped Oreo cookies

2 cups sour cream

8 ounces good quality semisweet chocolate

5 Oreo cookies, halved crosswise to garnish, optional

1 Maraschino cherry, halved to garnish, optional

Butter sides only of a 9 or 10 inch spring form pan. Melt butter and combine with fine crumbs and cinnamon; sprinkle carefully over sides of pan. Gently press remaining crumbs onto ungreased pan bottom and refrigerate while preparing filling.

Preheat oven to 425°. Beat cream cheese until smooth, then beat in 1 1/2 cups sugar and the flour until well blended. Beat in eggs and yolks until mixture is smooth. Stir in 1/3 cup cream and 1 teaspoon vanilla. Pour half of batter into prepared crust. Sprinkle with chopped Oreo cookies and pour remaining batter over, smoothing with a spatula. Bake at 425° for 15 minutes. Reduce oven temperature to 225° and bake for 50 minutes, covering loosely with foil, if top browns too quickly. Meanwhile, blend together sour cream, 1/4 cup sugar and 1 teaspoon vanilla, and spread over top of hot cheesecake. Increase oven temperature to 350° and bake for 7 minutes. Cool quickly and refrigerate overnight.

Scald 1 cup cream, then add the semisweet chocolate and 1 teaspoon vanilla. Stir for 1 minute. Remove from heat and continue stirring until chocolate is melted. Refrigerate for 10 minutes. To decorate cheesecake, place on serving dish and pour glaze slowly over top. Quickly smooth some of the glaze over the sides. Be careful not to work it too much or you will lose the shine. If desired, arrange Oreo halves, cut side down, around outer edge of cake. Place cherry in center. Refrigerate until ready to serve. Serves 12 to 16.

Mrs. Garrel Fleming (Ginny Puryear)

Pecan Cheesecake

1½ cups graham cracker
crumbs
½ cup butter, melted
¼ cup sugar
5 (8 ounce) packages cream
cheese, softened
5 eggs, room temperature

1⅔ cups packed light brown
sugar
1½ cups chopped toasted
pecans
1 teaspoon vanilla extract
Whipped cream to serve,
optional

Preheat oven to 325°. Combine graham cracker crumbs, butter and ¼ cup sugar. Press into bottom and sides of a 10 inch springform pan. Set aside.

Using an electric mixer, beat cream cheese, eggs, and brown sugar in large bowl. Add pecans and vanilla, and stir until thoroughly combined. Spoon into prepared crust, spreading evenly. Bake at 325° for 1 hour. Turn off oven. Let cake stand in oven with door open until top is brown and cracked, at least 30 minutes. Cool slightly. Refrigerate at least 2 hours before serving. Decorate with whipped cream if desired.

Mrs. Don Davis (Pat)
Fiesta Chairman 1976-1977, Guild President 1983-1984

Amaretto Cheesecake

¼ cup butter, melted
1½ cups fine vanilla wafer or
graham cracker crumbs
1 cup plus 3 tablespoons sugar,
divided
3 (8 ounce) packages cream
cheese, softened

2 teaspoons Amaretto liqueur
3 eggs
½ cup whipping cream
1 cup sour cream
Pinch of sugar

Preheat oven to 350°. Combine butter, cookie crumbs and 3 tablespoons sugar, then press into a 10 inch springform pan. Mix together cream cheese, 1 cup sugar, liqueur, eggs and whipping cream until well blended. Pour over crust and bake at 350° for 45 minutes. Combine sour cream and a small amount of sugar. Spread over hot cheesecake and bake an additional 5 minutes. Remove from oven. Let cool, then refrigerate at least 4 hours.

You can also use chocolate wafers for your crust and add ⅓ cup cocoa to your filling to make a chocolate Amaretto cheesecake.

Lael Byers

Cheese Pie

2 (8 ounce) packages cream cheese, softened	1 teaspoon vanilla extract, divided
3 eggs	2 cups sour cream
3/4 cup plus 5 tablespoons sugar	1 (10 inch) graham cracker crust

Preheat oven to 375°. Combine cream cheese, eggs, 3/4 cup sugar, and 1/2 teaspoon vanilla until smooth. Bake at 375° for 15 minutes. Remove from oven and turn temperature up to 475°. Mix together sour cream and 5 tablespoons sugar and 1/2 teaspoon vanilla. Spoon it on top of pie. Bake at 475° for 5 minutes. Serve very cold.

Mrs. Ron Tobin (Bonnie)

Yorkshire Cheesecake

Crust:

1 1/2 cups flour	3/4 cup butter
6 tablespoons sugar	2 egg yolks
1 teaspoon grated lemon peel	1/2 teaspoon vanilla extract

In medium bowl combine flour, sugar and lemon peel. With pastry blender, cut in butter until crumbly, then stir in egg yolks and vanilla. Refrigerate 30 minutes. Meanwhile heat oven to 400°. Press 1/3 of chilled dough onto the bottom a 9 inch springform pan and bake 8 to 10 minutes. Cool. Press rest of dough around sides of pan to within 1 inch of top.

Filling:

4 (8 ounce) packages cream cheese, softened	1/2 teaspoon grated lemon peel
	1/2 teaspoon grated orange peel
1 cup finely grated very sharp Cheddar cheese	4 eggs
	2 egg yolks
1 3/4 cups sugar	1/4 cup beer
1/2 teaspoon vanilla extract	1/4 cup whipping cream

In a large bowl beat cream cheese until fluffy. Add Cheddar cheese and beat about 5 more minutes. Add sugar, vanilla, and grated peelings. Add eggs and egg yolks, beating well after each addition. Stir in beer and cream. Turn oven up to 500°. Pour cheese filling into pan and bake 10 to 12 minutes or until top is a light brown. Then, reduce heat to 250° and continue baking for 2 hours or until top is firm and cake tester inserted in center comes out clean. Cool on wire rack, then remove sides of pan and refrigerate.

Mary Coneway

White Chocolate Cheesecake

Crust:

1½ cups graham cracker crumbs

1 to 2 tablespoons sugar

5 tablespoons unsalted butter, melted

Mix all ingredients together in a large bowl. Press onto bottom and sides of a 9 inch springform pan. Refrigerate until set.

Filling And Topping:

4 (8 ounce) packages cream cheese, softened

½ cup unsalted butter, softened

¾ cup sugar, divided

3 tablespoons flour

4 large eggs, at room temperature

10 ounces imported white chocolate, melted

5 teaspoons vanilla, divided

Pinch of salt

2 cups sour cream

Shaved white chocolate to garnish, optional

Preheat oven to 325°. Combine cream cheese and butter, beating until smooth. Add flour and ½ cup sugar, beating until well blended. Add eggs, one at a time, blending well after each addition. Add chocolate, 4½ teaspoons vanilla and salt. Beat for 1 to 2 minutes. Turn mixture into prepared crust. Bake at 325° for 1 hour. Remove from oven long enough to prepare topping. Increase temperature to 350°.

For topping, blend together sour cream, ¼ cup sugar and ½ teaspoon vanilla. Pour over hot cheesecake and return to oven to bake an additional 7 minutes. Cool quickly, letting stand 2 hours at room temperature, then refrigerate at least 12 hours. Yields 16 servings.

Mrs. Garrel Fleming (Ginny Puryear)

Cheesecake Tarts

2 (8 ounce) packages cream cheese, softened

¾ cup sugar

2 eggs

1 tablespoon lemon juice

1 teaspoon vanilla extract

24 vanilla wafers

24 paper baking cups

1 (21 ounce) can cherry or blueberry pie filling

Preheat oven to 375°. Beat together cream cheese, sugar, lemon juice and vanilla until light and fluffy. Set paper baking cups in muffin pans and place a vanilla wafer in each. Fill two thirds full with cream cheese mixture. Bake at 375° for 15 to 20 minutes or until set, no more than 20 minutes. Put 1 tablespoon pie filling on each tart. May be refrigerated up to 24 hours ahead. Yields 24 tarts.

Mrs. Rick Mincher (Debbie)

No-Bake Chocolate Cheesecake

1/2 package chocolate wafers, crushed	1/2 cup sugar, divided
1/4 cup butter, melted	2 eggs, separated
8 ounces cream cheese, softened	6 ounces semisweet chocolate chips, melted
1 teaspoon vanilla extract	1 cup whipping cream, whipped

Preheat oven to 325°. Combine crushed wafers with butter and pat onto bottom of a 9 inch springform pan. Bake at 325° for 10 minutes. Combine cream cheese, vanilla and 1/4 cup sugar. Stir in beaten egg yolks and chocolate. Beat egg whites to soft peaks, then gradually fold in 1/4 cup sugar. Combine with chocolate and fold in whipped cream. Pour into crust and freeze. Remove from freezer approximately 40 minutes before serving. Remainder re-freezes beautifully.

Mrs. Stephen Miller (Kaye)

Microwave Cheesecake

Crust:

2 cups graham cracker crumbs	1/2 cup butter, melted
1/2 cup sugar	1/2 teaspoon cinnamon

Combine crumbs, sugar, butter and cinnamon in a 2 quart pyrex pan and press firmly on bottom of dish. Cook in microwave on HIGH for 2 minutes.

Filling:

3 (8 ounce) packages cream cheese, softened	2 teaspoons vanilla extract, divided
5 eggs	2 1/2 cups sour cream
1 1/3 cups sugar, divided	Fruit pie mix to serve

Beat cream cheese until smooth and stir in eggs, one at a time, mix in 1 cup sugar and 1/2 teaspoon vanilla. Pour into crust and bake on MEDIUM for 15 to 20 minutes, turning every 4 minutes. Combine sour cream, 1/3 cup sugar and 1 1/2 teaspoons vanilla. Blend well and pour over cheesecake. Return to oven and cook on HIGH for 1 minute and 15 seconds. Chill. You may spread any fruit pie mix on top to serve. Yields 16 servings.

Mrs. Lee F. Looney (Cindy)

• To soften brown sugar, place it in a dish with a slice of apple and microwave for 15 seconds.

Bavarian Apple Torte

Crust:

1/2 cup butter, softened	1/4 teaspoon vanilla
1/3 cup sugar	1 cup flour

Cream together the butter and sugar, then stir in vanilla. Add flour, mixing well. Spread dough on bottom and 2 inches up the sides of a greased 9 inch springform pan.

Filling and Topping:

8 ounces cream cheese, softened	1/2 teaspoon vanilla extract
1/2 cup sugar, divided	4 cups peeled, cored and sliced apples
1 egg	1/2 teaspoon ground cinnamon

Preheat oven to 450°. Combine cream cheese and 1/4 cup sugar; add egg and vanilla, blending well. Spread filling evenly over pastry. Sprinkle apples with 1/4 cup sugar and cinnamon, stirring well. Spoon apples over filling. Bake at 450° for 10 minutes, then reduce the temperature to 400° and bake another 25 minutes. Cool before removing from pan. Serves 8 to 10.

Mrs. Larry Hall (Jane)
Fiesta Chairman 1982-1983

Flan Almendra

1/2 cup sugar	3 egg yolks
1 2/3 cups sweetened condensed milk	1 teaspoon vanilla extract
1 cup milk	1 cup slivered almonds, coarsely ground
3 eggs	

Preheat oven to 350°. Sprinkle sugar evenly in a 9 inch cake pan and place over medium heat. Using oven mitts, caramelize the sugar by shaking pan occasionally over the heat until the sugar is melted and is a golden brown. A little stirring may be necessary when using a gas burner. Allow to cool. Sugar may crack slightly.

Combine remaining ingredients and beat on high speed for 15 seconds. Pour over caramelized sugar. Cover pan with foil and place in larger shallow pan containing 1 inch of hot water. Bake at 350° for 55 minutes or until knife inserted near center comes out clean. Remove pan from water. Let cool on wire rack at least 30 minutes. Loosen edges with spatula and place serving plate on pan and invert. The almonds will rise to the top forming a crust. Serves 8.

Mrs. Ron Tobin (Bonnie)

My Favorite Flan

1¾ cups sugar, divided	2 (12 ounce) cans evaporated
2 tablespoons water	milk
3 whole eggs	1 teaspoon vanilla extract
3 egg yolks	Toasted almonds to garnish

Preheat oven to 325°. Place 1 cup sugar in a saucepan and cook over medium heat until it has a "wet" look. Stir constantly until a syrup is formed. Add water and stir until golden brown. Pour into a 10 inch pyrex pie pan and let cool while you prepare the custard.

Mix eggs and ¾ cup sugar, then beat until light yellow. Warm the milk, but do not boil. Add to the egg mixture and continue to beat. Add vanilla. Strain through a sieve into pie pan lined with carmelized sugar. Bake at 325° in a pan of hot water for 45 minutes. Unmold while hot on rimmed serving platter and garnish with toasted almonds. Serves 8.

Mrs. Henry Mayes (Kathy)

Easy Southern Rice Pudding

2½ cups milk	1 teaspon vanilla extract
⅔ cup instant rice	½ cup raisins
2 eggs	Brown sugar to serve, optional
½ cup sugar	

Preheat oven to 300°. Scald milk with instant rice. Beat eggs and mix in sugar and vanilla. Add to milk mixture. Fold in raisins. Pour into a well buttered 9 inch baking dish and bake at 300° in a pan of hot water for 30 minutes. Serve hot or cold, sprinkle with a little brown sugar.

Mrs. Henry A. Pate (Patricia)

Snow Pudding

1 teaspoon unflavored gelatin	3 eggs, separated
¼ cup cold water	2 cups milk, scalded
1 cup boiling water	Pinch of salt
1⅓ cups sugar, divided	1 teaspoon vanilla extract
¼ cup lemon juice	

Soak gelatin in cold water. Dissolve in boiling water. Add 1 cup sugar and lemon juice and set in refrigerator. Stir occasionally and when quite thick, beat with whip until frothy. Add egg whites, beaten stiff, and continue beating until stiff enough to hold its shape. Beat egg yolks, add ⅓ cup sugar and salt. Pour small amount of scalded milk over egg mixture and mix well. Pour egg mixture into milk and cook a few minutes over low heat, stirring constantly. Pour custard into serving bowl or individaul bowls and top with meringue. Serves 6.

Mrs. Rowland Firth (Susan)

English Trifle

1	(12 to 14 ounce) pound cake		Pinch of salt
1	(10 ounce) jar raspberry jam	2	cups milk
½	cup medium dry sherry	2	teaspoons vanilla extract
¼	cup brandy	1	pint fresh raspberries or strawberries
5	egg yolks	1	(29 ounce) can sliced peaches, drained
6	tablespoons sugar	1½	cups whipping cream
1	teaspoon cornstarch	1	tablespoon powdered sugar

Cut pound cake into 1 inch slices and coat each with jam. Line bottom of Trifle bowl or deep glass container with cake, then pour sherry and brandy over top. Cover lightly and stand at room temperature for 1 hour. Whisk together the yolks, sugar, cornstarch and salt. Heat milk almost to a boil, stirring constantly. Very slowly, pour milk into egg mixture. Transfer to a heavy saucepan and cook over medium heat until custard coats the spoon. Remove from heat and add vanilla, stir. Let cool.

Reserve 10 raspberries for garnish and arrange remainder on cake. Pour custard over top. Whip the cream, adding the powdered sugar. Whip until firm. Reserve ½ whipped cream for garnish and pour remainder over the custard. Decorate with berries and reserved cream. You can make two layers of cake, fruit, custard and cream, repeating the layers. Serves 12.

Mrs. Elliot Silverstone (Dianne)

Chocolate Mousse Supreme

¾	cup unsalted butter	1½	teaspoons vanilla extract
1¾	cups sifted powdered sugar	4	squares unsweetened chocolate, melted
6	eggs, separated	1½	cups chopped pecans
¼	cup milk	2	cups whipping cream, divided
1½	teaspoons rum extract, Grand Marnier or other liqueur		

Cream butter, gradually add sugar and beat until light and fluffy. Add egg yolks, one at a time, beating until smooth after each. Blend in milk and flavorings. Add chocolate until uniform. Whip one cup cream and fold into mixture. Fold in chopped pecans. Beat egg whites until stiff but not dry and carefully fold into chocolate mixture with a spatula. Refrigerate at least 4 hours or overnight. Whip remaining cream to serve with mousse. Serves 6.

Mrs. Don Davis (Pat)
Fiesta Chairman 1976-1977, Guild President 1983-1984

Chocolate Mousse

6 ounces semisweet chocolate chips	3 large eggs, separated
2 tablespoons liquid strong coffee	1 teaspoon rum or vanilla extract
1/3 cup sugar	1/2 cup whipping cream
	1 tablespoon powdered sugar

Melt chips in double boiler with coffee and sugar. Stir well. Remove from heat. Add egg yolks, one at a time, stirring well after each. Add vanilla and cool slightly. Beat egg whites until stiff, but not dry. Blend small amount of whites into chocolate. Fold chocolate into remaining egg whites. Pour into individual cups or wine glasses and chill at least 3 hours. Whip cream and powdered sugar until well blended and stiffened and serve on top mousse. Serves 6.

Mrs. Howell Ridout (Debbie)

Cold Lemon Soufflé

1 package unflavored gelatin	1/4 cup lemon juice
1/4 cup cold water	Grated rind of 1 lemon
3 eggs, separated	1 1/2 cups whipping cream
1 egg white	Blanched unsalted almonds,
1 cup sugar	toasted to garnish
1 teaspoon vanilla extract	

Soak gelatin in cold water. Heat in a double boiler over hot water until clear. Beat egg yolks until pale and lemon colored. Add sugar gradually, beating until light. Add juice, rind and vanilla. Beat cream until stiff and in a separate bowl beat the egg whites until stiff. Add gelatin mixture to yolk mixture and fold in whipped cream and whites. Chill, and top with almonds to serve. Serves 6.

Susan Hasslocher
Guild President 1984-1985

Strawberries Romanoff

8 ounces seedless raisins	Pinch ground nutmeg
2 ounces brandy	8 ounces light brown sugar
4 cups sour cream	1 quart whole unsweetened
1 teaspoon cinnamon	strawberries

Purée raisins with brandy in a blender. Add sour cream, cinnamon, nutmeg and brown sugar. Blend well. Place strawberries in serving bowl and add sauce to suit your taste.

Dee Vargas

Hot Apple Cobbler
With Cinnamon Ice Cream

½ cup butter	1 cup milk
1 cup flour	4 cups sliced apples, peeled
1½ cups sugar	1½ cups brown sugar
½ teaspoon salt	1½ teaspoons cinnamon
3 teaspoons baking powder	¼ teaspoon allspice

Preheat oven to 350°. Melt butter in a 9x13 inch pan. Sift together flour, sugar, salt and baking powder. Blend with milk. Pour over melted butter. Spread apples over the top and sprinkle evenly with brown sugar, cinnamon and allspice. Bake at 350° for 1 hour. Crust will magically appear and cover the entire surface of the cobbler. Serve hot with cinnamon ice cream.

Cinnamon Ice Cream:

1 quart vanilla ice cream, softened	3 teaspoons cinnamon
	½ cup sugar

Soften ice cream and stir in cinnamon and sugar. Refreeze.

Mrs. Allan L. Williams (Rose Betty)

Aunt Jen's Peach Cobbler

5 cups sliced peaches	6 tablespoons butter, divided
½ cup plus 2 tablespoons sugar, divided	2 teaspoons baking powder
1 cup plus 2 tablespoons flour, divided	½ teaspoon salt
	⅓ cup shortening
1 teaspoon cinnamon	⅓ cup milk

Preheat oven to 425°. Place peaches in an 8 inch square pan. Combine ½ cup sugar, 2 tablespoons flour, and cinnamon; sprinkle over peaches and dot with 4 tablespoons butter. Sift together 1 cup flour, baking powder, and salt. Cut in shortening, adding enough milk to hold ingredients together. Pat out dough on a lightly floured board to fit pan. Place dough over peaches. Dot with 2 tablespoons butter and sprinkle with 2 tablespoons sugar. Bake at 425° for 30 minutes.

Mrs. Bill Balcezak (Sharon)

Fried Apple Pies

Pastry:

2   cups flour
1   teaspoon salt

1/2   cup milk
1/2   cup oil

Combine flour and salt. Combine milk and oil, stirring well. Pour milk mixture into flour mixture and stir until just blended. Shape dough into a ball.

Apple Filling:

3   medium apples, peeled and chopped
1   tablespoon water
2/3   cup sugar

1   tablespoon flour
1/8   teaspoon ground cinnamon
1/8   teaspoon ground nutmeg
Oil for frying

Combine apples and water in a saucepan. Cover and cook over low heat for about 10 to 15 minutes or until tender. Drain off accumulated liquid. Combine sugar, flour and spices, stir well. Add to apples and cook over medium heat 10 minutes or until thickened. Roll pastry to 1/8 inch thickness and cut out eight (5 inch) circles. Spoon about 2 1/2 tablespoons apple filling on each circle. Moisten edges and fold pastry in half, making sure edges are even. Press edges together with a fork dipped in flour to seal edges. Heat 1 inch of oil. Fry pies in hot oil until golden, turning once. Drain on paper towels. Yields 8 pies.

Mrs. John M. Davis (Alice)
Fiesta Chairman 1973-1974

Bread Pudding With Rum Raisin Sauce

1/2   loaf sourdough French bread
1   quart milk
3   eggs

2   cups sugar
2   tablespoons vanilla extract
1   cup raisins
1/2   cup butter, melted

Preheat oven to 325°. Soak bread in milk and crumble finely. Add eggs, sugar, vanilla and raisins, mixing well. Pour butter into a 3 quart baking dish and add pudding mixture. Bake at 325° for 45 minutes. Serves 12.

Rum Sauce:

1/2   cup butter, softened
1   cup sugar

1   egg
1/4   cup rum or whisky

Cream butter and sugar. Add egg and rum and cook until thick. Warm before serving and dip over pudding.

Mrs. C. Jay Middlebrook (Linda)

White Chocolate Crepes With Raspberry Sauce

1   cup unbleached flour
1   teaspoon baking powder
1   cup milk
2   large eggs

4   ounces white chocolate, finely grated, divided
2   pints fresh raspberries or individually frozen
1   cup fresh raspberry sauce

Combine flour and baking powder in a blender or processor until just mixed. Add milk and process until smooth. While machine is running, add eggs, one at a time. Add 2 ounces white chocolate, grated, and process briefly, scraping down sides of bowl. Continue processing until mixture is fairly smooth. Let set for 20 minutes. Heat the crepe pans and butter lightly. Pour a scant 1/4 cup of the batter into a buttered 7 inch crepe pan tilting the pan to coat the bottom. Cook until crepe is lightly browned on one side, then flip and cook until freckled. Fill each crepe with raspberries and roll. Place two on each serving plate and top with 2 tablespoons fresh raspberry sauce. Garnish with 2 ounces white chocolate, grated. Serves 8. *Crepes can be prepared ahead, then wrapped carefully with plastic wrap and frozen.*

Mrs. Garrel Fleming (Ginny Puryear)

Pumpkin Roll

1   cup sugar
3   eggs
2/3 cup pumpkin
1   teaspoon cinnamon
1   teaspoon ginger
1   teaspoon salt
3/4 cup flour
1/2 cup chopped pecans

Powdered sugar to sprinkle on towel
8   ounces cream cheese, softened
4   tablespoons butter, softened
1   cup powdered sugar
1   teaspoon vanilla extract

Preheat oven to 375°. Mix together sugar, eggs, pumpkin, cinnamon, ginger, salt and flour. Spread on a greased and floured 15x10 inch jelly roll pan with sides. Sprinkle with pecans. Bake at 375° for 15 minutes. Turn out on cloth sprinkled with powdered sugar. Roll up like a jelly roll. Cool.

Combine cream cheese, butter, 1 cup powdered sugar and vanilla. Unroll jelly roll and spread with filling. Reroll and chill. Slice and serve. Serves 12 to 15.

Susan Goodsell

Salad Cracker Fruitcake

2	cans sweetened condensed milk	1	(15 ounce) box golden raisins, cut into small pieces
1	pound marshmallows	1	(6 ounce) package chopped dates
1	pound unsalted saltine crackers, crushed	1	(3½ ounce) can coconut
1	pound candied cherries, cut into small pieces	1	pound chopped pecans
1	pound candied pineapple, cut into small pieces		Juice of 1 lemon

Heat milk, but do not boil. Add marshmallows and stir until dissolved. Combine crackers, fruit and add coconut and pecans, mixing well. Add lemon juice to milk mixture and pour over fruit and cracker mixture. Stir well. Pour into a large foil lined pan. Use enough heavy duty foil to fold over and cover cake. Press mixture down well. Refrigerate at least 3 days before cutting. Store in the refrigerator. This keeps for weeks. *I ususally make this only at Christmas. It is sticky, chewy and delicious. This tastes nothing like a regular fruitcake.*

Mrs. Bruce Knierim (Pam)
Fiesta Chairman 1981-1982

Frozen Lemon Soufflé

2	eggs, separated	1	cup whipping cream
7	tablespoons sugar, divided	4	fresh mint leaves to garnish
	Juice and rind of 2 lemons		Grated lemon rind to garnish

Cut collars out of parchment paper or waxed paper to fit four individual 4 ounce ramekins. Wrap a collar around each and secure with tape. Beat egg yolks with 3 tablespoons sugar until mixture is thick and lemony in color. Add lemon juice and grated rind and continue to beat until mixture is smooth and creamy. Whip cream with 2 tablespoons sugar until stiff and fold into beaten egg yolks. Beat egg whites until soft peaks form and and continue to beat, gradually adding the remaining 2 tablespoons sugar, until smooth, glossy and stiff. Add to whipped cream mixture and fold together very gently. Fold lemon mixture into prepared ramekins, 1 inch above the rim. Freeze at least 2 hours before serving. Remove from freezer 30 minutes before serving and when ready to serve, remove collars. Garnish with grated lemon rind and fresh mint. Serves 4.

Ada Smyth

Frozen Toffee Dessert

2 to 3 packages ladyfingers
6 chocolate covered toffee
candy bars
1 quart coffee flavored ice
cream, softened

2 cups whipped cream
2 tablespoons brandy
2 tablespoons creme de cacao

Line botton and sides of a 9 inch springform pan with ladyfingers. Crush candy, and reserve some for topping. Combine candy and ice cream. Pour into pan. Combine whipped cream and liqueurs and spread over ice cream layer. Sprinkle with crushed candy. Freeze. Serves 12.

Mrs. Charles Boner (Grace)

Fudge Ice Cream Pie

1/4 cup white corn syrup
2 tablespoons brown sugar
3 tablespoons butter
2 1/2 cups crisp rice cereal
1/4 cup peanut butter

3 tablespoons white corn
syrup
1/4 cup fudge ice cream
topping
1 quart vanilla ice cream

Combine 1/4 cup corn syrup, sugar and butter in a saucepan. Bring to a boil and remove from heat. Add cereal and press into a buttered 9 inch pie pan. Blend peanut butter, 3 tablespoons corn syrup and fudge topping. Spread one half the mixture over crust and freeze. Reserve remaining peanut butter mixture to put on top. To serve, soften ice cream and allow pie to stand at room temperature 10 minutes. Spoon ice cream into pie shell. Warm remaining peanut butter mixture and drizzle over ice cream. Serves 8.

Mrs. Paul Loftin (Liz)

Rabon No-Cook Vanilla Ice Cream

3 to 4 eggs, separated
1 1/2 cups sugar
1 can sweetened condensed
milk

1 teaspoon vanilla extract
8 cups milk

Beat egg whites until stiff but not too dry. Beat egg yolks until creamy and light in color. Combine and slowly add sugar and condensed milk. Add vanilla and milk, be sure to scrape sides of bowl. Freeze in a 1 gallon freezer container according to manufacturer's directions. Yields 1 gallon.

Lana DeWeese

Leon's Rum Raisin Ice Cream

1	cup raisins	2	eggs, slightly beaten
2	cups rum	4	cups milk, scalded
2	tablespoons flour	4	cups half and half cream
2	cups sugar	2	teaspoons vanilla extract
1/8	teaspoon salt		

Soak raisins in rum for 6 to 8 hours. Drain raisins, saving rum. Mix flour, sugar and salt, then add beaten eggs. Gradually pour in milk and cook in a double boiler for 10 minutes, stirring constantly. Cool. Add cream and vanilla and raisins. Freeze in a 1 gallon freezer container according to manufacturer's directions. When ice cream is firm, pack with ice and salt to freeze.

Rosanne Henna

Homemade Peach Ice Cream

4	eggs	1/4	teaspoon salt
4	cups whole milk	3	cups whipping cream
2	cups sugar, divided	6	cups mashed fresh peaches

Over low heat cook together eggs, whole milk, 1 cup sugar, salt and cream until it makes a custard. Cool. Add peaches that have been sweetened with 1 cup sugar. Freeze in a 1 gallon container according to manufacturer's directions. Any leftovers may be kept in ice trays in your freezer for several weeks. Yields 1 gallon.

Mrs. Henry A. Pate (Patricia)

White Chocolate Ice Cream

1	cup water	10	ounces white chocolate,
3/4	cup sugar		melted
6	large egg yolks	2	cups whipping cream
1	tablespoon vanilla extract		

Blend together water and sugar in a heavy saucepan. Cook over low heat until sugar dissloves, swirling pan occasionally. Bring to a boil and boil 5 minutes. Combine egg yolks and vanilla, beating on high speed until light and fluffy, about 7 minutes. Slowly add hot syrup to yolks, beating constantly until thickened and completely cool, about 10 minutes. Gradually add chocolate and continue beating until cool, another 7 minutes. Stir in cream. Cover and freeze at least 5 hours or overnight until set. May be stored in freezer several days if well covered. Yields 1 quart. *This is a wonderfully dense and creamy mixture that does not require an ice cream maker.*

Mrs. Garrel Fleming (Ginny Puryear)

Rocky Road Ice Cream

²/₃	cup cocoa	2	ounces semisweet chocolate,
2	cups sugar, divided		shredded with coarse grater
4	cups milk	2	cups miniature
2	teaspoons vanilla extact		marshmallows
¼	teaspoon salt	½	cup chopped pecans or
4	cups whipping cream		almonds

In a large saucepan, mix cocoa and 1 cup sugar. Gradually stir in milk and cook over low heat until sugar and cocoa dissolve. Cool to room temperature, then stir in vanilla, salt and cream. Set aside. Stir chocolate, marshmallows and nuts into cocoa mixture. Pour into ice cream freezer container and freeze according to manufacturer's directions. The marshmallows rise to the top, so stir the marshmallows evenly through the mixture before serving or ripening.

Mrs. Ron Tobin (Bonnie)

Peppermint Ice Cream

4	cups milk, scalded	2	cups half and half cream
3 to 3½	packages pure sugar	1	cup whipping cream
	peppermint candy		Milk to top off freezer container
4	eggs, slightly beaten		

Melt candy in milk and add eggs. Cook and stir over low heat until slightly thickened. Pour into 1 gallon freezer container; add half and half and whipping cream. Finish filling with milk to 3 inches from top. Freeze according to manufacturer's directions.

Susan Hasslocher
Guild President 1984-1985

Perfect Chocolate Sauce For Ice Cream

1	cup sugar	1	(5 ounce) can evaporated
2	tablespoons unsweetened		milk
	cocoa		Ice cream, your favorite flavor

Mix sugar and cocoa in a microwave bowl with cover. Cook on HIGH for 1½ minutes. Add milk. Mix well. Cover and cook on HIGH for 3 to 4 minutes or until mixture bubbles and coats a spoon. Cool for approximately 20 minutes. Serve on ice cream. Yields 1½ cups sauce.

Mrs. Allan L. Williams (Rose Betty)

Quick And Easy Microwave Fudge

3   cups powdered sugar
½   cup unsweetened cocoa
¼   cup milk

¼   cup butter or margarine
1   tablespoon vanilla extract
½   cup chopped nuts

Sift together powdered sugar and cocoa into microwave proof glass pan. Add butter in thin slices around dish, then add milk. Cook in microwave on HIGH for 2 to 3 minutes. Remove and add vanilla and nuts. Stir well until smooth and pour into buttered 5x7 inch pan. Set in freezer for 20 minutes. Yields 35 pieces.

Mrs. Wallace Bender (Dana Buckley)

Texas Pralines

1   (1 pound) box light brown
    sugar
1   cup whipping cream

2   tablespoons butter
1   cup pecan pieces

Combine brown sugar and cream. Microwave on HIGH for 6 to 7 minutes. Stir well. Microwave on HIGH for another 7 minutes. Add butter and pecans. Microwave on HIGH for 2 to 3 minutes. Stir or beat well. Drop by spoonsful on foil only. Yields 48 to 50 small pralines.

Mrs. Fred Thom (Diana)

Pralines

3   cups sugar
1   cup buttermilk
½   cup margarine
1   teaspoon baking soda
1   teaspoon vanilla extract

¼   cup white corn syrup
Pinch of salt
1   pound pecans, broken into
    large pieces

Combine all ingredients except pecans in a very large saucepan. Cook to a soft ball stage or 230° on a candy thermometer. Remove from heat and let set for 2 minutes. Beat until thick and creamy. Add pecans. Drop by teaspoonfuls onto buttered pans. Yields about 60 candies.

Mrs. Kerry G. Merritt (Nancy)

• *Nuts should be kept frozen to retain best flavor until ready to use.*

Peanut Brittle

2 cups sugar
1 cup corn syrup
1/2 cup water

2 cups raw Spanish peanuts
1 teaspoon vanilla extract
1 teaspoon baking soda

Combine sugar, corn syrup and water. Cook in a saucepan until syrup spins a thread. Add peanuts, and cook until peanuts and mixture turns a golden brown, a hard crack stage. Remove from heat, then add vanilla and baking soda. Stir slightly. Pour into a large well buttered dish. Cool and break into pieces. *It is best never to make peanut brittle on a humid or muggy day.*

Mrs. Charlie Cantwell (Winn)

Microwave Caramel Corn

1/2 cup butter
1 cup brown sugar
1/4 cup corn syrup
1/4 teaspoon salt

1/4 teaspoon baking soda
1/2 teaspoon vanilla extract
3 quarts popped corn

Combine in a 2 quart bowl the butter, brown sugar, corn syrup and salt. Cook on HIGH until mixture boils, then cook 1 minute longer. Remove and stir in vanilla. Add baking soda and stir until it starts to foam about 10 seconds. Pour over popcorn and mix with wooden spoon until all popcorn is evenly coated. Cook 1 minute more on HIGH to set. Cool. Break into pieces.

Elsa Elizondo

Microwave Peanut Brittle

1 cup raw Spanish peanuts
1/2 cup corn syrup
Dash of salt
1 cup sugar

1 teaspoon vanilla extract
1 tablespoon butter
2 teaspoons baking soda

Place peanuts, syrup, salt and sugar in a 2 quart bowl. Cook on HIGH for 7 minutes, stirring twice. Add vanilla and butter, and cook on HIGH 1 minute more. Remove and add baking soda. Stir until it foams. Pour immediately onto a buttered cookie sheet, tilting to spread evenly. Cool and break into pieces.

Elsa Y. Elizondo

Party Mints

About ½ box plus 2½ cups
    powdered sugar
1   egg white
2   teaspoons butter

½ teaspoon peppermint
    flavoring
3   drops food coloring

Sift powdered sugar onto clean waxed paper. Measure 2½ cups powdered sugar and put into large bowl. Add egg white, butter and flavoring. Mix until creamy. Add drops of food coloring, any color. Knead with hands. Shape into 1 inch balls. Put them on waxed paper. Flatten with fork and let stand.

Mrs. Fred Markham (Marilyn)

Popcorn Cake

1   cup unpopped popcorn
1   pound salted peanuts
1   pound plain M&M candies

½ cup butter
1   (1 pound) bag large
    marshmallows

Pop corn, and place in a large greased bowl with peanuts and candies. Mix well. Remove unpopped corn. Melt butter and marshmallows together and drizzle over popcorn mix. Mix well with a greased spoon. Press with buttered hands into a generously greased tube or bundt pan. Let cool 2 hours before cutting with a serrated knife. This can also be pressed into a greased 9x13 inch pan and cut into squares.

Becky Allen

Coconut Chocolate Drops

2   squares unsweetened
    chocolate
1   can sweetened condensed
    milk

1   (7 or 8 ounce) package
    flaked coconut
½ cup chopped walnuts

Preheat oven to 350°. Melt chocolate in double boiler, then stir in milk, coconut and walnuts. Drop by rounded teaspoonsful on greased cookie sheets. Put in oven and immediately turn off heat. Leave in oven 15 minutes. Yields 4½ dozen.

Mrs. Danny Pounds (Charlotte)

Chocolate Nut Cups

1   cup semisweet chocolate
    chips
1   cup peanut butter chips

1   tablespoon vegetable oil
1   cup salted Spanish peanuts

Combine chips and oil. Melt in microwave oven for approximately 1 minute or in a double boiler over hot water, stirring until chips are melted. Remove from heat and stir in peanuts. Cool slightly, and drop by teaspoonsful in decorative paper nut cups. Chill in refrigerator until firm. Store in a covered container in the refrigerator. Yields about 4 dozen.

Mrs. Larry Deinlein (Betty)

Krispie Chocolate Balls

3   cups crisp rice cereal
1/2 cup butter, softened
1   (16 ounce) box powdered
    sugar

2   cups crunchy peanut butter
1/2 bar paraffin
12 ounces semisweet chocolate
    chips

Mix together the cereal, butter, powdered sugar and peanut butter. Roll into small balls. Melt together the paraffin and chocolate in a double boiler over boiling water and quickly dip balls into mixture. Place on waxed paper to set.

Mrs. Paul White (Suzanne)

Buckeyes

1   cup margarine or butter
2   cups peanut butter
5   cups powdered sugar

12 ounces semisweet chocolate
    chips, melted

Melt margarine in a large saucepan. Mix in sugar and peanut butter. Butter a 9x13 inch pan. Spread peanut butter mixture in bottom and top with melted chocolate. Cut into squares while chocolate is still warm. Store in the refrigerator. Yields about 24 squares.

Mrs. A. W. Roesler (Linda)

SUBSTITUTIONS

IF YOU'RE OUT OF:	USE:
1 cup cake flour	1 cup all-purpose flour less 2 tablespoons
1 cup self rising flour	1 cup all-purpose flour plus 1 1/4 teaspoons baking powder plus 1/4 teaspoon salt
1 teaspoon baking powder	1/4 teaspoon baking soda plus 3/8 teaspoon cream of tartar
1 tablespoon cornstarch	2 tablespoons all-purpose flour
1 cup all-purpose flour	3/4 cup whole wheat flour
1 cup sugar	1 cup packed brown sugar or 2 cups sifted powdered sugar
1 cup honey	1 1/4 cups sugar plus 1/4 cup liquid
1 ounce chocolate	3 tablespoons unsweetened cocoa plus 1 tablespoon butter
1 cup milk	1/2 cup evaporated milk plus 1/2 cup water
1 cup buttermilk	1 tablespoon lemon juice or vinegar plus enough milk to measure 1 cup
1 cup sour cream	1 cup plain yogurt
1 cup half and half cream	1 cup undiluted evaporated milk or 3 tablespoons butter plus 7/8 cup milk
1 cup whipping cream	1/3 cup butter plus 3/4 cup milk
1 cup cream, whipped	4 ounces frozen whipped topping, thawed or 1 envelope dessert topping, prepared
1 whole egg	2 egg yolks
1 tablespoon snipped fresh herbs	1 teaspoon dried herbs, crushed or 1/2 teaspoon ground herbs
1 medium onion	1 tablespoon minced dried onion or 1 teaspoon onion powder
1 clove garlic	1/8 teaspoon minced dried garlic or 1/8 teaspoon garlic powder
3 fresh medium tomatoes	1 (16 ounce) can tomatoes, cut up
3 cups tomato juice	1 1/2 cups tomato sauce plus 1 1/2 cups water
1 cup catsup	1 cup tomato sauce plus 1/4 cup sugar and 2 tablespoons vinegar
1 teaspoon Worcestershire sauce	1 tablespoon soy sauce plus dash of hot pepper sauce
1 teaspoon lemon juice	1/2 teaspoon vinegar
1/2 pound fresh mushrooms	6 ounces canned, drained
1 tablespoon prepared mustard	1 teaspoon dry mustard
1 teaspoon allspice	1/2 teaspoon cinnamon and 1/8 teaspoon ground cloves

AVERAGE CAN SIZES

No. 1 = 11 ounces (1 1/2 cups)

No. 2 = 20 ounces (2 1/2 cups)

No. 2 1/2 = 29 ounces (3 1/2 cups)

No. 3 = 46 ounces (5 3/4 cups)

No. 10 = 6 1/2 pounds (13 cups)

ESTIMATING INGREDIENTS

Apples:	3 medium	2½ cups chopped
Bacon:	8 slices cooked	½ cup crumbled
Bananas:	3 medium	2 cups, mashed
Bell Pepper:	1 large	1 cup diced
Bread:	1 slice fresh	⅓ cup lightly packed crumbs
	1 slice dry	⅓ cup dry fine crumbs
Cabbage:	1 pound	4½ cups, grated
Carrots:	1 pound	3 cups, grated
Cheese:	1 pound	4 cups, grated
	4 ounces	1 cup, grated
Coconut:	3½ ounces	1⅓ cups
Coffee:	1 pound	5 cups, ground
Cornmeal:	1 pound	3 cups
Crackers:	25 saltines	1 cup, crushed
	15 grahams	1 cup, crushed
Eggs:	5 whole	1 cup
	8 whites	1 cup
Flour:	1 pound	4 cups
Lemons:	1 medium	2 to 3 tablespoons juice
	1 medium	1 tablespoon grated rind
Macaroni:	1 cup uncooked	2¼ cups cooked
Onion:	1 medium	½ cup chopped
Oranges:	1 medium	2 to 3 tablespoons
	1 medium	2 to 3 tablespoons grated rind
Rice:	1 cup uncooked	3 cups cooked
	1 cup precooked	2 cups cooked
Sugar:	1 pound brown	2¼ cups packed
	1 pound granulated	2 cups
	1 powdered	3½ cups
Whipping cream:	1 cup	2 cups, whipped

STANDARD MEASURES

Pinch	less than ⅛	4 cups	1 quart
3 teaspoons	1 tablespoon	4 quarts	1 gallon
4 tablespoons	¼ cup	1 ounce	2 tablespoons
5⅓ tablespoons	⅓ cup	8 ounces	1 cup
8 tablespoons	½ cup	16 ounces	1 pound
16 tablespoons	1 cup	32 ounces	1 quart
2 cups	1 pint		

Index

E

EGGS AND CHEESE

F

Sampler
P.O. Box 5705
Austin, Texas 78763

Please send me _____ copies of *Sampler*. I have enclosed $14.95 per copy plus $1.50 postage and handling. Texas residents please add $.92 per book for sales tax.

_____ Texas Residents - $17.37 each
_____ Non Resident - $16.45 each

Enclosed is $ _____ payable to _____

Name _____

Address _____

City _____ State _____ Zip _____

- -

Sampler
P.O. Box 5705
Austin, Texas 78763

Please send me _____ copies of *Sampler*. I have enclosed $14.95 per copy plus $1.50 postage and handling. Texas residents please add $.92 per book for sales tax.

_____ Texas Residents - $17.37 each
_____ Non Resident - $16.45 each

Enclosed is $ _____ payable to _____

Name _____

Address _____

City _____ State _____ Zip _____

- -

Sampler
P.O. Box 5705
Austin, Texas 78763

Please send me _____ copies of *Sampler*. I have enclosed $14.95 per copy plus $1.50 postage and handling. Texas residents please add $.92 per book for sales tax.

_____ Texas Residents - $17.37 each
_____ Non Resident - $16.45 each

Enclosed is $ _____ payable to _____

Name _____

Address _____

City _____ State _____ Zip _____